W9-AET-387

A DAY FOR THE HUNTER

A DAY FOR THE PREY

CHICAGO STUDIES IN ETHNOMUSICOLOGY

A Series Edited by Philip V. Bohlman and Bruno Nettl

EDITORIAL BOARD
Margaret J. Kartomi
Hiromi Lorraine Sakata
Anthony Seeger
Kay Kaufman Shelemay
Bonnie C. Wade

A DAY FOR THE HUNTER

A DAY FOR THE PREY

Popular Music and Power in Haiti

GAGE AVERILL

The University of Chicago Press ❖ *Chicago and London*

Gage Averill is associate professor of music and
Latin American studies at Wesleyan University and
was the Haitian music columnist for *The Beat Magazine* for eight years.

The University of Chicago Press, Chicago 60637
The University of Chicago Press, Ltd., London
© 1997 by The University of Chicago
All rights reserved. Published 1997
Printed in the United States of America
06 05 04 03 02 01 00 99 98 97   1 2 3 4 5
ISBN: 0–226–03291–4 (cloth)
ISBN: 0–226–03292–2 (paper)

Library of Congress Cataloging-in-Publication Data

Averill, Gage.
  A day for the hunter, a day for the prey: popular
    music and power in Haiti / Gage Averill.
  p.   cm.—(Chicago studies in ethnomusicology)
  Includes discography (p. 255), bibliographical
    references (p. 245), and index.
  ISBN 0–226–03291–4 (Cloth)—ISBN: 0–226–
    03292–2 (pbk.)
  1. Popular music—Haiti—20th century—
    History and criticism.   2. Power (Social
    sciences)—Haiti—History—20th century.
  I. Title.   II. Series.
  ML3486.H3A94   1997
  781.63'097294—dc20   96–34209
                                        CIP
                                        MN

⊗ The paper used in this publication meets the
minimum requirements of the American National Standard for Information Sciences—Permanence of Paper for Printed Library Materials,
ANSI Z39.48-1984.

To my wife, Giovanna Maria Perot-Averill

E, E! Ala yon ti peyi dwòl o
Chak fwa yo panse n koule

Yo wè n remonte
Yon jou pou chasè
Yon jou pou jibye

Hey, hey! What a strange country
Every time they think we're
    running
They see us get up again
A day for the hunter
A day for the prey

BOUKMAN EKSPERYANS,
"GANGA," 1995

Contents

Preface

This is a book about music and power, or more exactly about music in the discourse and relations of power. I contend that Haitian politics and more generally the struggle for power have insinuated themselves into every arena of musical expression. Popular music, as a discursive terrain, is a site at which power is enacted, acknowledged, accommodated, signified, contested, and resisted. Emerging in the context of power relations, popular music bears the traces of those relations. A popular Haitian aphorism has it that *Ayiti se tè glise* (Haiti is a slippery country), and this is nowhere truer than in the convoluted landscape of Haitian politics. What I attempt in these pages is to communicate some of the subtle and complex interactions of music and power in Haiti and to point in some possibly productive directions for understanding why they are so often yoked together.

Encounters in Music and Power

My perspectives on Haitian popular music have developed through eight years of interactions, conversations, observations, and readings, and my account of music and power in Haiti reflects those experiences. To clarify the contingent and subjective nature of my knowledge about these issues, let me begin by recounting a few brief anecdotes culled from my field notes and embellished with "head notes" (memories).

On my first night in Haiti in 1988, unable to locate my contact and having lost all of my luggage (sent to Suriname by mistake), I checked into a hotel and wandered into a nearby bar. There I met two American women who were working for a U.S. AID (U.S. Agency for International Development) reforestation project in the south of Haiti, and we started drinking beer and talking. They were concerned that peasants in their area, even those working for the project, seemed disillusioned with—and resistant to—the project. The peasants were engaging in sabotage, "poaching" of trees for charcoal, work slowdowns, spreading of rumors, and a variety of other tactics that the peasants called *mawonaj*. I was surprised by the peasants' adaptation of this term, which I knew only in relation to its original meaning: escape from slavery. Its use as a rubric for a class of tactics of resistance and subterfuge suggested a reinterpretation of the term over the course of a history of resistance to agents of oppression (whether foreign or national) against whom outright warfare was impossible. The AID workers also divulged that area *rara* bands were singing disparaging songs about the project and this was undermining their credibility.[1] *Rara* is a processional music of peasants and the lower classes in Haiti, and because it was the beginning of *rara* season (roughly Lent), the bands could be heard at night just about anywhere in the country, including in the hills around us that night in Pétion-Ville. Outside, we heard a commotion, so we walked out into the street to find a small crowd pointing toward the horizon. Far off in the distance, north of Port-au-Prince, a very large building was burning, its flames visible from Pétion-Ville. It was Damien, the Agricultural Ministry and College, and tonight it was the target of *mawonaj*. We watched the fire rage on for some time while *rara* bands, their bamboo trumpets sounding like a chorus of owls in the hillsides, filled the night with sound. As we shall see, the arts of musical *mawonaj* figure prominently in this book.

It was a surprisingly long drive from Cap-Haïtien, the northern provincial capital, to the town of Bas-Limbé. Picking up four hitchhikers, who rode on our rental car's bumper, we bounced in near-total darkness down the dirt road leading from National Route 1 into Bas-Limbé, site of a *fèt chanpèt* (countryside festival) and host that night to one of Cap Haïtien's two venerable orchestras, Orchestre Septentrionale. This was in the middle of August, the month of *vakans* (vacation time), when towns all over Haiti hold *fèt chanpèt*s and *fèt patwonal*s (*patron's day* festivals). Septentrionale had just recorded a song at the time about this kind of event called "Plezi chanpèt" (Pleasures of the country festival). It beautifully illustrates the pleasures to be found in a *chanpèt*, the importance of the festival, and the money that it brings from the city to the countryside.

Sa k lòt bò ap rantre, sa k isit ap prepare	Expatriates are returning, locals are preparing
Tout moun pral fète	Everyone's going to the fete
Nan chanpèt yo mariye, nan chan-pèt yo divòse	At the *champêtre* they'll marry and divorce
Nan chanpèt yo rekonsiliye . . .	At the *champêtre* they'll recon-cile . . .
Mesyè mesyè mete grinbank sou nou	Mister, Mister, give us a buck [greenback]
Medanm yo mete gangans sou nou	Madams, lay some elegance on us
Si se djaz ou ye mete mizik sou nou	If you're with the band, lay some music on us
Se nan chanpèt pou n wè nèg ki bon matcho	At the fete we'll see some macho guys
Se nan chanpèt pou n wè fanm ki bay filin	At the fete we'll see women who can turn you on
Se nan chanpèt pou n wè djaz ki bay konpa	At the fete, we'll see bands play-ing *konpa*[2]

The yard for dancing at Bas-Limbé was surrounded with a chest-high block wall. There were cars parked randomly; many *taptaps* (pick-up trucks converted into brightly painted, covered buses); and female vendors selling sweets, *kleren* (cane liquor), and coffee. The ticket window was a hole in the block wall through which a number of people were trying to stick their hands. Joining the battle of the hands, I picked up tickets for our group of four, and we snaked single file through the crowd-control entrance. Inside, the atmosphere was much more *"relaks."* Tables dotted the grass in the dark, piled with bottles of Barbancourt rum and with bowls of *lanbi* (conch). The generator roared off to one side, providing the electricity to run the few lights and the band's PA system.

The twelve members of Septentrionale who were present finished tuning their instruments and launched into some older tunes in their patented rhythm, the *rit boul difè* (fireball rhythm), similar to *konpa* but with some Cuban influences and idiosyncratic touches. We joined in the slow dancing close to the stage. After a potpourri of romantic boleros, the band sang a recent song about the history of Haiti's hard-ships since the slave rebellion in 1791, with the following chorus:

Se yon mesaj ki pou pase de bouch an bouch	This is a message to pass from mouth to mouth

Pou tout moun konsantre nan priye	For everyone to concentrate on a prayer
Pou n wete malediksyon ki sou tè dayiti	To remove this curse from the land of Haiti[3]

In writing this song and others in a more socially engaged vein (called *mizik angaje,* or politically engaged music), Septentrionale joined many other bands and performers who were weighing in on the social transformations shaping the country. Only two years after the exile of the Duvalier family and still very much in a tumultuous period in Haiti's political history, most musicians were taking their roles as cultural leaders seriously.

Somewhere in the latter part of the song, a group of rowdy *tonton makout*-s (former members of the Duvalierist militia), who were at a table in the back of the enclosure, pulled out some guns and started firing into the air. This had been standard behavior for *makout*-s during the Duvalier years, when it was part of their mode of enjoyment, but it shocked many at the dance during a period where the *makout*-s were so on the defensive. With the crowd startled, the lead singer stopped the band and shouted into the mic, "No, no. Puts your guns back. There will be no firing guns here. This is for pleasure. Relax a bit. No guns, okay?" And relax they did; the music started up, the guns went back in the holsters, and people went back to slow dancing. This informal countryside festival was intended to be as far from a political event as one gets in Haiti, yet here I was struck by how close to the surface the political struggle was, how ready to spill over into any public event. In the era of *dechoukaj* (uprooting, i.e., basic change), musical pleasures were generally not very far from political pressures.

Perhaps more obviously political was an incident I recounted previously in an article on Haitian carnival.[4] At an outdoor Haitian music festival that I helped to organize in Miami at carnival time in 1989, the final band, Miami Top Vice, launched into a spirited carnival medley. I looked out into the crowd from the stage to see a number of men spread their arms to *lese frape* (let hit), an exuberant carnival behavior, and I realized too late that I had neglected to inform the police that this might occur. As officers dove into the crowd to arrest the men for "drunk and disorderly" behavior, the announcer grabbed the microphone, silenced the music, and encouraged the crowd to surround the police to demand the release of the Haitians. A police call for help (scarcely two months after the infamous Overtown riots in Miami) brought what seemed like every squad car and fire engine in downtown Miami to the scene within minutes. As we negotiated with the police for a tense half-hour, members of the crowd began to make use of the three-toned whistles passed out as free souvenirs by the sponsor, the Nutrament Corporation (manufacturer of a sports drink). Crowd members combined the three tones into hocketed patterns (in which the melody notes are distributed among many instruments) resembling those of *rara* and carnival bands. Empty Nutrament cans filled in for bells, and antipolice carnival songs (part of a traditional form of censure called *chan pwen*-s, or sung points) were composed on the spot. As I watched these makeshift carnival ensembles fire up the crowds, I was in awe of the power of the carnival music—even here in the Haitian diaspora—to animate a confrontation of this sort. In the sociopolitical space of the diaspora, the political issues were different, but the crowd was manifesting its access to the same tactics and tools of musicopolitical signification used in Haiti, the same weapons of musical *mawonaj.*

Thinking back on these three experiences and on many others like them, I am aware that throughout my research on Haitian music I was dogged by questions of music's role in enacting and negotiating authority, domination, co-optation, subordination, hegemony, and resistance. This book is an effort to grapple with these questions.

Background and Structure of the Book

My first experience of Haitian music was a recording of revolutionary songs by the group Atis Endepandan that I played on my radio show in Madison, Wisconsin, in the mid 1970s. I found the guitar work and the percussion on the recording (which I later learned was an evocation of traditional *rara* bands) fascinating and a bit impenetrable, and I kept coming back to it over the years. The next time I heard something comparable was on a recording by Verna Gillis of *rara* bands from Haiti and the Dominican Republic when I was starting graduate studies in ethnomusicology at the University of Washington in 1984.[5] Unable to find anything of substance on *rara*, I decided to make it my dissertation topic and to travel to Haiti to research *rara*. But politics intervened in the form of the overthrow of Jean-Claude Duvalier in 1986, which was accompanied by conflict in the streets for months afterward as the popular forces *dechouke*-d (uprooted) the regime and its supporters. Concerned about the safety of American researchers in the countryside, my granting agency withdrew my fieldwork grant and I was without a project. The uprooting process in Haiti, *dechoukaj*, hit close to home when I went to visit a Haitian friend (and Creole tutor) in Seattle. He was packing his bags for Haiti to try to save his father's life. His father, a prominent general under the Duvalier dictatorship, had been blamed for a massacre of peasants in the south of Haiti and had been apprehended by a crowd, roughed up, and imprisoned—*dechouke*-d. My friend handed me a cassette he had prepared for me of something I had never encountered before—Haitian commercial popular music called *konpa*.

In the months that followed, I decided to revise my project to focus on commercial music, with an emphasis on a genre study of *konpa*, which was nearly unknown in the United States. I spoke with ethnomusicologist Jocelyne Guilbault, who was beginning a study of *zouk*, a popular music of the French Antilles, and who suggested a collaboration on Creole musics of the Caribbean if I were to go ahead with the idea. My theoretical interests at the time centered on issues of class, race, and ideology, and I had already finished a small pilot study of the music of the Dominican Republic using such a framework. The ethnomusicological literature on popular music, class, nationalism, and related issues was anemic at best at the time, but a few books that came out in 1984–85 served as inspiration: Wallis and Malm's *Big Sounds from Small Peoples: The Music Industry in Small Countries*, David Copelan's *In Township Tonight*, and Manuel Peña's *Texas-Mexican Conjunto*, all of which demonstrated a concern for the political economy of popular music. The other "invisible hand" guiding my work was the research of my adviser, Christopher Alan Waterman, into Yoruba *jùjú*, which was not yet consolidated into his book, *Jùjú: A Social History and Ethnography of an African Popular Music*.

I decided to try to create an ethnography and political economy of Haitian popular music that would, to quote George Marcus, "[probe] the experience of its subjects while adequately representing the larger order in which they are implicated."[6] Although I was less concerned at the start with social history, every interesting issue I stumbled onto in Haitian music seemed to be deeply immersed in historical discourses, and, slowly, social history joined ethnography and political economy as the guiding paradigms for my research.

A community-based ethnography appeared out of the question for a study of Haitian popular music. Although Haitian popular music was initially centered in the capital city of Port-au-Prince, for decades it had evolved in a complex interaction of locales, including Port-au-Prince and its suburbs, provincial cities and towns in Haiti, cities of the Haitian diaspora, foreign markets, and the many smaller urban areas of Haiti. The transnational character of the Haitian diaspora was impressed on me in my first interview on the subject of Haitian music with the director of the Haitian American Chamber of Commerce in Miami. He interrupted our conversation repeatedly, with one ear always on the daily broadcast from Haiti over one of the sixty Haitian radio programs in Miami. Many experiences like this led me to question how immigrants variously "belonged" to Haiti and the United States and how Haitian popular music articulated this pattern of transnational belonging. The Haiti of the title of this book should be read as inclusive of the Haitian diaspora and of the global commercial markets within which Haitian music is consumed. For these reasons, I borrowed the transnational "tour" by Haitian musicians as the spatializing metaphor for my research, aiming for a "system ethnography."

Within this market, I identified the major concentrations of Haitians: Port-au-Prince (and the provincial cities of Haiti), New York City, and Miami, Florida, which were also the major concentrations of Haitian commercial musicians, and these became the principal sites of my ethnographic research. In the eight years I have been working on Haitian music, I have been to Haiti seven times (for visits from two weeks to three months), and have visited and worked regularly in Miami and New York. My research has consisted of viewing and often recording musical performances, conducting interviews, witnessing recording sessions, participating in carnival and *rara* processionals, taking drumming lessons, rehearsing and performing with *konpa* bands, attending Vodou ceremonies, visiting festivals and patron's day celebrations all over Haiti, and poring over archival materials.

The political struggle affected my research in Haiti dramatically at times. There were days when I was stopped and searched at army checkpoints four or more times. Under a constantly insecure political climate, with armed thugs (*zenglendo*-s) active at night, nightlife often dried up and performers found it difficult to make a living. There were three coups (not including sabotaged elections, unsuccessful coups, and "managed" transitions) in the eight years leading up to the writing of this book, and these typically resulted in occasional gunfire in the district in which I stayed in Port-au-Prince. In a period of epochal change that has crystallized political conflicts, any collective event, whether carnival or a concert, could turn ugly if provoked, as at a

Manno Charlemagne concert I attended where the audience was pelted by bottles thrown from outside the theater. In short, the country was in chaos, and new musical movements (the "new generation" and a new "roots music" movement) were emerging, all of which influenced the shape and direction of my work (away from a genre study and solidly toward issues in the political economy and social history of Haitian popular music).

Although my dissertation, *Haitian Dance Band Music: The Political Economy of Exuberance* had been published in 1989, my research into Haitian popular music and my involvement in Haiti intensified. I returned to Haiti to participate as an election monitor for the Organization of American States, for carnivals, for *rara* research, and for festivals. Over the following six years, while teaching at Columbia University and Wesleyan University, I published a number of articles that picked up and elaborated on threads in the dissertation. One group of articles dealt with spatial issues: the circulation of musical influence among Creole Caribbean popular musics, the role of music in creating and sustaining a transnational Haitian culture, and the globalization of the Haitian music industry.[7] Another set of articles dealt more explicitly with political themes: class, race, and authenticity; carnival politics; Afrocentric identity movements in music; and music and militarization.[8] While the latter group of articles, spanning more than six years in publication dates, provided opportunities to work through some of the issues in this book, I came to view this book as a means of cooking all of the issues of music and power together in a single stew pot.

Although the literature on music's relationship to politics, class, race, nationalism, ideology, and transnationalism was impoverished at the outset of my study, that is certainly no longer the case. Deborah Pacini Hernandez's fine book, *Bachata: A Social History of a Dominican Popular Music,* explores the "unique relationships between popular music, social identity, and class in the Dominican Republic," overlapping with this work in many of its concerns. Another scholar of Dominican music, Paul Austerlitz, has published *Dominican Merengue in Regional, National, and International Perspectives,* which, in addition to its concern with social geography, also considers the influence of nationalism on the trajectory of the genre and grapples with the thorny issues of racial ideology in the Dominican Republic.[9] The material by both authors on the role of music in the Trujillo dictatorship provides a helpful cross-cultural comparison for the material in Chapter 3. Studies of *zouk* by Jocelyne Guilbault and of calypso by Donald Hill have examined their subjects through the media and industries responsible for their development and dissemination; both represent an increasing awareness that expressive culture cannot be studied apart from commerce.[10] More germane from the standpoint of politics is the book *Race, Class, and Political Symbols: Rastafari and Reggae in Jamaican Politics,* by Anita M. Waters, although it is restricted largely to the use of music in the national elections between 1967 and 1983. The guiding question for Waters seems to have been, "Why would a political party identify itself with a millenarian cult, whose beliefs are sharply at odds with a majority of the electorate, and whose membership never exceeded 3 percent of the population?"[11] Her conclusions are relevant to the issue of the use of Haitian "roots music" in the progressive electoral politics of the 1990s, an interaction I chronicle in Chapter 5. Robin Moore has placed the work of Fernando Ortiz in Cuba within a framework of the ideological impact of *afrocubanismo,* and he has looked at the racial dynamics of the appropriation of rumba and other expressions of lower-class black culture in the middle class *teatro vernáculo.*[12] All of this scholarly activity has provided a more meaningful field of knowledge and a basis for comparison on which to interpret the Haitian material.

During the years I was carrying out research for this study, I often felt as though I were living multiple lives, with a full-time academic career; a public ethnomusicology practice as a journalist, critic, and popularizer of Haitian music; and involvement as a musician and band director. My music journalism career began by accident when I tried to convince the Miami *New Times* to initiate coverage of Haitian music in Miami and they responded by assigning me to write a cover story.[13] To my astonishment, the article produced tangible effects, including a temporary increase in visits to Haitian clubs by outsiders, a *konpa* festival, some new bookings for Haitian bands, and a program of Haitian music in the schools. Arriving in Haiti a few weeks after publication of this article, I found that it had preceded me and had circulated among musicians, giving me instant entrée. These experiences exposed me to the possibilities for combining academic research with public journalism. After my first year of research, the editor of the *Beat,* a magazine of "Reggae, African, Caribbean, and World Music," asked me to write an article on Haitian music in 1988, which was later reprinted by the Haitian daily newspaper *Le Nouvelliste.* After the article appeared, the *Beat*'s editor wrote to say something to the effect of, "By the way, we have assigned you to do a regular column, called "Haitian Fascination." Your next contribution will be due. . . ." And thus I found myself as the only regular chronicler of Haitian music in English, with a column in the principal outlet for the growing "world beat" market.

The column led to an invitation to coproduce and annotate an album of Haitian music with movie director Jonathan Demme and with Haitian record producer Fred Paul for A&M Records, which provided the first mass exposure for Haitian music in the U.S. market. After that, I wrote liner notes for a number of Haitian bands (Boukman Eksperyans, Coupé Cloué, Magnum Band, and Boukan Ginen), attempting to help American audiences understand the material better. My research also led to a number of shows on Afropop International on National Public Radio. Although this activity created certain contradictions for me in tone (analytical vs. promotional vs. critical), it produced tangible paybacks for musicians with whom I was working. It also encouraged feedback from Haitian musicians and producers, who often read, commented on, and critiqued my articles ("Gage, you fucked up . . . Agenor is a tennis player, not a human rights activist!") in a way that would never have occurred with academic articles alone. The requirements of media and presenting projects also helped to keep me current, whereas the demands of an academic position conspired mightily to isolate me in the classroom and office.

As for the contradictions of tone that my work embraced, I would like to recount an anecdote. In my first Miami *New Times* article, I wrote, "Without a doubt, *compas* is one of the most dynamic, most sensuous, and most irresistible of Third World dance musics," a statement with a clear "promotional" tone that infused the entire article. The local festival that developed as a result of the article (called Miami Discovers *Compas*) used this sentence in their promotional literature, identifying its author as an ethnomusicologist; it came out as "*Compas* is considered by ethnomusicologists [*sic*] to be one of the most dynamic and irresistible of Third World dance musics." A year later, I received a mailing from a Haitian organization with an article in Creole on *konpa* which recycled the formula once again. "Gwo sosyològ save yo konsidere mizik konpa kòm yon'n nan mizik ki gen fòs nan peyi sou devlope yo. Kè moun pa ka reziste." A literal translation of this yields, "Big [prominent] scholarly sociologists consider *konpa* music as one of the [most] forceful musics in underdeveloped countries. People's hearts can't resist." Here, a young, unknown ethnomusicology student was transformed into a "prominent scholarly sociologist," and his promotional quip was enshrined as academic doctrine. Apart from the flattering boost to my lowly status at the time, this feedback loop emphasized the dangers resulting from the inevitable collision of roles and rhetorical stances.

Throughout my research, I was striving for a highly dialogic, persistent, and engaged encounter with another culture and its music. From all of the above, it must be apparent that my work took on a rather distinctive tone, which I jokingly came to call "gonzo" ethnography. The reference to Hunter S. Thompson is playful, yet not entirely off the mark. Much of my research was done at bars, at Carnival, and at country festivals, all of which serve as locales for the dedicated pursuit of simple pleasures. Like others in attendance at these events, I drank my share of rum, Prestige beer, and *kleren;* partied; ate; danced and sang. Another tenuous similarity is a degree of partisanship and engagement in the issues that I have been unable or unwilling to part with. It is nearly impossible to work in Haiti and not to be touched by the misery and suffering of a large portion of its people. While suspicious of simplistic and dogmatic solutions—and especially of know-it-all outsiders—I nevertheless engaged in a degree of cultural and political critique that has filtered through all or most of my writings, including this book. Finally, my research and feedback methodology evolved to take advantage of my music journalist alter ego.

I believe that dialogic ethnography implies a subject position that allows the ethnographer to engage in a sympathetic, culturally informed dialogue of cultures without suspending entirely his or her own critical judgment. My service as an election observer during the 1990 elections was in this spirit, and I have also spoken at rallies and have at times publicly criticized the military governments that were ostensibly my hosts in Haiti. I don't claim to have resolved all (any?) of the contradictions raised by my engagement in these issues, my closeness to the subject matter, or my multiple "hats." While I don't consider objectivity to be my ideal subject position, I have struggled mightily to allow conflicting voices to emerge in this text and to represent adequately and respectfully the range of views and political positions that I've encountered. I have tried to allow the musical practitioners to speak loudly, often, and contradictorily when necessary in this narrative while attempting neither to deepen gratuitously any of the various polemics myself nor to mediate these discourses.

In order not to mislead, allow me to clarify what this book is *not*. This is not a stylistic history of Haitian music: I have not described in detail what makes Haitian *méringue, konpa,* or *mizik rasin* sound the way it does, nor have I included musical transcriptions, in part because I want this book to be fully comprehensible and useful to non-musicologists. It is also not a general history of popular music in Haiti. Many musicians and groups that might figure prominently in such a history make only a passing appearance in this account, if they appear here at all. I will have to pay my debts to the generations of extraordinary Haitian musicians elsewhere. This book is closer to a social history of Haitian commercial music, but it is a lean one at that, pared down to address the role of music in the distribution and exercise of power in society and culture. This book is ethnographically informed, but it is far from an ethnography in the strict sense. Perhaps it could be described as an ethnographically informed social history of the relation of Haitian popular music to power and politics.

I hope this does not sound dull and dry. I am well aware that social scientists often transform the object of their interest into something entirely alien, unrecognizable to those whose lives it touches. My experiences with Haitian music have been anything but dull and dry, and my intent is to represent some of the richness of the experience and of this extraordinary musical world in the pages of this book.

The structure of this book is simple. I have chosen the years 1915–95 as the outside limits of its narrative because they mark a coherent period from the beginning of the first American occupation of Haiti to the end of the second. This has been the "American Century" in Haiti as it has been in much of the world, and the two occupations have helped to further the integration of Haiti into a global political economy saturated by American influence.

I have broken this time span into four chapters, each bracketing a period with a particular relationship of music to power and politics. The Duvalier family figures prominently in this division (as they do in almost all political histories of Haiti in this century), because the Duvalier dictatorsip so thoroughly imprinted itself on relations of power. The chapters follow this division into political regimes: pre-Duvalier, the reign of François Duvalier, the reign of Jean-Claude Duvalier, and post-Duvalier. There was a risk in choosing this scheme: It may suggest to some readers that I am concerned primarily with the relationship of music to the state or, more narrowly, to dictatorships, whereas I am equally concerned with the issues of power in its more dispersed, local, subtle, and "capillary" forms.[14] The ordering of chapters and subsections follows a general chronological impulse, but I am not concerned with presenting a year-to-year or month-to-month account of developments. Instead, many of the subsections develop themes that dislodge a strict chronology. Chapter and subsection headings generally employ a two-part device. The first half of the heading consists of a quotation, whether from a song or interview (more often the former) from Haitian musicians, which is balanced by a descriptive title of my own. This conceit is intended to call attention to the problematic nature of interpretation, reminding the readers that this book itself is constructed in a dialogue of cultures.

Every chapter contains a case study. I have employed these case studies to allow me to "zoom in" to examine people, events, repertories, and institutions in greater detail while varying the texture of the book a bit for its readers. Case studies cover the 1949 Port-au-Prince Bicentennial, the polemic between two founding figures of *konpa,* songs about the plight of the "boat people," and music in the elections of 1990. The last case study allows me to inject a small, but concentrated, dose of first-person narrative. The use of the first person is restricted somewhat in the rest of the text, as I am dealing with a historical subject (1915–95) from the vantage point of ethnographic experience in the period from 1986 to 1995. I realize that this gives the book a certain trajectory or narrative arc: The earlier chapters have a more "background"-like feel, whereas the narrative texture thickens and perhaps becomes more vivid as we approach the ethnographic present.

Acknowledgments

Legba, ouvri baryè pou mwen. In Haitian Vodou ceremonies, the trickster deity, Legba, opens the gate for the others to enter. By way of an opening ceremony, I would like to honor all of the people who have, in myriad ways, opened the gate for me, starting with scholars of African diasporic music and culture such as Robert Farris Thompson, Henry Louis Gates Jr., Roger D. Abrahams, Harold Courlander, Richard Alan Waterman, Melville J. and Frances S. Herskovits, Sally and Richard Price, George Simpson, Fernando Ortiz, and many others.

For encouraging me to go on to graduate school in ethnomusicology, I want to thank Professors Lorraine Sakata and Daniel Neuman; their unflagging confidence buoyed me all the way. During my second year of graduate school at the University of Washington, I convinced Christopher Alan Waterman to serve as my dissertation adviser, and he has been a forceful presence in my work ever since.

My graduate studies and my early research in Haitian music were generously funded by the Mellon Fellowships in the Humanities. In addition, Wesleyan University provided me with a timely faculty research grant. I thank Dieter Christensen at Columbia University for taking a chance and giving me my first real job in academia, which just happened to be in the liveliest city in the world for Caribbean music. In the following year, I had the job offer of a lifetime from Wesleyan University, where I have been snugly ensconced ever since. Thanks to my Wesleyan colleagues (current and former), especially Mark Slobin, Kay Kauffman Shelemay, Ann Wightman, Richard Ohmann, Alex Dupuy, and Su Zheng, who have helped to cultivate a lively intellectual and creative climate that is everything academia should be.

I want to take this opportunity to thank some people with whom I have worked closely over these years. Let me begin with Ralph Boncy,

who has an encyclopedic knowledge of Haitian music and with whom
I have had a long and rewarding dialogue (including co-authorship of
some columns in the *Beat*). My collaboration with Jocelyne Guilbault
on her important *zouk* project was an exciting first foray into dialogic
research and writing. My editor (aka Minister of Information) at the
Beat, C C Smith, wrote (with Gerard Tacite Lamothe) a fine series of
articles on Haitian popular music and provided me full access to her
interview transcripts (and has put up with my last-minute, Fed-Exed
submissions for eight years). Michael Largey was an invaluable help
during my first visit to Haiti, and we have shared many adventures
and misadventures. Jonathan Demme was the driving force behind
Konbit: Burning Rhythms of Haiti, the first recording project I worked
on, and he has been a tireless advocate of Haiti and Haitian music
ever since.

I am deeply indebted to the following people who patiently ex-
plained things, gave lessons, and consulted with me: Frizner Augustin,
"Papa Jube" Altino, Jean-Girard Azard, Theodore "Lolo" Beaubrun Jr.,
Mimrose Beaubrun, Lionel Benjamin, Chiko Boyer, Cinna Octavius
"Ti-Blanc" Charles, Joe Charles Jr., Pierre "Bobo" Ciné, Eddie "Didi"
Crevecoeur, Giselle Débrosse, André Déjean, Fred Déjean, Raoul Denis
Jr., Robert "Bobby" and Jacqueline Denis, Emerante de Pradines
Morse, Ronald "Aboudja" Derenoncourt, Marc Duverger, Serge Du-
viela, Dernst Emile, Eddy François, Ricardo "Ti-Plume" Franck, Jean-
Robert "Pòki" Herisse, Jean-Yves "Fanfan Ti-Bòt" Joseph, Farah Juste
Desgranges, Dr. Jean-Claude Desgranges, Henry Juste, Jean-Gesner
"Coupé Cloué" Henry, Jean-Michel "Eliphète" Isnas, Wagner Lalanne,
Henri-Robert Lamothe, Wilfrid "Tido" Laveaud, Nikol Levy, Claude
Marcelin, Robert Martino, Farol Mésidor, Maurice Morissette, Alfred
Michel, Emeline Michel, Guy Montreuil, Guesley "Ti-Gous" Morisseau,
Richard and Lunise Morse, Holly Nicolas, Lochard Noël, Alix "Tit"
Pascal, André "Dadou" Pasquet, Fred Paul, Max Paul, Jean-Baptiste
"Baba" Pierre, Réginald Policard, Gabriel Romulus, "Azouke" Sanon,
Jean Sebon, Jules "Toto Nécessité" Similien, Harold Staco, René St.
Aude, Jean-Michel "Zouzoul" St. Victor, José Tavernier, Fito Ulysse,
Jean-Claude Verdier, Jeff Wainwright, Herby Widmaïer, Joël Widmaïer,
and Mushy Widmaïer.

Many people have improved this book (or sections of the book in
progress) with their perceptive comments and criticisms: Mark Slobin,
Gerard Béhague, Richard Ohmann, Thomas Turino, T. M. Scruggs, Jeff
Todd Titon, Gerdès Fleurant, Chris Waterman, Alex Dupuy, Ann Wightman, Les Gay, Lydia Goehr, Dieter Christensen, Jocelyne Guilbault,

Jean Robertson, Martine Pierre-Louis, Deborah Pacini Hernandez, Veit Erlmann, Khachig Tölöyan, Anne Rasmussen, Ingrid Monson, Roberta Singer, Julian Gerstin, and my editors at the University of Chicago Press—T. David Brent, Matthew Howard, Mark Jacobs, and Kathryn Kraynik. I am especially grateful for the input and encouragement of my fellow scholars of Haitian music and culture, such as Gerdès Fleurant, Leslie Desmangles, Nina Glick Schiller, Lois Wilcken, and David Yih.

There are many people whose interest in Haitian music has in one way or another enriched this book: Sean Barlow, Dan Behrman, Kathleen Burke, Jean Nonez, Mark Dow, Verna Gillis, Anthony Seeger, Al Angeloro, Ray Allen, Chris Migliaccio, Tony Hardmon, Jim Mullins, Anneka Wambaugh, Michele Wucker, Jordan Levin, Mary Luft, Daisanne McLaine, Rudy Stern, Chantal Regnault, Jean Jean-Pierre (Mapou Productions), Ned Sublette, and Dolores Yonker. Kera Washington served for a semester as a research assistant for this book. And there are others whom I just want to thank for their encouragement and help somewhere along the way: John Baily and Veronica Doubleday, Peter Manuel, Martha Ellen Davis, Cynthia Schmidt, Sean Williams, Dan Sheehy, Philippa Coughlan, Lise Waxer, L'Ecole Ste. Trinité, Hôpital St. Croix, Jean-Jean Fabius, Radio Metropol, the staff and management of *Haïti-Observateur*, Pierre Jean-Pierre, Maurice Moses and his family, Jean Jean-Pierre, James "Smitty" Smith, John Jost, Paul Samuel, and a group of people too numerous to mention who have put me up, treated me to meals, and lavished on me all of the hospitality for which Haiti is justly famous.

I have been sustained by the love and encouragement of my entire family, especially my wife and partner, Giovanna Maria Perot-Averill, who deserves extra recognition for her unbounded understanding and for everything she has done to see this through. I want to thank my mother, Mary Janet Higgins, and my entire family-in-law, the Perots—Elton, Vicky, Josie, Jean-François, Estrella, Sunny, and Cimarron—for their unflagging support and for all the calls to check up on how this book (and its author!) was coming along.

Parts of this book have appeared over the last seven years in my column ("Haitian Fascination") in the *Beat* magazine and in the following other publications:

"'*Mezanmi, Kouman Nou Ye?* My Friends, How Are You?' Musical Constructions of the Haitian Transnation." *Diaspora* 3(3): 253–72 (1994).

"*Anraje* to *Angaje*: Carnival Politics and Music in Haiti." *Ethnomusicology* 38(2): 217–48 (1994).

"'*Se Kreyòl Nou Ye'*/We're Creole": Musical Discourse on Haitian Identities." In Gerard H. Béhague, ed., *Music and Black Ethnicity: The Caribbean and South America*. Coral Gables, FL: University of Miami North-South Center (1994). Books published by North-South Center are distributed by Lynne Rienner Publishers, 1800 30th St., Suite 314, Boulder, CO 80301.

"*Toujou Sou Konpa*: Issues of Change and Interchange in Haitian Popular Dance Music." In Jocelyne Guilbault et al., *Zouk: World Music in the West Indies*. Chicago: University of Chicago Press (1993). © 1993 by the University of Chicago.

"Haitian Dance Bands, 1915–1970: Class, Race, and Authenticity." *Latin American Music Review* 10(2): 203–35 (1989). Reprinted by permission of the University of Texas Press.

"Haitian Music in the Global System." In Alvina Ruprecht and Cecilia Taiana, eds., *The Reordering of Culture: Latin America, the Caribbean and Canada in the Hood*. Ottawa: Carleton University Press (1995). Excerpt reprinted with permission of the publisher.

A Note on Translation

Under the 1987 Haitian Constitution, both French and Creole (Kreyòl) are considered official languages of Haiti. Until the codification of Creole orthography by the Institut Pédagogique National d'Haïti (IPN) in 1979, Creole texts were represented in a variety of often idiosyncratic spellings. Unless otherwise noted, I follow the IPN system, relying on the *Haitian Creole-English-French Dictionary* of the Indiana University Creole Institute (Valdman 1981) to resolve spelling and usage questions. To signify pluralization of Creole terms within English text blocks, I use "-s," avoiding the Creole plural marker (-yo). I have not altered the Creole spellings in quoted material and in song titles taken from album jackets, which remain in their original and which may represent earlier or idiosyncratic Creole orthographies.

I quote song texts in an effort to present the richness of the interpretive universe in Haitian musical discourse and to analyze ideological subject positions, rhetorical gestures, signifying tropes, and so on in the texts. In order not to violate copyright protection on the lyrics, I keep the quoted passages only as long as is necessary to demonstrate my point and, in all cases, short in relation to the entire song. Omitted lines from within the body of the quoted song text are signaled with an ellipsis. All translations are my own unless otherwise noted.

1

Introduction
"A Message to Pass from Mouth to Mouth"

My decision to write this book on music and power might itself cause some consternation in Haitian circles. Some Haitian musicians will feel, understandably, that it focuses too much on conflict, and that this might fuel outsiders' perceptions that everything in Haiti is Sturm und Drang. This book is narrowly focused, it is true, and excludes far more than it includes. The emphasis on power follows from my own theoretical interests, from my experiences in a period of political turmoil in Haiti, from the debates raging in Haitian lay and academic circles over the political future of the country, from my perception that an audience for this book will be broadly familiar with and interested in Haitian politics, and from a conviction that the intersection of culture and power possesses a broad theoretical appeal throughout the humanities and social sciences. As Dirks, Eley, and Ortner have stated, "The complex and problematic relations between social movements and disorderly popular culture, involving distinctions of class and gender, ethnicity and race, roughness and respectability, are becoming central to the contemporary problematic."[1] The same authors emphasize the "degree to which power itself is culturally constructed" through "knowledge making, universe construction, and the social production of feeling and of 'reality,'" in other words through discourses.[2] Power is far from being the property of the powerful; it is a pervasive quality that adheres to every action and interaction. It is sought, undermined, despised, ignored, resisted, and negotiated. In contrast to the term "power," "politics" might best be viewed as the strategies and tactics for gaining, maintaining, and increasing power, especially (but not exclusively) in its more formal and public dimensions.

With my emphasis on strategies, tactics, and intentional social practice, it is clear that I believe that individuals and social groups can carve out for themselves a degree of what is often called "agency"— that they are not entirely imprisoned in social, political, psychological, sociobiological, or historical structures. In this perspective, I have been enormously influenced over the years by the writings of Anthony Giddens and Pierre Bourdieu, representing a turn in the social sciences which is sometimes dubbed poststructuralism. Giddens advocates a "theory of action which recognizes human beings as knowledgeable agents, reflexively monitoring the flow of interaction with one another." [3] Bourdieu has stressed the role of strategy in action: "To substitute *strategy* for the *rule* is to reintroduce time, with its rhythm, its orientation, its irreversibility." [4] I will have cause occasionally in this book to make use of Bourdieu's concept of "habitus," which he conceives of as dispositions which are social in nature, but individually reproduced, and which are generative (with individuals engaging existing matrices of perceptions and motivations to deal creatively with every new situation). Habitus is learned and internalized, but it is a social, not an individual, product.

I am concerned with the production of political meaning in music, and the production of meaning is a semiotic process. I am in general agreement with Jean-Jacques Nattiez's goal of recuperating semiotics from structuralism and restoring the role of the author and the reader, which is to say restoring the role of time, history, and praxis. [5] Nattiez engages in a tripartition of the interpretive process in expressive culture: *poiesis* (processes of creation), *trace* (material product), and *esthesis* (perception, apprehension, interpretation). One strength of this model is that it stresses the separation of composerly intention from readerly interpretation. Given that this bears an at-least-superficial resemblance to an economic model of production and consumption linked by commodities (material traces of production), I believe that Nattiez's trifurcation of the semiotic process provides a means of linking the political economy of expressive culture to analysis of the symbolic language and activity of expressive culture. However, I would like to take this model a step further in the direction of linking it to power. The creation of symbolic expression (in Nattiez's phrase, the poietic process) takes place in a particular historical, political, and economic context, as does the process of perception and interpretation (esthesis), and this model allows for what can be a radical separation in time and social circumstances between the two processes. By imagining these semiotic processes each nested in contexts of institutional, social-hierarchical, cultural, economic, political, and ideological relations, we can begin to imagine how power comes to bear on every process of cultural creation and interpretation—on every trifurcated semiotic process. The notion of the separation of production and reception/perception—and the concept of the "trace"—are critical to understanding how certain signifying tropes work in Haitian political music, and to understanding how the entire aesthetic of indirect signification (which emphasizes a creative space of interpretive difference) works. Although I do not employ Nattiez's terminology, this hybrid model that I have sketched underlies the argument I make in this book.

In this Introduction, I concentrate on developing a grounded framework for the operation and circulation of power in Haiti (grounded, that is, in the perceptions, terminologies, and discourses of Haitians) and a grammar for the musical signification of power.

Toward a Grounded Haitian Politics

Before proceeding to elaborate a framework for musicopolitical signification in Haiti, I want to look at the way power and politics are played out in Haiti and the way they are perceived and conceived, beginning with issues of class and race. Haitians of all classes and backgrounds are aware of class distinctions and social stratification, and they have developed an elaborate terminology to articulate these differences. Many of the terms (or at least their English equivalents) will be familiar to the reader, yet it should not be assumed that their meanings map directly onto their Euro-American cognates.

The term *klas* in Haiti does not refer to a position determined strictly by relationship to the means of production, but admits numerous criteria, including family background, geographic origins, wealth, education, phenotype, and comportment and is thus more akin to the Weberian concept of status group, which proceeds from the position of actors within structures of authority.[6] At the most superficial level, Haitians divide the country into two basic status groups: those with access to power and money (*lelit*, the elite) and those without (*pèp* or *mas*, the people or masses). In informal discourse, these categories are more often *rich* (rich) and *pòv* or *malere* (the poor or poverty stricken). In its popular use, the term *lelit* may incorporates both the *boujwazi* (bourgeoisie) who have large businesses, traditional wealth, extensive property, or have important positions in the government and the *klas mwayen* (small entrepreneurs, lower military echelons, professionals, artisans, and state functionaries). The *boujwazi* can be subdivided (in part along racial lines) into the traditional lighter-skinned ruling class (*boujwazi tradisyonèl milat*) made up of well-known families (*gran fanmi*), the numerically smaller group of wealthy blacks (*boujwazi tradisyonèl nwa*), and *arivist*-s, a higher stratum of government managers, most of whom are of middle-class origins and came to power with problack governments after World War II. Import-export merchants, many of whom are of Levantine origins (Syrians, Lebanese, and some Jews), constitute an identifiable subgroup of the elite and are usually identified as the *bòdmè* (literally: seaside, an area near the wharf in Port-au-Prince where there is a concentration of stores owned by members of this group). The poor and powerless in Haiti have many names for the wealthy and powerful, the most common of which include *gwo nèg* (big guy, translated by me as "big shot") and its synonyms, *gwo zotobre* and *gwo zouzoun*. These terms may identify someone who has an exaggerated sense of self-importance as well as someone of elevated status.

For the purposes of precision throughout this book, I will use the alternate tripartite distinction: *lelit/boujwazi, klas mwayen,* and *pèp* as a starting point for further distinctions. Government functionaries, bureaucrats, and ministerial level appointees are often accorded their own class subgroup (of the middle class) in Haiti, the *klas politik,* in part because the government has such a large payroll and in part because they constitute a social group *for themselves,* striving to protect their self-interests by maintaining and expanding the parasitic state.

The terms for the masses (*pèp* or *mas*) cover rural peasants, *abitan,* urban *proletaria, klas ouvriye* (urban working class), and structurally unemployed slum dwellers, *lounpen* (from lumpen proletariat). The *abitan* are commonly subdivided by geography: *moun mòn* (mountain people) and *moun plenn* (generally more prosperous plains dwellers). The highest stratum of peasants, those with ample lands and a role in local affairs, are called *peyizan eze* (well-off peasants). Categories are also employed for the middle-level peasants (*abitan mwayen*) and those at the bottom, *peyizan pòv*. Sometimes a geographic typology transcends the status group typology (although it is equally biased), with the resulting classification into either *moun lavil* (city people) or *moun andeyo* (people "out there").

Haitian concepts of class are thoroughly interpenetrated with those of color. Before the triumph of the revolution in 1804, Haitians were divided into three major racial categories; white, black, and mulatto (*milat*), which overlapped considerably with legal status categories of *lib* (free), *esklav* (slave), and *afranchi* (freed slave) or *gens de couleur.*

Early generations of mulattoes, related by blood to slaveholders, were often freed, while most blacks remained enslaved until the abolition of slavery at the time of the French Revolution. The three general racial categories were far more elaborate in practice, based first on the percentage of African and European blood, but complicated by characteristics such as the coarseness of hair, the width of the nose, and other facial features. Many complex categories of phenotype are in common use today, for example, *nèg/nègès, nwa* (black), *marabout, brin, grimo/grimèl, grifonn, wouj* (red), *jonn* (yellow), *milat/milatrès*, and *blan* (white).[7] In day-to-day discourse, these are often used descriptively and not pejoratively, but they are still attached to status considerations that privilege light skin, straight hair, and fine features, at least among the upper classes who control access to jobs and resources. A popular saying, *Nèg rich se milat, milat pòv se nèg* (A rich black is a mulatto, a poor mulatto is a black), admits a degree of movement between perceived racial categories, but speaks more to the treatment and status afforded those with wealth. Racial categories were further complicated by the original Haitian constitution (1804), which asserted that all Haitians were henceforth to be considered *nèg*. *Nèg* thus became synonymous with "person" in one meaning of the word, with "Haitian" in another, and with "black" in its original meaning. Similarly, *blan* translates both as "white" and as "foreigner."

Under the threat of the reinstitution of slavery under Napoleon, blacks and mulattoes joined forces to pursue independence and to end institutionalized slavery on Saint Domingue. However, after the assassination of the black Haitian Emperor Jean-Jacques Dessalines, the country split in two, the North ruled as a monarchy by King Henri Christophe and the South as a republic under the mulatto General Pétion. Although the country was later reunited, an internecine struggle based on racial conflict and mistrust became a persistent theme in Haitian society and politics. Haitian mulattoes gravitated to the cities, where they evolved into a very isolated merchant elite which controlled the country's political life. Under pressure from *caporalisme agraire* (militarized agriculture, an attempt, especially in the North, to reimpose a slavery-like system to maintain plantation exports), former slaves drifted into the mountains. They squatted on government land and practiced subsistence agriculture (with ancillary production of coffee and other market crops for sale in the cash economy). The substantial social, political, and cultural gulf between urban and rural Haiti has only increased in the twentieth century as economic powers formerly exercised by the provincial capitals were centralized in Port-au-Prince. Because of its isolation from the rest of Haiti and its power, the capital is often called the "Republic of Port-au-Prince."

The basic class contradiction in Haiti was complicated by the exclusion of the black landowning elite—along with the masses—from political power on the basis of color. In response, the black elite manipulated the color question to establish strategic alliances throughout the nineteenth century with peasants against the politically entrenched mulatto elite. What resulted was a complex manipulation of the *question de couleur* to obtain and maintain access to the Haitian state. In the 1880s, this contest became embodied in the two political parties: the Parti Liberal and the Parti National. The Liberals represented the mulatto position and advocated "power to the most capable," while the National Party was a predominantly black movement operating under the slogan "the greatest good to the greatest number."[8] This prototype of race-based political affiliation leads to much more sophisticated use of racial identity politics following the American occupation of Haiti in 1915, and this will be covered in Chapter 2.

I have referred to the cultural gulf between the classes, and I should elaborate on this before proceeding. Haiti is (arguably) a diglossic country. The elite and educated middle class speak French in more formal and official contexts and use Creole widely for informal discourse (jokes, insults, and in friendly or familial contexts). Haitian peasants and the urban proletariat, on the other hand, are typically monolingual Creole speakers and are predominantly illiterate. In addition, the Creole spoken in Port-au-Prince is quite distinct from remote country Creole, called *Kreyòl rèd* (hard Creole). In terms of religious practice, the lower classes are far more likely to serve the Afro-Haitian *lwa* (deities) in a complex of religious practices and beliefs sometimes called Vodou (either solely or in some combination with Catholicism), while the upper classes are predominantly Catholic and Protestant. Perhaps most important, the cultural antennae of the urban upper classes have always been pointed at Paris (and more recently the United States). Institutions such as the Catholic church, the government, schools, and so forth have always been self-consciously French in orientation, a neocolonial pattern not reproduced in the countryside, where Afro-Haitian social and cultural forms are stronger.

Haitians satirize the disproportionate importance of the state in Haiti with a proverb, *Apre Bondyè, se leta* (After God, the state). In classical Marxist political economy, the capitalist state was viewed as an arm of the bourgeoisie, a means of protecting class domination. But in many postcolonial nations, the state assumed a more independent and central function. For example, in Haiti, control of the state has always conferred the right to amass wealth through a monopoly over coffee and tobacco exports. It also conferred the right to distribute spoils—especially army and government jobs—to one's extended family, friends, and supporters. The state has typically answered to a small fraction of the population while siphoning customs receipts and taxes from the peasantry, returning little of value to the public in the form of infrastructure or services. Because of this, Haitian government has been characterized by analysts with such terms as "kleptocracy," "predatory state," and "parasitic state." [9]

Most poor Haitians have regarded politics as a game played for personal gain (and at the nation's expense) by a small group in Port-au-Prince dubbed the *poli-ti-kay* (a pun that phonetically substitutes Creole words meaning "little house" for part of the word "political"). Cynicism about politics is nearly universal among the poorer classes, as is evident in this short Vodou song text: *Dèyè do m pa gen je, politik se lizay o* (I don't have eyes behind my back, politics is just deceit), for which a singer explained that "doing" *politik* was equivalent to fooling someone. [10] One Haitian proverb recognizes that political squabbles among the *poli-ti-kay* can be fierce: *Lè de gwo nèg ap regle zafè yo, piti rale kò w* (When two big shots are settling their affairs, little folks get out of the way!). Political folksinger Manno Charlemagne treated the exclusion of the poor from politics in his song "Zanj" (Spirit/Angel):

La politique ç'est pour les anges	**Politics is for the spirits**
Ç'est pour les gens qui ont un nom	**It's for people who have [well-known] names**
Et ç'est pour la grande société.	**And for High Society.** [11]

I am of the opinion that the urban elite never achieved anything like hegemony in rural Haiti. While Haitian peasants have strategically adapted to the monopoly of the elite on affairs of state, there is no solid research to show that they accepted an ideology that justified domination (on the basis of elite superiority) or the "naturalization" of their subordination. To the contrary, there is ample testimony in informal discourse (especially proverbs, peasant songs, and folktales) that reveals a sophisticated class analysis and an ironic and playful commentary on the rationales and mechanisms of their subordination. The following are all very well-known proverbs (often showing up in musical texts) among Haiti's peasants: *Malere toujou bouke, lelit toujou nan vakans* (The poor are always broke, the rich are always on vacation); *Gwo nèg se leta* (The big shot is the state); *Sa malere di pa janm gen valè—betiz gwo nèg se bon pawòl* (What the poor say never has value—a big shot's nonsense is considered wisdom); *Fèzèdnat la fè nat, men se li k domi atè* (The mat maker makes the mat, but he ends up sleeping on the ground); *Pale fwanse pa lespri* (Speaking French doesn't make you smart). This list could go on. Many proverbs transform class relations into relations between animals, such as *Bourik travay pou chwal galonen* (The donkey works so that the horse can run around), and often between animals with a predator-prey relationship: *Rayèt pa janm gen rezon devan poul-la* (The cockroach has no rights in front of the chicken).

Haitian proverbs also testify to the social construction of these relations of domination and to the possibilities for their reversal: *Lè mapou tonbe, kabrit manje fèy* (When the mapou tree falls, the goat eats its leaves); *Lè poul mare, ravèt fè l eksplikasyon* (When the chicken is tied up, the cockroach taunts/lectures her). These proverbs (like the title of this book, taken from a Boukman Eksperyans song) speak to the dreams of restitution among people who understand their own predicament and who live under normal circumstances in one or another form of accommodation or overt and covert resistance. The support that peasants and the poor have given to politicians espousing their cause (from Emperor Solomon in the nineteenth century to Daniel Fignolé, François Duvalier, or Jean-Bertrand Aristide), and the delight they have taken in goading or frightening the elite, testify to a spectacular failure of elite hegemony. Under normal circumstances, peasant accommodation to the power of the army and elite is dramatized through public deference that masks a private tally sheet of resentments: *Rayi chyen, di dan-l blanch* (Hate the dog, but say his teeth are white).[12]

The tally sheet of resentments may, however, be expressed in a range of tactics of *mawonaj* to which I alluded. As I have mentioned, *mawonaj* has been deeded to contemporary generations as a term for strategies and tactics of everyday resistance. Since the discussion I had with U.S. AID workers mentioned earlier, I have heard the term *mawonaj* used many times to refer to the unspectacular, but very patient and often-successful, tactics used by the politically and economically powerless in Haiti to carve out a space for autonomous existence and to undermine the strategies of those with power and money, be they the Haitian state, foreign aid donors, or employers. Leftist guerrillas fighting the dictatorship of François Duvalier in the 1960s used the term

People in Mountain (handwritten)

mawonaj interchangeably with guerrilla warfare. In response, Duvalier erected a statue to the "Unknown Maroon" to incorporate this symbol of resistance into the symbolics of his regime.

The long history of oppressions experienced by lower-class Haitians—slavery, colonialism, feudalism, racism, class oppression, authoritarianism and totalitarianism, the sexism experienced by Haitian women, imperialism, and neocolonialism—has been an incubator for slow hatching a culture of resistance. The Haitian version of the pan-African trickster tales, the stories of Bouki and Ti-Malis, celebrate just this kind of wily resistance of the dispossessed. Ti-Malis is a small, urban hustler and trickster figure who regularly outwits the larger and stronger Bouki, a dim-witted country peasant. As Harold Courlander wrote of the tales, "The prime conflict remains the smart against the stupid, and the small and weak against the large and powerful."[13]

The emphasis on the everyday tactics of resistance begins to dislodge the focus on music and power from the state-populace nexus to the relations of power in which daily interactions, situations, and contexts are submerged. The model of power in Haiti that emerges from many different types of informal discourse is a very spatial model. To say someone *gen dèyè* (has behind) is to imply that there is someone more powerful backing him or her up. There is a popular Haitian proverb that can mean many things in many different contexts: *Dèyè mòn, gen mòn* (Behind mountains are mountains), but one of its common meanings is that behind every person, there is someone more powerful. To have someone who can get things done for you, someone who is better placed or connected, is to have a *moun pa w* (literally, someone for you). In the absence of well-developed institutions regulating the public sphere, Haitians have practiced the politics of alliance, alignment, influence, and connections, linking themselves to more powerful people who are in turn linked to others, all the way to the president or one of his rivals. This is a spatial, radial vision of the distribution of power in society. Although I pay a great deal of attention in this book to musics of resistance and contestation, I will argue that one of music's most important political functions is a status-quo-affirming one enacted through myriad musical rituals of alliance and obeisance.

In Haitian electoral politics, political parties coalesce around charismatic leaders, and these parties serve as the vehicles for their own political interests, almost never institutionalizing their appeal along broad interest-group lines. Instead, parties remain closely tied to their

founders' characters, personalities, and political fortunes. This pattern
is a product of both the radial nature of politics and a pervasive social divisiveness.

From the internecine struggles among the *poli-ti-kay* for control of
the state, to the polemics that motivate the competition between commercial musical ensembles, to the fierce struggles of territorial *rara*
bands, Haitian social life is steeped in divisiveness. This deeply rooted
habitus is a matter of great concern and discussion among Haitians,
and it has emerged as a topic in Haitianist academic critiques. A Haitian proverb traces this pattern to the slave trade and to the practice
of selling one's compatriots into slavery, *Depi nan Ginen, nèg rayi nèg*
(Ever since Africa, blacks have hated blacks). In an investigation of
language conflicts among Haitian immigrants in New York, Susan Buchanan employed a Haitian expression, *krab nan panye* (crabs in a basket), that Haitians themselves use to describe status-seeking factionalism: "Everyone struggles to reach the top of the basket, but the struggle
ensures that no one reaches the top; in other words, people are competing to remain equal. This pattern unfolds in Haitians' accusations
that *tout moun vle chèf* (everyone wants to be boss). . . . Groups split
over the issue of leadership as individuals break away from established
groups to expound their own philosophies and ideas."[14]

Divisiveness is especially intense in part because Haiti has been
trapped in a spiral of diminishing resources, but cultural habitus fa-
vors these kinds of interactions as well. The expression *Chyen ki gen
zo nan bouch li pa gen zanmi* (A dog with a bone in its mouth has no
friends) speaks to the jealousy and anger directed in peasant societies
at those who amass wealth and land and thus threaten the status quo
in a zero-sum game. Buchanan speaks of a *mentalite lakou*, a middle-
class inheritance from Haitian peasant culture, where one is taught to
trust only those of one's extended family (a *lakou* is a "yard," an extended residential unit). Karen McCarthy Brown, too, points to a sharp
contrast between the relations of cooperation and trust that characterize familial (and fictive familial) relations and those of suspicion and
competition that adhere to relations outside the family.[15]

Vodou songs are full of what Yih terms the "adversary" theme in
Vodou.[16] A close textual analysis of these songs reveals that many of
the adversaries, gossipers, malefactors, plotters, and hypocrites mentioned have local referents, residing with the protagonist of the song
in the same *lakou* or in nearby *lakou*-s. For example, I worked with
one traditional *rara* band in Carrefour du Fort on the *lakou* called Kay
Similien. The band, Briyant Solèy (Brilliant Sun) had been *kraze*-d

(broken up) for over a decade after a particularly bad run-in with a rival band, and their *sanba* sang this song in protest and commemoration,

Yo pran lan Briyant	They attacked Briyant Solèy
Sere l anba dlo	They hid it under water
Se sa m pa vle	I don't want this
Yo ban mwen kou-a	They gave me a blow
Kou-a fè mwen mal o	This made me ill
Malgre sa m anvi lape o	Despite all, I still want peace[17]

A nearby *rara* band, Modèle d'Haïti, based in Carrefour du Fort, had their own adversary song, which some members linked to the plots being hatched by enemies of President Aristide:

Konplo, wo yo fè konplo	A plot, they're hatching a plot
Konplo, wo yo fè konplo	A plot, they're hatching a plot
Danbala Wèdo, wo yo fè konplo	Danballah Wedo, they're hatching a plot
Wo yo fè konplo, sa ma di avè	They're hatching a plot, that's what I'll tell them[18]

As we will see in later chapters, various roots music groups of different epochs popularized *rara*-style songs in the same vein (e.g., Jazz des Jeunes's "Kote moun yo?" [Where are the people?], or Boukman Eksperyans's "Pwazon Rat" [Rat poison]. One of the many examples of popular songs constructed in the adversarial rhetorical style is André "Dadou" Pasquet's "Pa pale la" (Don't talk like that):

Pandan map fè efò	While I'm making an effort
Map chèche pen kotidyen	Searching for my daily bread
Medizan malpalan ape pale	The backbiting slanderers are talking
Yo gen je yo pa sa we	They have eyes but can't see
Yo gen zorèy yo pa tande	They have ears but can't hear
Pa pale la, pa pale la	Don't talk like that, don't talk like that[19]

The habitus of social division we have seen operating in political parties and in peasant society has had an incontestable impact on sociomusical organization. The most conspicuous products of this were the famous rivalries that propelled the commercial music industry during the Duvalier years that I cover in Chapters 3 and 4. Factionalism was also a part of the internal life of most bands. Schisms often occurred from internecine strife or competition, especially with the maturation of a subordinate band member who felt capable of leading his own group. Haitians describe this behavior with another proverb, *De kòk kalite pa rete nan menm baskou* (Two fighting cocks can't stay in the same yard). Conflicts over ownership of band names often spill over into public disputes and polemics, with more than one band claiming ownership of a name. These competitions have provided commercial music with heightened fan loyalties, drama at Carnival time, and topics for adversarial song lyrics.

The habitus of social division is a prominent feature on the landscape of Haitian power and politics. It has shaped musical praxis, but it is also a feature that *angaje* musicians—indeed all musicians concerned about the unity of progressive forces and the health of the Haitian political system—have combatted. Chapter 5 is full of calls by musicians for uprooting these historical patterns and for unifying progressive forces. To point to the politics of divisiveness, of connections, and of "big shot" patronage—as I do—is not to argue that these are permanent features of Haiti's sociocultural makeup nor to adopt a common cynicism regarding Haiti's history and its future, but rather to demonstrate the habitus with which efforts at democracy, unity of popular forces, and nation building have to contend.[20]

Sounds of Praise, Celebration, Derision, and Protest: A Grammar of Musicopolitical Signification

Haitian power relations and politics have given rise to a specific configuration of musical practices that intersect with power, show deference, subvert and resist it. What I will attempt to sketch in the following section is a descriptive grammar of these practices of musicopolitical signification.

Haiti has a fascinating history of praise and honorific music, much of which has been devoted to the various authoritarian figures who have ruled Haiti since independence. Michael Dash pointed to the tendency for Haitian poetry to degenerate into "court poetry and propaganda for the various presidents of Haiti," which he calls *"littérature commandée"* and *"littérature courtisane."* [21] During the colonial era, the drum regiments of the colonial army would salute distinguished persons and visitors with a type of music called a *serenad*, after which the musicians would be compensated with food, drink, or remuneration. This set of gestures comprising songs of praise and remuneration for musicians is found in the performance today of *ochan*. Whereas *serenad* only marginally survives, the practice of *ochan* is nearly ubiquitous in Haiti. The term *ochan* comes from a command used in military drumming, *"aux champs,"* meaning "to the fields," but *ochan* ended up as a performance designed to pay homage to patrons, dignitaries, and even *lwa* (spirits). The *ochan*—which is typically far more European in melody, rhythm, and text than most repertories in Haiti—negotiates relations of power. It symbolizes the contract between the powerless and the more powerful. When a group gathers to sing and play an *ochan* for a patron or a political figure, it is the power of the group they are trading for patronage and protection—the very audible power of numbers of people at least momentarily allied with the patron.[22]

Koudyay constitutes another event inherited from the colonial military that is used to reinforce relations of power through patronage and performance. The term *koudyay* comes from the French *coup de jaille*, a spontaneous bursting forth, and was used to label celebrations of military victories, coronations, and political successes. Characterized by mass exuberance, a *koudyay* in contemporary Haiti is a "spontaneous" celebration in the streets, usually sponsored by an important person, party, or institution when an atmosphere of delirious revelry is desired. Various festive elements (food, drink, music) are supplied by the patron, and the crowds supply the spirit. *Koudyay*-s are sponsored by those in power to show support for a leader on a tour, to intimidate opponents, to take people's minds off problems, to demonstrate electoral or grass-roots strength, and to solidify support. A bandleader summarized one of these strategies: "When there's a problem, the political problem for example, everybody is concerned with politics, but if the rulers or the head of the country would like to remove something from the consciousness of the people, they offer the people . . . a [*koudyay*]. It's the same thing with Carnival."[23]

In its desired ambience, a successful *koudyay* is indistinguishable from Carnival, and the full range of carnivalesque modes of behavior and enjoyment are accessible (see the section "Motion, Emotion, and Commotion" below). *Koudyay*-s have a powerful political effect in a country as poor as Haiti, where the masses are desperately in need of good times and a reason (and means) to celebrate. The problem for the sponsor or patron is that the alignments resulting from *koudyay* politics, in which the poor demonstrate temporary, contingent, participatory support in return for a festive release, are notoriously ephemeral.

Tenèb constitutes a small link in the chain connecting sound to power in Haiti. Deriving from the French word for shadows, *tenèb* designates a type of mass, anonymous protect in sound. I heard my first *tenèb* in downtown Port-au-Prince, where I was living in a house only a few blocks from the palace. At noon, the noise of car horns was the first noticeable sign. These were at first discrete rumbles emanating from one direction or another, but as it grew, the origins of the sounds were indeterminant. Car horns were joined by pedestrians clattering sticks along metal fences, by people blowing into conch shells and over bottles, by young boys banging on hubcaps, and by the sound of *kola* merchants drumming on their bottles with spoons. Anonymity was provided not by shadows but by mass participation. Because so many people were involved over such a distance and because no laws were being broken, the authorities could do nothing. *Tenèb* is predicated on the very simple and widespread correlation of sound with power. *Tenèb*-s are not music per se, although musical instruments are often used. Rather they constitute a collective performance of sound-as-power and a demonstration of the ability of popular forces to coordinate large numbers of people successfully. The same correlation of sound-as-power motivates the acoustic production of military parades, carnival bands, and bands competing on the basis of their sound systems. The ability to fill space with sound demonstrates one kind of power that can be harnessed for praise or protest.

Before discussing singers as social critics, I would like to look at Haitian attitudes about popular and commercial musicians in general. The profession of musician was belittled by the middle class, who saw musicians as *tafyatè*-s (drunkards) and *vakabon*-s (vagabonds). For the Haitian middle class, which has always had upwardly mobile aspirations, a choice to pursue a musical career was tantamount to professional suicide and was strongly resisted by parents. The stories that musicians tell of family attitudes are often quite similar: "I have to tell you that in Haiti, being a musician was never something that families could accept socially; it was really bad. They thought that playing music meant there was no future for you, because they know that you're a drinker and a womanizer. The first day that my father heard I was playing music, the guy was mad, mad, mad. I can remember my father's words, Why didn't you just tell me to buy you a conga instead of school books. Then I wouldn't have wasted my money and my time!'"[24]

The traditional view of musicians works against a view of them as purveyors of serious social consciousness: "It's not like the government is after them. Because a musician in Haiti is someone after women, after whiskey and rum. It's like the guy is nuts, he has nothing in his head. That's the way we musicians look. So a guy like this cannot be a politician, because politics is too serious. So nothing happen like this to musicians in Haiti."[25] Troubadour Coupé Cloué sang about this attitude in "Souvenirs d'enfance" (Memories of a childhood): "I recall when I was young / My parents didn't want me / Hanging out on the music scene / So anytime I had a gig to play / I had to sneak out the back door / But whenever I came home / They'd beat the hell out of me with a stick."[26]

For many decades, commercial singers in Haiti were classed as *chanteurs de charme* (singers of charm, romantic crooners) or *chanteurs de chocque* (singers of "shock," harder-edged, upbeat dance music), essentially received categories from Euro-American popular music. A third category consisted of singer-composers, often with guitars, who sang Haitian *mereng* in pan-Latin style, sometimes backed up by a small string-based trio or quartet. These singers and their music are called *twoubadou*-s (from *troubadour*) in Haiti. As I make clear in the next chapter, their music is a hybridization of Haitian *mereng* and Cuban *son*, but it is considered autochthonous to Haiti and very traditional. Troubadours are expected to communicate truthfully and with irony, humor, and a lot of strategic ambivalence and wordplay. They are appreciated (or forgiven) for their ribald and off-color lyrics, and such performers (Kandjo de Pradines, Ti-Paris, Moulin, Dodòf Legros, and others) have developed a reputation over generations as the consciences of the nation.

The role of the troubadour in popular music is parallel to that of the rural *sanba*-s and *simidò*-s, the song leaders of work brigades and *rara* parades, or their counterpart in Vodou ceremonies, the *oudjenikon*. These singer-composers are required to comment perceptively and often harshly on important people, current community events or scandals, and struggles of local (e.g., land tenure) or national significance. They expose sexual dalliances, report on and analyze plots and conspiracies, ridicule physical and character flaws, and censure those who profit excessively at their neighbors' expense.

Songs that censure, recriminate, criticize, and cast aspersions (usually indirectly) are called *chan pwen*, which literally means "point song," and singers are said to *voye pwen* (send a point) in song or simply *chante pwen* (sing a point). Like the *ochan*, it is a practice that spans sacred and secular contexts. Michel Laguerre characterizes the

chan pwen sung in Vodou ceremonies as "challenge" songs, "songs created to spell out ambiguous and conflicting situations between individuals, often those belonging to separate Vodou temples."[27] According to
Karen McCarthy Brown, "A *pwen* may consist of words, gestures, ritual objects, or herbs rubbed into a small cut in a person's skin. In
all cases, the point represents the condensation and appropriation of
spiritual powers."[28] Thus, one meaning of *pwen* is a class of "magical"
spells whose power works over distances. The art of *chan pwen*—
which can imply sending an "opinion" or point of view in the midst of
an argument or conflict, as well as sending the power of song against
someone else—is part of the traditional musicopolitical arsenal of
the musician.

The critique of the "point," whether sung or spoken, has parallels
in other African diasporic verbal traditions, such as the trading of
"dozens" in the United States, the "fatigue" that one Trinidadian calyp-
sonian may level at another, or the use of depreciatory and often obscene ritual chants in Cuban Santeria to provoke a deity to possess an
initiate when the deity or *oricha* has been reticent in appearing.[29] By
extension, the lengthy duels in song by leading Haitian commercial
musical groups (see Chatper 3) can be seen as a dialogue of *chan pwen*-
s, with each band prodded to improve upon the previous *chan pwen*
of which they were the intended target. Suzanne Comhaire-Sylvain
described the circulation of a *chan pwen* in Port-au-Prince: "In the
majority of cases, the person targeted is named, but one can also pro-
ceed by allusion when a direct attack is estimated to be dangerous: the
apparently harmless song flies from mouth to mouth because everyone
has *the* key to it. The song makes the rounds of the bals, the streets,
and enters into homes. It has achieved its goal."[30]

It is in possessing the semiotic power ("the key") to unlock the
meanings of the *pwen* that the audience takes such delight. Comhaire-
Sylvain also discussed a type of song which achieves its popular meanings not through the intent of the composer but through the interpretive creativity of the audience: "I made a study of one such example of
this genre: a Carnival song, seemingly obscene enough, had such success thanks to its captivating and simple melody that all the popular
orchestras adopted, even the common dance bands were playing the
melody and learned some variations on it. Schoochildren got hold of
it. In my neighborhood, kids seven or eight years old were using it as
a game song melody. . . . This song had taken on a seditious meaning
and [it was] prohibited by the police. A drunkard who was singing it
was thrown in prison."[31]

We will see many variations on this "excorporation" of meaning by the masses. This account by Comhaire-Sylvain testifies to a fact of life in urban Haiti that might seem odd in such a class-segregated society: Songs of "humble" origin (not just the meanings of the songs but the ways they mean) can circulate swiftly through many middle-class and even elite contexts. As a result, *voye pwen* (sending a point) has passed into popular musics through various mechanisms throughout the twentieth century, including the performance practice of troubadours, carnival (and the centrality of *voye pwen* as a centerpiece of carni-valesque critique), and various neotraditional movements in popular music.

There is a Haitian expression that cautions, *voye wòch, kache men* (Throw the rock, but hide the hand). The musical texts composed by *sanba*-s and *twoubadou*-s delight in the arts of indirect signifiation; in sending the point, but hiding the message. H. L. Gates convincingly links similar signifying practices in African-American oral literature to African rhetorical traditions such as the Signifying Monkey tales and to *oriki* (praise poetry) for the Yoruba / Fon trickster deity Esu-Elegbara. According to Roger D. Abrahams, signifying is, "the language of trickery, the set of words or gestures which arrives at 'direction through indirection.'"[32] Gates's argument is a cultural one in line with a history of scholarship on African retentions. An alternate, but not contradictory, line of reasoning connects indirect signification to a universe of guerrilla cultural strategies of historically powerless peoples, or to what James C. Scott calls the "infrapolitics of the power-less" and the "politics of disguise and anonymity."[33] A productive syn-thesis would suggest that the strategies of indirect signification in Hai-tian music are part of a family of "masked" practices of subordinated peoples all over the world, but in a particular form of the African dias-pora saturated with African cultural specificities and retentions.

The pleasure that a group takes in singing along with a *pwen* is not in receiving a critique in its entirety but in deciphering the critique and combining it with the unspoken, shared community knowledge of what has occurred. In other words, the purpose of the *pwen* is not to let people know that something has occurred, but to signify about the event, to engage in rhetorical tropes that expose the humor and the drama in the situation.[34] The intended target is often not named, but his or her identity is left vague or even misnamed. Euphemisms, double entendres, metaphors of various kinds, coded messages, hom-onymic puns, and allusions are all deployed to thicken the play of the text. These tropes of indirect signification increasingly make their way into urban popular music between the 1930s and the 1990s from their "home" in traditional rural and lower-class forms.

Many peasant and urban lower-class songs, especially (but not exclusively) those originating in carnival and *rara*, can be characterized by their incessant play with obscenity and vulgarity (*betiz*).[35] *Betiz* may deal with sex acts, especially intercourse or anal intercourse, or dwell playfully on male and female genitalia. The goal may be to humiliate a named or implied subject, but often the joy in public, collective transgressions of upper-class and Catholic speech norms is reward enough. Thus, *betiz*, which Elizabeth McAlister calls "sexualized popular laughter," can function much like a *pwen* or it can function more to signify the "liberated" or nonrepressed character of lower-class speech in carnivalesque contexts.[36] *Betiz* gets some of its political efficacy from the common tropes in Haiti by which relations of power are sexualized and gendered (with anal intercourse standing for a humiliating triumph of one over another). Like the act of *voye pwen*, *betiz* lyrics make their way into popular music through years of exposure at carnival, through the texts of *twoubadou* singers, and through the incorporation of peasant themes and rhetoric in roots music fusions from the 1940s on.

Betiz may be said to reside in a wide variety of Haitian traditional song forms, but it is most closely associated with the songs addressed to the family of deities known as the Gedes. The Gedes (including Bawon Samdi/Papa Gede, Grann Brijit, Gede Nibo, Bawon Lakwa, and others) are spirits who guard the secrets of death and the cemetery and also have a special relationship to crossroads. The dance of the Gedes is the highly sexual *banda*, with its accentuated rolling of the pelvis, and the Gedes have a privileged position from which to interject humor and sexuality into all of their interactions. *Betiz* then is the proper realm of the Gedes, the trickster deities (like the Ti-Malis trickster of Haitian folklore), and it too is a source of rhetorical power, related to the life-giving power of Papa Gede's sense of humor and sexual prowess.[37] Karen McCarthy Brown extends the Gedes' purview to the entire range of indirect signification: "Although Gede himself is rarely present during Haiti's popular Carnival season, Gede-style political commentary prevails. In a country that has known severe and almost constant political repression, Gede's ambiguous, many-layered humor is often the only safe avenue of protest."[38]

Peasants and the poor in Haiti habitually "poach" popular songs from the commercial music industry and reinterpret them to produce new texts and meanings. I will call this "excorporation," after Fiske, because it bears a relationship (in part, a relationship of opposition) to the more commonly understood process of incorporation covered below.[39] Excorporation signifies on the original text through parody or pastiche. This process is all the more effective when a powerful emblematic symbol such as a national anthem is excorporated and parodied. Excorporation constitutes the movement of a product of expressive culture in social space, being claimed by a social group subordinated to the group (and system) that produced it originally. Much movement of expressive culture in social space is metaphorically upward (in class terms) rather than downward, with middle-class musicians in the commercial music industry incorporating peasant and working class musical expressions and gestures (rhythms, song texts, melodic contours, proverbs, signifying tropes, stylistic devices, instruments, vocal qualities, compositional ideas, etc.) into commercial music. This is a persistent theme in my account of Haitian music from the 1920s onward. Although the ideological rationales for such incorporation vary over time (and by artist), in nearly every case the artists draw on the sedimented meanings and associations of traditional music to resist some form of perceived oppression. Traditions are constantly being reinterpreted and juxtaposed to the evils of the present system; what results is a traditionalism of resistance, capable of serving many ideological masters. The persistent incorporation of traditional music, especially music of Vodou, has been a vehicle for the movement of peasant signifying practices and musicopolitical vocabularies into commercial music. Every chapter of this book will cover at least one roots-oriented musical movement. As these movements incorporate Vodou, they variously strive to "ennoble" it, folklorize it, politicize it, or advocate it, but every one of these movements has deployed Vodou for its own purposes, and has reinterpreted Vodou in its own image.

Motion, Emotion, and Commotion: Audiences and the Politics of Pleasure

The powerful appeal of music—its engagement with human emotions—is the reason it serves effectively as an instrument of politics and a medium of power. Music creates strong associative memories and nostalgically evokes those memories. It is the accompaniment par excellence to courtship, and it helps make memorable collective experiences that move and profoundly affect their participants. My writings on Haitian popular music have always been motivated in part by my interest in understanding this potential of music to set human emotions in motion. I believe that Haitian popular music aesthetics are closely linked to those of neo-African traditional music and that both link proper performance to the desired emotional effect and their ability to "heat" the space of the event.[40]

Despite the importance of novelty in the commercial music industry, Haitian popular music serves as an essential connection with nostalgic sentiments, an indexical sign pointing to its times, and a key to unlocking pleasurable memories of the past. Owing to associations for the listener with places, people, and events, popular songs become repositories of cultural meaning apart from their content but dependent rather on their context. Audiences invest these musical commodities with associational value, and they can have political effect, especially when political regimes are invested with nostalgic appeal. The Haitian saying *Lane pase toujou pi bon* (Last year was always better) testifies to a persuasive cultural fiction (or truth) that Haitian history records a continuous decline in quality of life. Some long for the idyllic bourgeois life during Ayiti Toma (an ideal of life before the twentieth century), others look to the *bèl epòk* (beautiful period) during the tourist booms after WWII. Still others remember the early Duvalier period with a nostalgia for strong-arm leadership. The musics associated with each of these periods can feed sentimental political nostalgia.

One of the ways that music's pleasures beguile is as the soundtrack of courtship. Consider the nomenclature for couples dancing. Cheek-to-cheek dancing is described as *tèt kole* (heads glued), but when bodies are pressed against each other, the dance might be described as *kole kole* (pasted together). If the hips are swaying into each other with a figure-eight motion, it may be termed *kole mabouya* (*mabouya*, the name of the largest lizard in Haiti, is used to describe an undulating hip sway, a gentle version of the movement associated with Gede's dance, the *banda*), and very sexually suggestive dancing with the hips locked together is called *ploge* (plugged). These dances, intimately coupled to the music's pulse, feel, sway, and groove, link music to sexuality and courtship.

One of the most critical roles of music in sacred and secular ritual is to produce a sense of collectivity within "virtual" time, outside the flow of time associated with day-to-day living. In John Blacking's words, "Music halts change temporarily by harnessing time through the non-utilitarian repetition of events."[41] The synchrony experienced by audience members at a Haitian concert, dance, carnival, or other events is largely based in the expectation of (and desire for) collective participation and for an alignment with an event that "heats things up."

Carnival and *koudyay* enthusiasm is described in terms such as *debòde* (overflowing, exuberant, furious), *anraje* (worked up, turned on, crazy, enraged), or the colorful *antyoutyout* (exuberant, excited). Carnival participants achieve these states in a progressive escalation of music and movement. Musicians try to *chofe* (heat) the crowd with exhortations to respond physically. Revelers are encouraged to *lage kò-w* (let go of yourself) and to *mete men nan lè* (put hands in the air). Haitian Carnival balances between a celebration and a *deblozay* (fracas, blow-up) in which images of disorder (*dezòd*), chaotic mess (*gagòt*), and chaotic sound (*tenten*) characterize an event in which the desired ambience teeters just short of chaos. Recalling the sense of the term *debòde* (to the brim), one friend used a Haitian proverb to describe carnival: *Pise krapo kab fè rivye desann* (The frog's piss is all that's needed to make the river overflow). This ambience conveys carnival's most important political meanings, which are formed in relation to the aforementioned struggle over individual and collective bodies. When a band has a crowd *anraje* or *antyoutyout*, it has achieved a certain kind of persuasive power. At this point, the crowd may join enthusiastically in a *pwen*, ridiculing the elite, the government, a prominent figure, or someone else in the limelight. Crude obscenties may abound, and carnival and *koudyay* songs may delight with anatomical references to penises, vaginas, clitorises, and buttocks.

To *lage kò* (let go) allows a reveler to disregard other bodies, to *lese frape* (let it hit); in other words, to collide with those around him- or herself and to career through the crowd without concern for health or safety. At the street level, violent modes of interaction are a natural outgrowth of *anraje* exuberance, *lese frape*, ritualized combat, competition, and polemic. Exuberant modes of carnivalesque enjoyment, and the centrality of obscenity and vulgarity, have always produced upper-class "moral panics," a conflict over carnival aesthetics that parallels the conflicts of taste mapped onto class by Bourdieu in which images of strength, dirt, and disorderly deportment mark the "natural body" of working-class tastes and the source of bourgeois and petite-bourgeois revulsion.

The goal of "heating up" a crowd is in accord with a pervasive Vodou outlook (among the lower classes at least). When carnival or *rara* bands practice before going on the road, they are said to "*balanse bann-nan*," literally, to balance the band. Karen McCarthy Brown has made an elegant effort to unpack the meanings of *balanse,* an act that she calls "Gede's art form."[42] To *balanse* can mean to weigh choices or it can mean to rock back and forth (as in a contredanse step). In Vodou, Brown asserts, to *balanse* "means to swing ritual objects from side to side or to hold them as you turn yourself around and around. Such balancing "heats up," or enlivens, the object. . . . In the language of Vodou, balancing involves using forces that contradict each other to *raise life energy.*"[43] Seen in this way, the practices of the carnival band or the attempts to "heat up" a dance crowd share an orientation—even a philosophy—that the proper function of sacred or secular ritual is to build life force. Every conversation that I have had with Haitian performers about event evaluation has linked the success of an event to the interaction between performers and audience, geared to actualizing deeply rooted, persistent structures of pleasure, feeling, and enjoyment: "Money don't make the band play good, people make the band play good. You have to come to please—not for business. When you come to please . . . things become *cho* [hot]."[44]

The Haitian Music Industry and the Institutional Structure of Music Production

The aesthetics of popular musical production, the pleasures of its consumption, and the ideological content of its texts all emerge in relation to the institutional structure of the music industry, and it would be a serious mistake indeed to consider the ideology of popular music apart from its material form. While I haven't attempted a full political economy of Haitian music in the confines of the present work, I do want to sketch a portrait of the industry, its peculiar local physiognomy, and its connections to global industries in order more properly to contextualize Haitian popular music.[45]

Local music systems have developed within the loosely interconnected system of globalized capitalism. The worldwide export from the developed capitalist countries of what Leslie Sklair calls the "culture-ideology of consumerism" has been "the fuel that powers the motor of global capitalism."[46] Various types of local and undercapitalized culture industries evolved in dependent relation to the global system; the Haitian commercial music industry provides a particularly vivid example of a culture industry in the periphery. In the early part of the century, Haiti's small elite, negligible middle class, and impoverished rural peasantry failed to inspire major investments in its recording industry, even during the American occupation. Trailing far behind the industrialized countries in access to recording technology, Haiti wasn't typical of the Caribbean or even of many developing regions. Recording projects began in India in 1902, and 14,000 records had been recorded for Gramophone in Asia and North Africa before 1910.[47] In Cuba, the first recordings were made soon after 1910, and by the mid-1920s, American and British companies had a substantial catalogue of Cuban recordings of such groups as Sexteto Habanero and the Septeto Nacional.

In 1937, German-Swiss immigrant Ricardo Widmaïer recorded Jazz Guignard at his Port-au-Prince radio station HH3W, pressing a small number of 78 rpm recordings as gifts for friends, but the recordings were never released commercially. Using a field cylinder recorder, anthropologist Harold Courlander preserved peasant folk and liturgical music from the 1930s until the 1950s and recorded a series of noncommercial albums for Folkways Records, including one of parlor *méringues* by the Duroseau family chamber group in 1951. In addition, a few exploratory recordings of artists like Auguste "Kandjo" de Pradines, Dodòf Legros, and Emerante de Pradines in the 1940s allowed Port-au-Prince department stores to stock a few local 78s along with their imported recordings, but none of these recordings were widely distributed in Haiti, and they can scarcely be considered to have constituted a local recording industry.

With the advent of magnetic tape in the early 1950s, recording costs plummeted, and Haitian entrepreneurs began to produce a respectable number of 78 rpm recordings. The Ensemble aux Calebasses, under Nemours Jean-Baptiste, recorded its first commercial release around 1956. Most of the recordings in the 1950s and 1960s, in the early days of bandleader Nemours Jean-Baptiste's *konpa-dirèk*, were done by Herby Widmaïer at Radio d'Haiti, the new station of his father, Ricardo. Joe Anson, Haiti's first record magnate, stocked the records in his shop on Avenue Jean-Jacques Dessalines, and they became the platform on which he built his Ibo Records label. After a falling out with Duvalier in the late 1950s, Anson moved to New York, giving the incipient music industry a transnational structure in its earliest years.

In the mid-1960s, Marc Duverger, a beauty parlor operator in New York City, decided to open a record store in Brooklyn for the Haitian expatriate market. He, like Joe Anson before him and producer Fred Paul and others after him, imported raw musical materials (tracks and mixes) from Haiti for pressing and distribution in the United States and exported them back to Haiti. Duverger remarked on the miniscule size of this market at the time: "It's too bad at the time there was not much money in Haitian music. Sometimes we sell 500 records, 1,000 records. This was not too many years ago! You could sell maybe 5,000, 6,000, maximum 10,000. The problem is clear: not too many people working in Haiti. I would fly [to Haiti] each time, do my recording, pay the studio, and come home."[48]

The underdevelopment of the Haitian music industry is partly a function of the dependent nature of the economy as a whole within the global political economy, but it also reflects peculiar features of Haitian capitalism. Much Haitian economic activity revolves around the import-export trade and *achte-revann* (buying goods and reselling them at a slight profit to others who turn around and do the same thing). These practices require minimum investment and produce a quick, if only incremental, return. Haitian music entrepreneurs have downplayed marketing, distribution, resource development, and capital reinvestment in the search for short-term gain. Thus, the political economy of record production was, and still is, dominated by strategies of risk reduction. Musicians complain that producers "don't push the music" (that they don't pay for sufficient time in the studios to produce a quality product and that they fail to promote and distribute albums widely). According to trumpeter Anderson Cameau, "These people, they see the music just like a grocery store business. They buy this, and they want to sell it and make one dollar or twenty-five cents on each record and that's it. Let's say we go to a producer, and he tells us he's going to give us $5,000 to make an album, and he pays for the recording, pressing, album cover, and put that album out. And after that, he doesn't owe you no money. Even if you sell 20,000 or one million, he doesn't care about you. Not even a gift or a pair of shoes!"[49]

In describing his dealings with producer Joe Anson, producer Fred Paul provided a window on the transactions among businesspeople in commercial music:

> I had the same customers that Anson had. At the time, Anson was play-ing tough. With this business, you can't distribute one record. You need to have a lot of things selling. Otherwise the guys will order from the other guy who has a lot of records, because it's better to make the *kou-paj* [major deal]. So I was selling Anson the records at let's say at $2, and he was selling me his at $2.50, but I had no choice . . . and one day I got to be—well, not a *gwo neg* [big shot], but I got a little bigger— and I came down with a big order, 1,000 records or so, two or three different numbers, and I told him: "I want to pay for your records at

the same price I sell you mine." He said no. I had already unloaded, and I loaded back up and I left. And two weeks later, Mrs. Anson called me, and we made arrangement! It wasn't easy, because I didn't have the money these people had.[50]

Many of the major producers started out with a store from which they developed their business. There are also many minor producers for whom the store is still the primary business and record production only a sideline. One often finds among store owners/music producers a mentality described by producer Jeff Wainwright as a *boutikyè* (shop owner) mentality,

> meaning that they have a boutique, and they make records to barter for other records and all kinds of other stuff. . . . You don't have a lot of companies that act like real labels, paying their bills and promoting their artists. They [Haitian producers] are always looking to stab you somewhere. If I ask them for money from my albums that they sold, there is nothing. So I have to wait. So basically my money is financing their project. When their project comes out, they're still not going to pay me. They're going to put me in a bind where I'll have to take a certain amount of their product and sell it to pay me back what they owe me. Four or five months go by and still no money. And I have to pay the artists. Until it changes, there will be a lot of debts and bad receivables and things like that.[51]

Haitian bands have traditionally recorded for a lump-sum fee, forsaking royalties. Some performers have come to regard the lump-sum fee as a hedge against exploitation, assuming that producers will underreport record sales anyway and that some will go bankrupt before paying their accounts. The lump-sum payment is clean and risk free, and yet it introduces a heightened alienation of the artists from the musical product. Whereas royalties imply a continuing ownership interest in intellectual and artistic product, the lump-sum system cuts the tie after the band leaves the studio.

The Haitian audience expects bands to produce one or two albums per year, often seasonally: one for *vakans* (summer vacation season, during which many bands tour the countryside) and the other for the Christmas and *kanaval* (carnival) season. Should a band fail to produce an album for a period of more than a year, audiences and the media typically question whether the band is "going down." The schedule of annual or semi-annual seasonal production, combined with the practice of selling albums to producers for flat fees, has encouraged among some musicians an assembly-line approach to music production, although this is certainly not unique in the world's commercial music (where it may be something closer to the rule).

Some Haitian bands formed their own production companies to produce, promote, manage, and keep books. These "vanity" labels have included: Shleu-Shleu Records, Tabou Combo Records and Tapes, Ti-Da Records (Magnum Band), Pas De Shah (Skah Shah), Superstar Records (D. P. Express) and Machiavel Productions (System Band). Although musicians achieve greater control of the production of their music, the problems of undercapitalization, spotty distribution, meager markets, expectations about number of productions, and lack of promotion were seldom redressed by this measure.

Until President Jean-Bertrand Aristide signed the Berne Convention in August of 1995, there were no grounds for enforcement of intellectual property rights in Haiti. Even with the Berne Convention in place, the experience in states like Thailand indicates that there is a large gulf between acceding to international conventions and enforcing them. Guitarist Robert Martino lamented, "There's no rights; there's no security. It's not like here in the States where you make a record and if the record is doing very good, you make money on it, or in France, where if your music is playing on the radio, you get paid for it. In Haiti, they don't pay you—shit, you have to pay them to play your music!"[52]

Haitian artists also lacked an organization representing their legal, economic, and creative interests. Most Haitian performers who sold records and toured in the French Antilles joined the Syndicat des Auteurs, Compositeurs, et Editeurs de Musique (SACEM) to reap the benefits in this portion of their market, and musicians initiated discussions with SACEM about extending SACEM's purview to Haiti. Haitian performers active in the United States increasingly register their songs with the American Society of Composers, Authors, and Publishers (ASCAP). The historic lack of copyright protection and enforcement in Haiti, and the rampant piracy that resulted, were always a disincentive to investing the time and money to attain something close to international standards of recording.

The informal or unofficial sector of the Haitian music industry—which includes piracy (unauthorized copying) and bootlegging (unauthorized recording)—dwarfs the legitimate industry in the insular market by a factor of perhaps four to one. Pirated and bootlegged tapes are available in stores and from street vendors in all municipalities of

Haiti at well below half the cost of long-playing records or compact discs: "There are some people who buy a record of the band; they record the songs on a cassette, and then they sell the cassette on the streets or in the stores. As for live recordings, anyone can come with their cassette machine, record the music we're playing, and then make a copy and sell it before the music is released on an album. There are no laws against this in Haiti."[53]

Many of the cassettes have handwritten covers and make no pretense at authorization or legitimacy. More recently, the ease of digital piracy has resulted in a rash of high-quality pirate compact discs for the diasporic and foreign markets which masquerade (and are sold) as legitimate recordings. Legitimate producers have never produced much in the way of cassettes for insular consumption, assuming that the cassette market is saturated with the cheap pirated versions. The pirate industry, then, is left as the only sector satisfying the large demand for cheap musical commodities under conditions of intense poverty.

Most Haitian music producers, then, fall into one of the four categories I've mentioned: pirates, *boutikyè* producers, vanity label producers, and the more professional domestic entrepreneurs. None owns production facilities; nearly all work with independent pressing plants in Canada or the United States. There are also few direct linkages to transnational music corporations. Such are the institutional, market, and political constraints faced by commercial musicians in Haitian music.

Responding to the conditions of the Haitian music industry, many musicians turned to external markets to survive and prosper, crossing over from geographically and demographically limited markets to more lucrative and deterritorialized ones. In a series of three articles (in 1993 and 1995), I charted how Haitian musicians have responded to three subsets of their market: diasporic, linguistic, that is, French and Creole, and global or world beat. The critical factor is that Haitian musicians see each of these markets as confronting them with peculiar marketing problems that place contradictory demands on performers. Musical commodities that are intended for wide circulation throughout these markets are often compromise texts; the musicians, along with their promoters, labels, and producers, have "read" the aesthetics of markets and have positioned their creations for success to the greatest extent possible given their resources, abilities, and creative sensibilities. The effort by musicians to cross over takes longer than is generally understood. The Ensemble Nemours Jean-Baptiste was already the most popular band in Haiti when they bragged openly on their album liner notes in the late 1950s of their appeal overseas: "Thus, this humor, this poetry, intelligently orchestrated, harmonized, gives to Haitian music its great originality. It is in hearing the Super Ensemble de Nemours Jean-Baptiste that the foreign connoisseur truly understands this. Nemours Jean-Baptiste, creator of the Compas Direct rhythm, has definitely launched Haitian music toward the conquest of the continents, because this rhythm . . . makes a sensation wherever it is heard, in the Americas as well as in Europe."[54]

In a song called *"Compas mondial"* (World beat), Nemours Jean-Baptiste wrote of the group's international markets:

Toupatou kontan pase	**Everywhere they're more than happy**
Yon sèl pawòl k yap pale	**They're talking about a single word**
Se konpa yo rekalme, Ayiti a letranje	**They ask for *konpa* in Haiti and abroad**
Sa son nesesite	**It's a necessity**
Se li tout moun admire	**It's what everyone admires**[55]

Over the years, the inability of Haitian bands to achieve lasting success in global markets has been ascribed to many factors: the unwillingness of Haitian producers to sign away their artists (stranding their artists in local markets because of a fear of losing control); artists' unwillingness to agree to the terms of the international labels owing to a special sensitivity to issues of exploitation, linguistic isolation (the comparatively small number of Creole speakers), prejudice against Haiti, and culture conflicts over contracts and monetary dealings. A member of the band Zèklè discussed a problem they had with a French label:

We were with Warner in France, but I realized that it was just a FISC [tax scheme] so they could have compensation for the next album they were making after ours. They just declare ours bankrupt, a loss, so the next one that comes doesn't pay taxes. They're just using it. They make the money that they spend on you by producing 10,000 albums. But this is not their interest. They want to make 400,000 of the next LP without paying taxes. A lot of little groups have been drained out because of this. Right now, they can't mess around with me because

I know the business too well. Automatically, you're not interesting [to them] anymore because you know too much. But that's the only way not to get swallowed up by the jaws, especially when you're coming from a little country like Haiti.[56]

Foreign validation is a recurrent theme in Haitian popular music, and Haitian commentary on this subject often implies that it is a matter of national honor and prestige that Haitian music compete favorably with musics of other developing nations in global markets.

Postscript: "Seductive Discords"

"The marimba band started a melody of strangely cloying and oppressive rhythm. A murmur ran round the room: "La Méringue!" The national dance of Haiti! Against a background of ponderous vibrations the tune sobbed through the smoky air in a monstrous abortion of the tango. It was a strange dance; it was more than a dance—it was a ritual performance, an ovation to love, the ultimate love symbolized in the pairs of bodies, male and female, so closely entwined as to be almost molten into one by the fierce heat of their desire. They swayed over the floor, flexing this way and that, eyes closed, mouths open, forgetting everything in the rapture of their embrace and the seductive discords of the music."[57] This description of a dance, from Richard A. Loederer's sensational travelogue *Voodoo Fire in Haiti*, reveals more of the author's prurient obsessions and repressions than it does of the event itself. "Marimba band" is a misnomer: It is likely that this was an ensemble of stringed instruments and percussion accompanied by a *malinba* (large box-like version of an instrument often dubbed an "African thumb piano"). Most disturbing are the qualifiers and metaphors the author employs: "strangely cloying and oppressive," "monstrous abortion of the tango," "seductive discords." These images of oversexed bodies and irrational encounters, of darkness, discord, and even death, are at the heart of generations of representations about Haiti by outsiders. These images derive from colonial accounts of African religions in the Western hemisphere, from colonial *ur*-texts such as Joseph Conrad's *Heart of Darkness*, from the panicked European rationalizations of Haiti's anticolonial (and antislavery) rebellion (c. 1804), and from the tales told about Haiti by generations of European and American colonists, travelers, missionaries, and tourists. These descriptions build up an intertextual solidity and begin to construct reality for those that follow. In 1937, Melville J. Herskovits wrote in the preface to his book, *Life in a Haitian Valley*, "Haiti has fared badly at the hands of its literary interpreters. Condescension and caricature have been called upon, especially in recent years, to provide a short cut to an understanding of the people and their institutions. . . . Haitian life has been told as a tale of mysterious forces in their most repellent aspects."[58]

I would be delighted to assure the spirit of Herskovits that the situation is radically different some sixty years later. However, the ability of these tropes to reproduce—even in sympathetic accounts—can be seen in this press release for an album by the Haitian band Rara Machine, based in New York City. This short description contains a virtual compendium of images of bodies out of control, using words such as *overpower, ecstasy, feverish, trance, irresistible, magic,* and so on: Band members "almost overpower the audience with their onstage energy, their ecstasy elevating to a feverish pitch as they seem to go into a trance. Listeners may not be able to stop dancing to the irresistible music of Rara Machine, but it won't be because of voodoo magic."[59]

One could fill many books with examples like these, and, indeed, Michael C. Dash has sampled and contextualized the American literature on Haiti in his insightful *Haiti and the United States: National Stereotypes and the Literary Imagination.* A similar effort to deconstruct American journalistic accounts of Haiti is to be found in Robert Lawless's *Haiti's Bad Press.*[60] During the second U.S. occupation of Haiti, 1994–96, U.S. tabloids carried stories of zombie soldiers, of satan's face rising over Haiti, and of Vodou curses on U.S. troops.

Harold Courlander, the dean of Haitian ethnographers, warned me at the start of my research in Haiti to steer clear of notorious "culture brokers," local specialists in shaping outsiders' impressions of Haiti. He had in mind the then-recent work of ethnobotanist Wade Davis, whose account of his research on zombies, *The Serpent and the Rainbow,* combined a heroic first-person narrative with controverted scientific evidence and with rather scanty ethnography (largely dependent on this type of culture broker) for a book that was adapted into a Hollywood horror movie by the director Wes Craven.[61]

During the period of the recent American occupation of Haiti, I had a stark reminder of the importance of words and of the role that they can play in shaping policy. A friend had sent an article of mine on Haitian Carnival to the pro-Aristide Haitian consul. The consul, thinking it might help explain carnival exuberance to the American military, apparently passed the article on to the American occupation forces. I confess that I experienced a few nervous moments imagining military strategists studying my article to plan security for the 1995 Carnival. There is no retreat from responsibility for one's words, especially on such a controversial topic as the crossroads of music and power.

"Living from Their Own Garden"
The Discourse of Authenticity

The U.S. occupation of Haiti (1915–34) accelerated the incorporation of Haiti into global commercial and cultural relations, introducing foreign musics such as American jazz and Cuban *son* to Haitian urban audiences. It also threw fuel on the fires of conflicts over class and race. In response, an emerging black middle class championed the culture and arts of Haiti's peasants, researching peasant culture through ethnology and popularizing it in literature, visual art (the "primitive" school), and music (Vodou-jazz). A succession of ideological currents (*indigènisme, noirisme, négritude*) challenged elite hegemony with nativist philosophies that later bore political fruit in the presidencies of Dumarsais Estimé and François Duvalier after World War II.

This chapter explores the contradictory musical consequences of the American occupation, including the popularization of jazz and Cuban musics (and their hybridization with Haitian *mereng*), and the production of a complex discourse over issues of class, color, nationalism, and authenticity that has conditioned Haitian popular music and culture to the present. The chapter closes with a case study of an event that represented the consolidation of the indigenous arts, the celebration of the bicentennial of Port-au-Prince under President Estimé.

"*Méringue* Opens the Ball, *Méringue* Closes the Ball"

In emerging Caribbean and Latin America nations of the late nineteenth and early twentieth centuries, local elites seized upon hybridized African-European musical genres and proclaimed them "national" musics. The national forms were an exercise in the symbolics of nationhood and a means of coming to terms with the multiracial character of the New World societies. After the 1804 revolution in Haiti, European figure dances (e.g., *contredanse*, lancers, and quadrille) and Kongo-influenced African recreational dances (e.g., *chica*, *banboula*, and *kalenda*) were hybridized into a couples dance called the *karabinyè* (after the Carabiniers rifle regiments in the Haitian army), a dance believed to have evolved into the *mereng* (*méringue*, in French).[1] The term *méringue*, a whipped egg and sugar pastry popular in eighteenth-century France, was adopted presumably because it captured the essence of the light, animated final section of the Haitian *kontradans*. The dance incorporated an emphasis on the gentle rolling of the hips seen in many Caribbean dances of Kongo provenience. In Haiti, this movement is sometimes called *gouyad* (verb *gouye*, from the French *grouiller*, to move or stir) or *mabouya*, the name of the largest lizard on the island. The Kongo influence was also revealed in the persistent rhythmic figure that structured the melodies of the *méringue:* a syncopated five-beat pattern (often spoken as "dak-ta-dak-ta-dak") borrowed from the *kata* (time line) for the Vodou rhythm *kongo* and the rhythm used for carnival and *rara* bands, *raboday*.[2]

Planters and colonialists from Santo Domingo, fleeing the upheavals and violence of the Haitian anticolonial rebellion, settled in Santiago, Cuba, or New Orleans on the North American continent, bringing with them the Haitian creolized *kontradans* (contredanse). In Cuba, the dance spread from the eastern part of the island to the entire colony, evolving over the nineteenth century into the *contradanza*, *danza*, and eventually the *danzón*. Cuban author and musical historian Alejo Carpentier explained, "The 'negros francesas' [Haitians] had also played a very important role in the formation of Cuban music . . . by bringing a fundamental rhythmic element that was slowly incorporated into many folkloric genres of the island: *el cinquillo*."[3] The rhythmic figure that Carpentier calls *cinquillo* is the same *kata* pattern discussed above, and it appears in all of the Cuban *contradanza* descendants: the Martinican *beguine*, the Dominican *merengue*, and later Haitian dance musics such as *konpa* and *kadans*. It is often heard in a two-part, asymmetric structure, with the second half equivalent to four quarter-note pulses.

The scholarly debate over the relationship of the *mereng* to the Dominican *merengue* has a great deal to do with the history of social tensions between the two countries which share the island of Hispaniola. Haitian music scholars and critics nearly universally consider the Dominican *merengue* an offspring of the *mereng* planted in Dominican cultural soil during the Haitian occupation of the Spanish-speaking eastern section of the island between 1822 and 1844. Nationalist and racist Dominicans shudder at the implication of Haitian influence on the country's most typical genre, and many reverse the arrow of transculturation, claiming only an Iberian (or even Native American) genealogy for the dance.[4] Bandleader Luís Alberti's denial is typical of Dominican perspectives on the subject, "I believe that our most popular dance rhythm, begging the pardon of some, has nothing to do with negro or African rhythms. The *merengue* appears to me to be closer to a mixture of Spanish influence with our peasant airs from the interior country, and the same could be said of its melodic features."[5]

In Haiti, the term *mereng* refers to many distinct musical forms with different class and geographic roots. The term is sometimes indiscriminantly applied to any song of peasant or proletarian origin in Haiti, and it still occasionally refers to a final section in some rural *kontradans*. In the urban areas, it developed as an elite parlor music and dance, called *méringue lente* or *méringue de salon* (slow or parlor *méringue*) or *méringue dansante* (dance *méringue*), and as a composed chamber or concert music. To Haitians of the "old school," these varieties of *mereng* offer a nostalgic bridge to "Haïti-Thomas" (Creole: Ayiti Toma), the Haiti of long ago, remembered as a period of graceful French colonial architecture, of bougainvillea and frangipani, and of August vacations by the sea or in the mountains. This is the type of *méringue* that is nostalgically glossed as *mereng byen balanse* (well-poised *méringue*).

Haitian music critic Georges Fidélia classified all Haitian music in the early twentieth century into two currents of *mereng*, representing Haiti's deeply divided class structure,

> The first current, of a truly satiric nature, was an effective means for the people (especially the lowest people who couldn't do it otherwise) to say with malice or at times brutality what was on their mind to those who kept them in misery. These works were almost all of political or social inspiration. The second current, composed nearly exclusively of (what is convenient to call) slow *méringues* or salon *méringues,* was the expression of the bourgeois society of the time. They would get together in the salon to listen to the piano. In the afternoon they had tea in the garden or on the veranda. This society was in the position back then to sing of the charms of the country, the joys of life and love, and all of the heady sweetness of tropical island idleness.[6]

The *méringue lente* was the only serious contender among Haiti's elite as a "national" music and dance form, and it was traditionally played as the last dance for elite soirees. The *mereng* quoted in the heading of this section has the following passage, testifying to the importance of the *méringue* in elite musical life,

Mereng ouvri bal	The *méringue* opens the ball
Mereng fenmen bal	The *méringue* closes the ball
San mereng nanpwen kanaval	Without the *méringue*, there is no carnival

Nineteenth-century art music composers, such as Michel Mauléart Monton, Occilius Jeanty, and his son Occide Jeanty (director of the Musique de Palais), following in the tradition of European romantic nationalist composers, incorporated Haiti's "folk" music into art music, composing *mereng* for *bals du salon* (salon dances), concerts, military *kò mizik* (military music corps), and municipal or school *fanfa* (fanfares or wind bands). *Kò mizik* and *fanfa* have, over the years, trained many of the best musicians in Haiti and have been responsible for generations of seasoned musicians who performed not only military and art music but dance music as well. In a *fanfa,* one typically finds brass instruments (trumpets, horns, and trombones), woodwinds (clarinets, flutes, and more recently saxophones), and percussion instruments such as the snare and bass drums. Regimental bands from all over Haiti traditionally spent half the year in the capital, a stay during which the musicians studied theory and technique.[7] The influence of the fanfares in Haitian popular music is one facet of a profound presence of militarism in Haitian life, a legacy of European colonialism, of military resistance to colonialism, and of the central role that the Haitian military has played in Haitian history and politics.

At the dawn of the American occupation, the better-off residents of Port-au-Prince partied at private balls as well as at public dances called *bastreng* or *douz edmi* (twelve and a half, the entrance fee for men, in centimes). The instrumental accompaniment for these events typically included either a piano or a small, French-inspired string orchestra called *òkès bastreng*, which comprised cello, bass, violin, clarinet and/or trombone. The repertoire included popular European couples and figure dances: mazurkas, polkas, waltzes, *lanciers* (lancers), *contredanses*, quadrilles, as well as *mereng*. Relatives of the *bastreng* ensemble could be found throughout the Caribbean region (e.g., the Cuban *charanga francesa* or the New Orleans Creole string orchestra).[8] Practices for the grand balls, called *piti siye pyè* (literally, little foot wipes), were held on Thursdays. Here, younger men and women of the elite learned the various popular dances to the accompaniment of a piano or accordion. As the cinema spread to Haiti, small theaters were opened that featured a variety of acts, including films, classical music, *mereng* performances, skits, readings, and other arts, and these were called *ciné-variétés* or *ciné-théâtres*. Urban popular culture for the elite and the incipient middle class in turn-of-the-century Haiti was cast very much in the image of European popular culture, with the addition of some local content (e.g., *méringues*).

"The Sounds of a Strange Band": Jazz and Cuban Music during the Occupation

The U.S. Marines invaded Haiti in July 1915 shortly after a mob cut up the body of Haiti's President Vilbrun Guillaume Sam. Public pronouncements from the United States cast the occupation as a "civilizing mission" to restore Haiti's political system after the revolving-door presidencies and political violence at the turn of the century. Using an inspired oxymoron, *Time* magazine later described how the Marines "landed at Port-au-Prince and began *forcibly soothing* everybody."[9] But the occupation had a more complex, hidden agenda. The United States wanted to solidify American domination of trade and finance, elbow the Germans out of Haitian affairs, and protect the sea lanes to the Panama Canal at the outset of World War I. To monopolize foreign trade quickly, the Americans floated a loan of $400 million to pay all of Haiti's debts to other countries (leaving Haiti owing only the United States). The occupation centralized Haiti's political and economic life in the capital city; created a powerful, combined army and police force called the Garde d'Haïti; quickened the pace of technological and infrastructural development in Haiti; and deepened Haiti's immersion in the global political economy.

Despite a veneer of local control, the American Marines took near absolute control of Haiti's government, armed forces, taxation, and administrative apparatus. They embarked on a massive public works program, eventually conscripting workers into *kòve* (work brigades). On the military front, the Marines sought to dismantle the *kako* brigades (northern peasant militias) that had overthrown a succession of governments in the preceding two decades. These same bands, led by Charlemagne Peralte, offered the Americans a taste of armed opposition in the years 1918–20. In 1920, Peralte was captured and executed, and his body was publicly crucified on a door by the Marines. For many Haitians, *kako* resistance and the American response had driven a wedge between American rhetoric and American action and called into question the motives of the invaders.

The occupation produced many overt cultural effects. American troops, along with elite Haitians returning from Paris, introduced urban Haiti to jazz, the Charleston, the fox-trot, and other novelties of the 1920s and 1930s. Although recordings could be purchased in the late 1920s in downtown Port-au-Prince at Mohr and Laurin's,[10] the Charleston craze was probably first introduced to Haiti by a group of bourgeois Haitian students nicknamed *"le tout Paris,"* who brought the dance back with them from school in Paris.[11] Among the musicians playing jazz in Paris was a handful of Haitian expatriates. The Paris-based group, Salnave and his band (Jazz de la Coupoule), led by saxophonist Bertin Dépestre Salnave, was the first Haitian-led group to be recorded.[12] Salnave had come to Paris in 1913 to study, as had many young boys of the Haitian elite. He pursued a degree in music at the Paris Conservatory but took up a career as a professional musician at the onset of World War I. He joined Will Marion Cook's orchestra in London in 1919 and played in jazz bands with such African-American musicians as Sidney Bechet for the rest of his life, often directing his own groups. Salnave's career in Paris suggests that Haitian jazz was developing in both Port-au-Prince and in Paris.

Jazz records were imported from the United States and Paris and played in dance clubs. The American soldiers were persuasive advocates of new American dance musics and helped to popularize tunes such as "Saint Louis Blues" and "Baby Face." One Marine observed, "It was during my stay that American jazz began to sweep through Haiti as it has swept through so many countries. Such gems as 'Charley My Boy,' 'Yes Sir, She's My Baby,' and other masterpieces of Tin Pan Alley began to be heard on every hand. The Haitians took to them with vim to the detriment of their native music."[13]

Local jazz bands formed in Port-Au-Prince in the late 1920s to play for audiences that included members of the Haitian elite and middle class as well as soldiers in the American occupation force. The names of the new wave of Haitian bands demonstrated the influence of Afro-American dance music: Jazz de Louis Scott, Jazz Duvergé, Jazz Dugué, Jazz Hubert, Surprise-Jazz, Dynamique Jazz, Jazz Annulyse Cadet.[14]

Eventually the creolized form of the word jazz, *djaz,* came to signify any large dance band. The instrumentation of early Haitian *djaz* reveals influences from such American classic jazz bands as King Oliver's Creole Jazz Band and from the older syncopated dance bands with which James Europe toured throughout France. Europe's earlier group, the Memphis Students, had incorporated folk instruments such as the banjo, mandolin, and guitar into the dance orchestra along with the saxophone, formerly a symphonic novelty instrument. Jim Europe's World War I regimental band is credited with having stimulated the French appetite for black American syncopated dance music, and the Paris connection is the locus for many of these transcultural influences.

Café-restaurants and clubs such as the popular Sea-Side-Inn specialized in French-style cabarets and café concerts. The Sea-Side-Inn featured Jazz de Louis Scott on Saturday evenings in addition to recorded fare played on phonographs. The Café Latino, where the foxtrot and shimmy were the rage, was popular with a late-night party crowd and infamous for the easy liaisons it offered with Dominican prostitutes. Starting around 1923, the American presence encouraged the opening of bordellos along the waterfront and in some of the seedier neighborhoods. These establishments also featured lighter-skinned prostitutes from the Dominican Republic, who were called *fi fwontyè* or *fi enpote* (frontier girls or imported girls). Because the prostitutes used dancing as a means of securing clients (and because these halls catered to American soldiers), the bordellos came to be known as "dancings."[15]

With the fad for American jazz, the Haitian *mereng* declined as a staple of elite and middle-class dances through World War II, although *mereng* compositions were often mixed into the *djaz* repertory. Haiti's Europhile elite saw, of course, that African-American dance music was extremely popular in Paris, but its meaning in Haiti cannot be reduced to simple mimicry. During the occupation, Haitian intellectuals encountered intellectual and expressive currents in U.S. black culture linked to the Harlem Renaissance movement. The writings of Langston Hughes, Countee Cullen, and others and the political movement of Marcus Garvey were all discussed by Haitian nationalists at the dawn of the *indigène* movement. "Hot," or syncopated, dance music, with rhythmic similarities to the *mereng,* struck a responsive chord among urban Haitians. The power relations between the United States and Haiti during the occupation certainly helped to popularize American dance music, but Haitian partisans of jazz also seemed to be exploring an African-American musical kinship, a relationship between musics of "diasporic intimacy."[16]

The notion of aesthetic kinship could also be extended to Cuban dance musics, which rivaled jazz for popularity in many clubs in the later years of the occupation. The Cuban sound was popularized in Haiti through radio broadcasts from Cuba, through commercial recordings by bands such as Septeto Nacional and Trio Matamoros, through Haitian tourism to Havana (and to Paris where the habanera was popular), and through Haitian cane cutters (who worked Cuban sugar harvests).[17] The nomadic cane cutters brought back with them the guitar-based song tradition that mixed in Haiti with indigenous song traditions (including topical *mereng*) and became known as *twoubadou* (troubadour) music. Because the Cuban influences were introduced by all classes, from landless peasants to elite tourists, the penetration of Haitian culture by *twoubadou* music was both rapid and profound. An early description of a *twoubadou* group occurs in the poem "Bouge," by Carl Brouard, from 1928, in which he speaks of "a strange orchestra":

> Melancholy prostitutes danced the meringue,
> dreaming of a distant past . . . far away, and their
> shoes clicked on the worn floor
> Melancholy, they turned . . . turned
> as in a dream to the sounds of a strange band: guitar,
> guïro, triangle, drum.[18]

As the poem suggests, the typical instrumentation for these groups consisted of one or more guitars, a *tanbou* (barrel drum) played with the hands like a Cuban conga drum, a scraped or shaken idiophone (*graj*, or scraper, and often a large box-like lamellaphone (related to the Cuban *marimbula*) called a *malimba* or *maniba*. In Haiti, the *malinba* has three to five flat metal keys suspended over a sound hole in a wooden box, and it serves as the bass instrument in the ensemble. Banjos occasionally supplanted guitars. The names chosen by the Haitian groups—for example, Les Quatres Troubadours (c. 1930), Quarteto Jean Legros, or Trio Quisqueya—show their debt to the Cuban trios and quartets.

The degree to which local song traditions hybridized with the Cuban guitar tradition is not widely recognized in Haiti. Because their music elided easily with rural styles of the *mereng* and because they are associated with peasant and lower-class musicians, they are often thought to be *natif natal*, or native born. They are grouped together with other secular, rural ensembles under the rubric *mizik tipik* (typical, i.e., traditional music) or *mizik anba tonèl* (music played under the arbors). Perhaps the most poetic name for this type of music and ensemble is *mizik grenn siwèl* ("nougat nut" music).

In the early 1920s, Haitian president Louis Borno, the "client-president" installed by the U.S. occupation forces, offered a remodeled, bourgeois Carnival patterned on French and Italian models that was meant to subordinate and undermine a popular festivity that combined the spirit of medieval European Carnival with neo-African expressive culture. He banned weekly preparatory parades called *egzesis* (from military "exercises") and ordered that floats adorned with queens take part in the procession. He pressed for the *bann apye* (bands on foot) to become more orderly and thematized. In the opinion of the editors of the newspaper *L'Essor*, "Our Carnival is in full development. The evolution of Carnival is already far from an African stage. It promises something splendid in the years to come."[19] After 1925, businesses such as Guilbaud Tobacco Manufacturing sponsored *cha mardigra*-s (Mardi Gras floats, often allegorical in nature). Elite social clubs held Mardi Gras balls, typically concluding with a rendition of the traditional *mereng* "Bonswa danm, mwen kale dodo" (Goodnight, ladies, I'm going to bed). A king and queen were first elected in 1927 by a new entity, the Carnival Committee. This elite Carnival aimed for a graceful and delicate display (organized by the government and social elite and observed by the masses) with exclusive entertainment (balls) sponsored by the establishment *for* the establishment. Fast *méringues*, derived from the celebratory military music called *koudyay*, were the musical focus of Carnival.

Radio played a small role in popularizing various currents in Haitian and foreign music during the occupation. Haiti's first *téléphone sans fil* (wireless telephone, i.e., radio station) went on the air in October 1926 with a dedication by President Borno and a musical program featuring Musique de la Gendarmerie, pianist Ludovic Lamothe, violinist Valério Canez, and a choir from Saint-Joseph de Cluny.[20] Radio HHK, located in back of the Palais des Ministères facing the park called the Champs de Mars, was under the direct control of the U.S. Marines. Owing to a lack of receivers in the country, the occupation government provided public speakers, first on the Champs de Mars. Initial programming consisted of a single hour on Thursday evenings devoted to news and entertainment in both English and French and a

Saturday morning educational program in Creole. Among the most popular features of the broadcasts were the concerts by the Musique du Palais that occupied part of the Thursday broadcasts. Marine Captain John Craige directed the station and employed a leading violinist, Fabre Duroseau, as emcee (Duroseau also played solo when performers didn't show). In his memoirs, Craige wrote, "Where to get talent was a problem. I pressed the Gendarmerie Band into my service. Then I visited persons who were known to possess musical talent. This was a fascinating job for it allowed me to interview members of the old, aristocratic families of Port-au-Prince. . . . It was a theory of Mr. Borno's government that our broadcasting station should present the Haitian people to the outside world as being conventional, commonplace, civilized folks, just like Europeans or North Americans."[21]

Because of the restricted hours of the programming (expanded for a short while in 1931 and then cut back owing to lack of money) and because of the paucity of receivers in the country, radio remained a marginal influence in Haitian life until after the occupation. However, RCA did begin broadcasting to Haiti in 1932, and a second U.S. Marine–run station was turned over to the Haitian government at the end of the occupation (Radio HHH).

"The Call of the Conch Shell": Resistant Traditionalism

The American occupation of Haiti challenged Haitian nationalism, class relations, racial ideologies, and international relations, creating a crisis for Haiti's intelligentsia and its political class. American military might was overwhelming, and few saw any real hope in armed resistance. Many in the elite openly welcomed the opportunity to reestablish order in Haiti's political life. Yet the invasion marked the first loss of Haiti's political sovereignty since the hard-won revolution, and many intellectuals and nationalists preceived it as a crushing blow to national pride and dignity. A deeply entrenched racial habitus also received a blow from the American presence. The American Marines (all of whom were white) had little insight into Haiti's highly nuanced racial categories and status gradations. While promoting the interests and the standing of the *boujwazi milat*, the Americans nonetheless made it clear that they regarded all Haitians as blacks and as inferiors. Rumors spread that the selection of the Marines for the occupation had been slanted toward racist southerners in order to humiliate the

Haitians. American attitudes and behavior appeared crude and boor-
ish to members of the Haitian *milat* elite, who had not previously been
on the receiving end of racial prejudice, and who, in turn, disparag-
ingly contrasted "Anglo-Saxon materialism" to Haiti's "Latin refine-
ment." In its challenge to Haitian nationalism and racial ideologies,
the occupation helped to inspire a counterhegemonic reaction to the
foreign presence, the *indigène* movement, that emphasized African cultural heritage and racial authenticity. This movement would have far-
reaching cultural and political consequences for the nation.

Haiti's black middle class had grown in number, owing in part to
campaigns of the National Party in the late nineteenth century to secure administrative and professional jobs for blacks. By the early part
of the twentieth century they had emerged as a potent political and
intellectual force. Members of this class's intellectual vanguard articulated some of the first nationalist responses to the occupation; writers
and poets registered grief, shock, and outrage at foreign domination
of Haiti in a new *littérature de combat*, or what the French would later
call a *littérature engagée*.[22] One member of the black middle class, Jean
Price-Mars, sounded the initial call for cultural and political revitaliza-
tion. His series of lectures, published in 1920 as *La Vocation de l'élite*,
castigated the Haitian elite for collaborating with the American occupation and for forsaking their moral obligation to lead the nation.

Having inspired a generation of rebellious, anti-authoritarian intellectuals with his first work, Price-Mars gave a second set of lectures
addressing cultural issues in 1920, later published as *Ainsi parla l'oncle*
(So spoke the uncle).[23] Price-Mars saw the elite's cultural imitation of
France as a stale and bankrupt exercise, destined to inculcate a sense
of inferiority in Haitians. To replace the Haitian cultural dependence
on France, he advocated a *mouvement folklorique* and a new concept of
cultural authenticity rooted in Haitian peasant experience and African
roots. He encouraged research into Haitian folklore or ethnology so as
to elicit scientific data on peasant life and culture that could inspire a
nativist Haitian expressive culture and movement. *Indigènisme*, for
Price-Mars, was a means of cultural and political assertion in the face
of foreign occupation, racial prejudice, and class domination by a Europhile elite.

Paradoxically, Haitian *indigènisme* owed a deep debt to intellectual
currents in Europe and the United States. In the aftermath of World
War I, European intellectuals and artists embarked on a period of soul
searching and artistic ferment, characterized by a rejection of rational-

ism. Among the responses to the disaffection with modernity (in the wake of the "modern" war) was a passion for the "primitive" and exotic arts—on display in museums of natural history—and for new mechanisms to express internal reality (expressionism, surrealism, dadaism, etc.). The *indigènistes* were influenced by currents of European primitivism, which viewed "primitive" cultures as existing in a state of harmony with nature and free of the anxieties and repressions that accompany modern living. In Europe this was reflected in sponsorship of expensive ethnological expeditions to Africa, in a passion for American jazz, and in a fascination with the power of primitivism.[24] The European sciences of ethnology and anthropology were founded on a hunger to observe, record, and analyze cultures considered primitive. The other foreign contribution to the genesis of Haitian *indigènisme* was the literary, musical, and political movement among American blacks that became known as the Harlem Renaissance which also exploited folk motifs and themes that built a bridge to an African past.

In Haiti, intellectuals saw in their own "primitives" (i.e., the peasants) an absence of the identity crisis that was so palpable for black intellectuals in the African diaspora. A return to their roots, for these members of the middle class, was balm for the spiritual homelessness of the postcolonial experience. For them, as for some Europeans, Africa (and African elements in Haiti's peasant class) came to stand for a state of paradisiacal innocence, fellowship, and spiritual harmony. Such Haitian *indigèniste* writers as Carl Brouard and Jacques Roumain celebrated the Haitian landscape, romanticized the mystic ecstasy and communion of Vodou ceremonies, ennobled the peasant, sprinkled their French-language texts with Creole, and expressed a mystical identification with Africa. In Brouard's poem "Nostalgie" (1927), he wrote, "Drum, when you resound, my soul screams toward Africa."[25] Oddly, the *indigène* writers at first seem fully to adopt the European construction of Africa (and by analogy, Haitian peasants) as "savage," reveling in this "savagery" as an antidote to European manners and mores. Their celebration of Africa was not a celebration of the highly civilized and culturally sophisticated African societies, but rather a rejection of civilization altogether through a myth of African primitivism.

It is interesting to note how often elements of Haitian traditional music show up in the *indigène* poetry. Whereas poetry and writing in general were tainted by their obvious debt to European high art, Haiti's peasant musics were considered pristine examples of African retentions. *Indigène* writers sought to write poetry with all the un-self-conscious Africanness of Haitian music. Poet Normil Sylvain wrote of poetry, "It is the sound of the drums announcing the dance from one hillside to another, the call of the conch shell. . . . it is the vibrant, sensual rhythm of a meringue with wanton melancholy, which must be incorporated in our poetry."[26] The "call of the conch shell" described by Sylvain is one of the most enduring symbols of *mawonaj* in Haiti and elsewhere in the Caribbean. Escaped slaves in the colony of Santo Domingo blew on conch-shell trumpets to signal escapes, rebellions, and secret assemblies.

In 1927, writers Emil Roumer, Jacques Romain, Daniel Heurtelou, and Philippe Thoby-Marcelin founded the influential *Revue indigène*, which, although short-lived, became the house organ for the new movement, followed soon thereafter by *La Ronde*. Literary artists were clearly in the forefront of *indigènisme* (it wasn't until after World War II that popular musicians, choreographers, and painters made an equivalent contribution), and the movement gradually raised the political consciousness of the middle class. Even the elite grew increasingly resentful of the often racist treatment of mulattos by white American soldiers (as early as 1918 they prohibited American membership in the exclusive Cercle Bellevue in response to the banning of Haitians from the American Club at Turgeau). By the end of the occupation, many of the tenets of the *indigène* movement had been broadly disseminated throughout the highly stratified urban population. Thus, the American occupation, which gave the traditional mulatto elite short-term economic and political advantage, had the long-term consequence of establishing the dominance of a new middle-class Africanist ideology. The emergent ideology of *indigènisme* contested the cultural and political hegemony of the *boujwazi milat* and struggled over the symbolic content of collective representations.

The *indigène* movement's concept of authenticity was implicitly a spatial model, positing a neo-African, sacred, rural peasant tradition at the center (this center imagined occasionally as a *poto mitan*, or center post, in a Vodou temple, a conduit for visits by the *lwa* to the world of the living) and secular, foreign, urban elite spaces at the margins. The ruling class in Haiti, more European in phenotype and in culture, was portrayed by the movement as less authentic, less representative of Haiti as a whole, than the middle class and black elite. Music, literature, skin color, and political ideology were all arrayed along this continuum of authenticity. When Haitians speak of the centrality of Vodou to the meaning of being Haitian, they see peasant culture as an extension of the African past into the present. The drum as its center (in the music of the Vodou cult) becomes a synechdoche for Africa and the call of African heritage.

"Go Home to Your Mother's House": Musical Opposition to the Occupation

One of the most prominent critics of the occupation was the director of the Musique du Palais, Occide Jeanty. Because the Haitian Army was commanded by the Marines, this left Jeanty in the unenviable role of head of the principal musical ensemble of the occupation froces. As a result of his stance on the occupation, Jeanty was removed from the directorship by President Sudre Dartinguave (1915–22) and took up the direction of the *orphéon* (male choir) of the coastal town pf Petit-Goâve. Jeanty, however, was a friend of politician Louis Borno, and after Borno assumed the presidency in 1922, Jenaty was placed once again at the head of the Musique du Palais, where he remained until the end of the occupation (1934). While continuing to play at official functions, Jeanty made use of the public concerts of the orchestra to rouse patriotic sentiment. A friend of Jeanty, port Jean Brierre, was interviewed by Michael Largey in 1988 and reminisced about Jeanty's political influence: "He was a leader in the resistance to the American occupation. Each time Occide Jeanty directed the musical ensemble from the National Palace, he had this piece . . . '1804' [the year Haitians secured their independence]. The crowd was electrified! When Occide played '1804,' the crowd was extraordinary. The crowd demonstrated so much that they forbade the performance of '1804'. . . . Occide didn't have the right to perform it on Sunday nights on the Champs de Mars [the public square in front of the National Palace]."[27]

In 1926, the police were forced to disperse a demonstration by a masked carnival entourage protesting the reelection of the collaborationist president Louis Borno. In 1928, the elite social club Cercle Bellevue canceled its carnival grand ball to protest the incarceration of some of its members by the American-led Garde d'Haïti soon after the club was shut down by order of the Minister of the Interior. In response to the worsening climate for the government, members of the elite who still supported the government (and the occupation) organized the Parti Progressiste (1925) and a social club called the Union Club, which opened in 1927 with a sumptuous ball in honor of the Bornos.[28]

Vocal protest in the expressive arts became more militant in the late 1920s. Suzanne Comhaire-Sylvain noted a popular song with the refrain *"Jolibwa nan prizon"* (Jolibois in prison), about a nationalist leader named Jolibois who had been jailed frequently during the occupation.[29] One of the most popular of the anti-American songs of the period was a *mereng* called "Angelique O," ostensibly about an unhappy courtship:

Ale kay manman-ou	Go home to your mother's house
Ale kay manman-ou	Go home to your mother's house
Ale kay manman cherie	Go home to your mother's house my dear
Pa vin ban m dezagreman	Don't come here to bother me
Tifi pa konn lave pase	The girl doesn't know how to wash or iron
Ale kay manman-ou	Go home to your mother's house
Andjelik O Andjelik O	Angelique O, Angelique O,
Ale kay manman-ou	Go home to your mother's house

By one account, the song was named after Angelique Cole, the wife of Colonel Cole, a U.S. Marine commander, but the *pwen* was clearly directed toward the entire American presence in Haiti.[30] It is a perfect example of *pwen* that disguises the intended subject through personification. "Angelique O" was the favorite song at Carnivals in the late 1920s, as a growing anti-Americanism confronted the foreign presence in Haiti. Because of their militaristic social organization, their size, and their enthusiasm, carnival bands can easily metamorphose into militant, political *manifestasyons* (demonstrations) in times of political crisis. One observer of the Carnival in Aux Cayes commented that for years the carnival groups had been becoming less numerous and more restrained, but that in 1929, "they were again very strong. The great resistance to the foreign occupation was expanding from day to day. The struggle was alive, harsh; and these bands constituted, then, the reservoir and the force of nationalism devoted to the service of the liberation of the national territory."[31]

A popular anti-American strike by students at the Damien Agriculture College and a protest over the alcohol and tobacco tax that led to a massacre of peasant protesters by U.S. Marines brought tempers to a head. President Hoover sent a fact-finding mission in early 1930 (the Forbes Commission), which had the misfortune to arrive just before Carnival. To protest the American mission, the carnival queen returned her crown to the commission and a general boycott of Carnival kept the crowds at bay. In place of the Carnival *kòtèj* (parade), a patriotic *manifestasyon* led by a women's organization implored God to enlighten the Americans.[32]

Like Musique du Palais director Occide Jeanty, singer Kandjo de Pradines (Candio in its French spelling) is remembered as an artist who opposed the occupation in its latter years. In his home city of Port-au-Prince and throughout the provinces, he was in great demand as a singer before, during, and after the occupation in clubs, at private parties, in theaters, and eventually at outdoor rallies. Kandjo was born in Paris of French parents, but he came to Haiti as a child after a bout with polio that left him crippled for life. His schooling included a strong course of music, and he became proficient on piano, guitar, and mandolin, among other instruments. At the age of fourteen, he was carried on his back to a Vodou ceremony, where the initiates were reportedly highly taken with the crippled French youngster. His condition was serious at the time, and he had no control over the left part of his body. After his experience, he wrote the Vodou-inspired song "Erzulie" about the well-known Haitian female deity of the same name, and this song became one of his most beloved compositions and a part of the Haitian folkloric repertory up to the present. By the age of nineteen, Kandjo had devoted himself to a musical career, and he was chosen to sing the premiere of the national anthem, "La Dessalinienne," in 1903.[33] His daughter, Emerante, discussed his evolution as a topical singer.

He wrote lots of different songs: political songs, satire songs, *merengues*, love songs. . . . After a while he was called to do songs for people like the churches, like when they thought there was too much deprivation on the people, they would call him to compose a song. He used to take whatever was going on in the country, he had a song about it. He wrote a very critical song about the nuns, because there was the first Haitian nun in Haiti, and, just because it had never happened before, they thought that something was wrong with her. She had a hard time, and everything went so bad that she had to leave. My father related the whole story to the public in a song with 26 verses. That song get into the town. Because when he did a song during the week—and he had a regular concert every Thursday—when the song went into the public, it was impossible [for the church] to bear it, to live with it, and so they called the president. That was in 1906. Then the president (Nord Alexis) said, "I cannot say anything about that. I would like to

call him and have him sing me the song 'cause I don't know it myself."
My father sing the song with the 25 verse (at that time), and after he
left the palace he added another verse![34]

The song about the nuns was called "Pa fè m sa" (Don't do me like
that) and contained the following couplets:

Tou sa yo pale	All that they say
Bon pou demaske	Is helpful for unmasking
Yo pase lan Bondyè	They use the name of God
pou ap fè mechanste	To do evil

Kandjo, like many urban, educated Haitians, had a mixed reaction
at first to the occupation, believing that outside intervention was necessary to get Haiti past the internecine strife of the early decades of
the century, and his songs of the early occupation period are reflective
and philosophical. For example, he sang,

Pouki? Paske nou gen tròp defo	Why? Because we have too many faults
E ke kote gen vyann toujou gen zò	And where there's meat, there are always bones
Fòs movèz fwa rann n egare	The pressure of these bad times dumbfounds us
Nou broule twòp tou sann adore	We burn too much, all saints adored
Se konsekans la nap apiye l	As a consequence, we're backing it
E se la tout verite la ye	And there it is, that's the truth
Eske sa bèl eske sa tris	Whether it's beautiful, or whether it's sad
Eske pou nou se yon soufis	Whether for us it's enough
Reflechi byen pou m di m sa l ye	Reflect well because I tell it as it is
Pita na vin di m	Later you'll come tell me
Si m mal obsève	If I observed badly or not[35]

Kandjo advocated building self-reliance as a way of becoming independent of the need for foreign control:

Blan pa vini pou li plante anyen	The foreigner doesn't come to plant anything
Se nou k pou gran manchèt a kou	It's up to us to sling a machete around our neck
Pou nou bat latè, chase lamisè	To beat the ground, to chase away misery
Plante lavi si nou vle jwenn lavi	To plant life if we want to pursue life[36]

Whatever he thought of the occupation at its start, Kandjo became disillusioned with American abuses, in particular with the exploitive economic treaty and with harsh American tactics during the strike at the agronomy school and in other crises. Perhaps his most important legacy, then, was the songs that emerged in the campaign to unseat President Borno, in which he joined forces with the anti-occupation movement. His topical and critical *méringue* "Senateur King," praised an American senator who had opposed the financial treaty imposed on Haiti (this song was banned by Borno's government). On many occasions the targets of Kandjo's barbs attempted to intimidate him, including one time in which he had to crawl over an embassy wall to obtain protection. Emerante de Pradines Morse related a story about her father's audience protecting him from danger: "You have to see the reaction of the public. If the public is for a singer, there is nothing the government can do, you know, about that. I saw that with my father when he make that . . . I think the song was "Pedale." [She sings:] "Pedale o pedale, Nou vle repedale, Men fò kapab ale" (Pedal, o pedal, We want to pedal again, But you have to be able to go). The police got a call from the palace, they invade the theater, and so the people come and brought him to his house. That's a Haitian trait among the lower class of people: If they are yours [for you], you can trust that there is nothing going to happen to you."[37]

"Ou pap repedale" (You're not pedaling again) parodied his earlier "Nap pedale" (We're pedaling), and in it he included a satiric chorus (laced with English words) that was a popular sing-along with his audiences:

Avè lafwa, lèsperans, le travay e linyon	With faith, hope, work, and unity
Aba lokipasyon	Down with the occupation
Yes, sirs, ponpe, sote	Yes, sirs, hop and jump
Ayiti restera nasyon	Haiti will remain a nation[38]

Kandjo fashioned a career that mixed bitter social satire ("Pa fè m sa"), patriotism, and tender local themes ("Erzulie") on a musical platform that combined French chanson, Haitian *mereng*, and Haitian traditional-style melodies. With his knack for capturing popular sentiments, he won for himself a devoted audience that spanned urban and rural environments (he sang at many rural *fèt chanpèts*) and all social classes. Although the term *twoubadou* was used at the time only for itinerant singers and small bands that played for hand outs, it later came to be applied to the type of populist singer of topical *merengs* personified by Kandjo. French by birth, Kandjo largely created this archetype of the Haitian troubadour.

Kandjo joined anti-Borno demonstrations, leading the singing of "La Déssalinienne," "Angelique O," and his songs critical of the government and its American backers. After the Forbes Commission recommended that President Borno step down and that the United States phase out the occupation of Haiti ahead of schedule, Borno dutifully complied, and a six-month provisional presidency was followed by elections that installed a mulatto politician, Stenio Vincent, as president (1930).

President Vincent and the United States were clearly committed to a gradual "Haitianization" of the administration of the country and to a phaseout of the occupation. Vincent's ephemeral popularity stemmed from presiding over the early end of the occupation and from the measures he took to drive Middle Eastern merchants out of the retail businesses. In response, a *mereng*, "Merci Papa Vincent," was sung at Carnival, at military events, and at private balls and dances:

Ki moun ki bay kòmès en detay-la?	**Who gave us the retail merchant business?**
Se Pwèzidan Vensan!	**It's President Vincent!**
Annou rele, mesi, Pwèzidan Vensan	**We'll call out, "Thank you, President Vincent!"**

As Vincent's political fortunes declined, his opponents parodied the song by inserting new satirical questions in the question-and-answer structure, such as, "Who made my skin show through my worn out pants? It's President Vincent!"[39]

The popular character of Carnival expanded during the Vincent years, and the public was allowed a delirious celebration at their own "outdoor ball" at Vallière Market. The carnival orchestra Otofonik G. B. de Hiram Dorvilmé was admitted to the *kòtèj* (parade) starting in 1931. Otofonik's instrumentation included bongo, *tchatcha* (rattle), friction drum tambourine, and *manman tanbou* (mother drum). In the days before amplified carnival bands, groups such as this were referred to generically as *òtofonik*, a creolized version of the word *Orthophonic* on the old Victrola 78 rpm records, because the megaphones that the lead singers used resembled the horns from old phonograph players.[40] Over the years, some of these groups, such as Otofonik G. B. from Rue Neuf and Titato (Tic-Tac-Toe) from the neighborhood Belair, became carnival stars, attracting thousands of revelers to their entourage. Many carnival bands also used flutes or brass instruments, as the groups were closely patterned on military *fanfa*.

In 1934, the last year of the American occupation, the mayor of Port-au-Prince instituted a competition for best *mereng kanaval*, and the winner was composer Ludovic Lamothe with a song called "Nibo."[41] A newspaper article at the time praised the "unbridled joy" elicited by this composition, which was without a doubt heightened by anticipation of the departure of the American Marines: "The author, in an inspiration that one could call unbridled, appears truly to have expressed the *ohé! ohé!* [carnival refrain] soul of the reveling crowd. The rhythm is erotic and inclines, in the first measures, to the most frenetic joy. We repeat that this is not a personal opinion; rather it is supported by the delirium that this captivating composition achieved with the public on the evening of Mardi Gras. Everyone, old and young, from the most serious to the most careless, was tingling with excitement [*avaient des fourmis dans les jambes;* literally, had ants in their legs, used here to suggest a compulsion to dance]."[42]

On the final day of the occupation, the Garde d'Haïti, accustomed to marching to "Semper Fideles" and the "Halls of Montezuma," instead asked their musical corps to play "Angelique O" as the troops marched in front of 10,000 people. At the ceremony, the "Stars and Stripes" was followed by "La Déssalinienne," the new Haitian anthem, and Haiti was once more a sovereign nation.[43]

Music and Ideology after the Occupation

In 1935, Ricardo Widmaïer launched Radio HH3W, a private station that developed a reputation as a performers' hangout. Widmaïer made what is presumably the first recording of a Haitian band (in Haiti), Jazz Guignard (led by pianist François Guignard), at the station in 1937 or 1938. Jazz Guignard included Haitian *mereng*-s in their repertoire, and they recorded "Ti-Célia" and "Kole Kole." The station exposed many new artists, including banjo player Annulysse Cadet, who headed up the Jazz Annulyse Cadet, and Dodòf Legros, who was featured in the *twoubadou* group sponsored by the station called Trio HH3W.[44] Ricardo's son, Herby, recounted the following story about the trio:

> My father, who was owner and director of the station, then told the boys, "Listen. You're drinking all the time . . . why don't you form a trio? You're good, do something serious with it." They said they didn't have the money to buy guitars. So my father bought them guitars— brand new guitars—and said, "Why don't you call the group Trio HH3W [calls letters for the station]?" It was with Dodòf Legros, my friend who died a few years ago, Domelasse Philippe, and a third guy [Alexandre Legros]. Dodòf was a nice guy, and he used to sing well too. He composed some very interesting songs. He had a lot of humor and sex but just at the right level. He was never in bad taste. So my father bought them guitars, but they played for two or three weeks; then there was a fight or something, and they broke the guitars over somebody's head. But I think he bought them new ones. Then they were called Trio Haïti after that, but before that it was Trio HH3W.[45]

Legros's trio was in the classic Cuban mold, but both jazz bands and Cuban-style ensembles reigned in the years between the end of the occupation and the end of World War II. Popular jazz bands of the period included Jazz Guignard (aka Super Modern Jazz Guignard, c. 1936), Baby Blue Jazz (c. 1938–42), Jazz de Geffrard Cesvet (c. 1940), and Jazz Chancy (c. 1941).

Antalcidas O. Murat, who became the most important figure in the indigenous music movement, is represented here in his two earliest groups: Baby Blue Jazz and Jazz Chancy, in which he applied his *fanfa* training on the trumpet and honed his arranging skills. Jazz Chancy opened the new dance hall in Pétion-Ville, the Miraflorès, in February 1942, while the long-lived Jazz Guignard did the same with another "dancing" in Carrefour in 1944 called Cabane Tito.[46]

Cuban-style *sones*, boleros, rumbas, and *guarachas* (often with Creole texts) formed the bulk of the repertory for a profusion of new trios, quartets, quintets, and sextets that plied the clubs, hotels, theaters, and radio stations of Port-au-Prince and Pétion-Ville. In 1941, violinist Velério Canez, himself a member of the Jazz de Geffrard Cesvet, complained that "the true rhythm of the Haitian *mereng* is no longer in fashion these days, to our misfortune. . . . Every day we hear Haitian melodies which are executed to the rhythm of the *bolero-son* or the Cuban *rumba.*"[47] The growth in size and instrumentation in many of the Cuban-style groups of the period demonstrates the increasingly sophisticated emulation of Cuban prototypes; as with the following three groups:

El Quinteto Estudiantino Haitiano (1938)

Hermann Camille	clavier/leader
Yves Lerebours	piano
Gaston Madère	*malinba*
Roger Fareau	flute

El Sexteto Estudiantino Haitiano (1940)

Hermann Camille	clavier/leader
Yves Lerebours	piano
Gaston Madère	*malinba*
Maurice Morisset	battery
Ulysse Cabral	vocals
Dieuveuille Dugué	trumpet

Orchestre Les Gais Troubadours (1942, formerly Jazz Cabral)

Hermann Camille	saxophone/leader
Yves Lerebours	piano
Gaston Madère	bass
André Desrosiers	bongo
Maurice Morisset	battery
Henri Mollenthiel	saxophone
Murat Pierre	saxophone
Michel Desgrottes	trumpet
Dieuville Dugué	trumpet
Kesner Hall	trumpet
Joseph Trouillot	vocals
Ulysse Cabral	vocals

In 1943, the Gais Troubadours played for the opening of the new home of the nightclub Cabane Choucoune in Pétion-Ville, with President and Mrs. Lescot among the thousand or so in attendance. The name Choucoune was a tribute to the song of the same name by Oswald Durand. The club had opened in 1940, but moved to its spacious new building, designed on an Afro-Haitian traditional concept of a large circular space with a massive wood pole in the center supporting a conical, thatch-like ceiling. The Gais Troubadours were the most popular wartime band in Port-au-Prince, opening many of the cinema shows. Part of the inspiration for the orchestra's new name, increased size, and Cuban orientation was the appearance in Port-au-Prince in 1942 of the leading Cuban ensemble, Sonora Matancera. The next major Cuban band to visit Haiti was Siboney (with the dancer Anita Vasquez), which booked a long engagement at the celebrated Cabane Choucoune from December 1944 until Carnival 1945.[48] Other Cuban and Latin orchestras followed, including the renowned Xavier Cugat Orchestra.

The Cuban and jazz movements in Port-au-Prince's popular music scene were the schools in which a new generation of Haitian musicians "cut their teeth." Dodòf Legros went on to become one of Haiti's most beloved *twoubadou* composers and directed his own ensembles, including the Ensemble Ibo Lélé. Murat Pierre, Jean Legros, Michel Desgrottes, Joseph Trouillot, Ulysse Cabral, and others all directed their own orchestras, and Raymond Gaspard became the guitarist for Nemours Jean-Baptiste, the originator of the *konpa-dirèk*. Their musical evolution in a Cuban idiom helps to explain the continuing powerful influence of Latin American music in the period of the *indigène*, or Vodou-jazz, orchestras as well as later, in the period of the *konpa-dirèk* and *kadans ranpa*. The Cuban-style groups mixed instrumentation from the Cuban *charanga* orchestras, *conjuntos* (with their core piano and trumpet sound), and rural *son* groups. The vogue for Cuban music also resulted in the incorporation of boleros, *guarachas*, and rumbas into the Haitian repertory (even into some Vodou drumming); these three genres are known in Haiti as *bolewo*, *gwalatcha*, and Afro-Cubaine. The popularity of Dominican prostitutes in Haitian dance halls before and after World War II helped to solidify the popularity of Spanish-language music, such as the Cuban *son* and the Dominican *merengue*, in those places.

The reign of Cuban music in Port-au-Prince was so complete that the publication *Haïti-Journal* felt it necessary to launch a campaign in favor of the *méringue* in 1945 and to inaugurate a *méringue* competition. With 217 entrants, first prize went to Antoine Duverger of Jazz Guignard for "Foufoune," second to thirteen-year-old pianist

Micheline Laudun (later Laudun Dénis) for "Méringue," and third to Walter Scott Ulysse of Les Gais Troubadours for "Choubouloute."[49]

Despite the increasing Cuban musical influence, the period following the occupation saw continued *indigène* intellectual ferment among the old and new generations. Starting in 1938, a circle of intellectuals, including Lorimer Denis, François Duvalier, and Carl Brouard, produced the journal called *Les Griots*, dedicated to popularizing Africanism and a form of *indigènisme* called *noirisme*. Griots are hereditary musician-storytellers in areas of West Africa who maintain clan and tribal genealogies and histories; the founders of the journal used the term to call attention to the role that intellectuals and artists could play as the conscience of the people. The Griots advanced notions such as the "black soul," pan-Africanism, and the right of "authentic" blacks to govern Haiti. The poet Morisseau-Leroy wrote, "Let the study of African art, researched in depth thanks to the work of ethnologists and confronted with the manifestations of the Haitian soul in popular songs, create for the poet a means of expression that is racially appropriate."[50]

Noiristes used the term "class" but linked it in a very mechanical fashion to race, such that François Duvalier and his collaborators could speak of the class *nwa*.[51] Their notion of black identity was essentialist and metaphysical. They argued that the psychobiological uniqueness of the African race required a non-European form of government with elements drawn from African kingships. Ensuing history reveals that the absolutist and authoritarian politics of the Duvalier dictatorship had their intellectual genesis in this *noirisme* of the Griots. Advocating black power, *noirisme* found kinship in the theories of culture generated elsewhere in the decolonizing African diaspora. Poets Aimé Césaire (Martinique) and Leopold S. Senghor (Senegal) made the unity of the black race an agenda for black intellectuals over the entire diaspora. Pan-Africanism and *négritude*, promoted in the journal *Présence Africaine*, simultaneously embraced and overshadowed Haitian *noirisme*, which took on the role of local variant of a transnational Africanist ideology.

In the same year that the occupation ended (1934), the Haitian Communist Party was founded by writer Jacques Roumain. Most of its early members had also been considered *indigènistes*, but they abandoned a racial theory for one based on class conflict. Roumain found the fixation of the "authentics" on race (and with a catalogue of wrongs committed against the race) to be troubling. Roumain accused doctrinaire *noiristes* of obscuring class relations in order to advance their quest for political power. Important communist literary figures such as Roumain and later Jacques-Stéphan Alexis and René Dépestre saw in the *noiristes* a Haitian reflection of European fascism, with its racial essentialisms, its grand mythologies, its populist appeal, its emphasis on strong leadership, and its easy villains. But with both groups (*noiristes* and communists) fascinated by the cultural life of the Haitian peasants, and with both sharing a common intellectual history and rhetoric, it is not always easy to differentiate the two political perspectives clearly.

Many black intellectuals viewed the presidency of the *milat* Elie Lescot during World War II (1941–46) as a continuation of the occupation by proxy. Lescot supported a Catholic church pogrom against Vodou temples and practitioners that began as a grass-roots movement of strict Catholics. Because the militants in the *campagne anti-superstitieuse* forced their fellow parishioners to sign oaths renouncing the practice of Vodou and belief in the African deities, the campaign also became known as the *renons* (renunciation). The anti-Vodou fever peaked in the years 1941–42; by then the Catholic church hierarchy and the president had weighed in on the side of the *renons,* and for a short while it was state policy to encourage it. During this time, partisans destroyed Vodou temples, drums, and other ritual paraphernalia. As one might expect, this move was very unpopular with the *authentiques,* who were already smarting over Lescot's appointment of a preponderance of mulattos to positions of power, a practice more blatant than even under the occupation. These unpopular policies helped to swing public opinion solidly away from Lescot and toward the *authentiques* by the end of the war.

In *Ainsi parla l'oncle,* Price-Mars had called for peasant Vodou music to be integrated into concert halls and salons. Price-Mars's suggestion to composers was to study the "plainchant" of the Vodou ceremonies to create a music that would "mark the capacity of the race for an individual art, generating ideas and emotions."[52] Art composers Ludovic Lamothe, Justin Elie, and Werner Anton Jaegerhuber, among others, created a modest, but fascinating, corpus of Vodou-influenced art music.[53] In a small country such as Haiti, with a disproportionately small elite and middle class, art music, popular music, and folkloric troupes often overlapped both in their audiences and in their performers. Velério Canez was a principal violinist in Pro Arte et Litteris (along with his wife, who played viola) and also played jazz with the Jazz de Geffrard Cesvet. Choral concerts presented by Werner Jaegerhuber

(c. 1939) featured singers in traditional dress singing such pieces as Ludovic Lamothe's 1934 carnival song "Nibo." Folkloric dance troupe director Lina Fussman-Mathon (later Mathon Blanchet) played piano at many of these classical concerts at venues such as the Rex Theatre. The Duroseau family of Cap Haïtien had a family philharmonic; played parlor *méringues*, contredances, and other light dance musics; and produced many important dance-band musicians. Spouses of many of these performers were active in music, folkloric performance, and theater as well. What emerges in all this is a portrait of an elite (and, to some extent, middle class) with a strong ethic of cultural participation, and with wide-ranging interests in high-status European art music, contemporary African-American popular and dance music, and nationalist expressions from *méringue* to Vodou-influenced chamber music.

The other emergent nativist expressions were the folkoric troupes, which had their origins in the children's classical choir directed by Lina Mathon Blanchet, the classical pianist just mentioned. In 1939, a group of visiting German artists suggested that the choir perform folk songs, and she added these—along with a few dances—to the group's repertory. Blanchet put together a men's choir, the Legba Singers, which President Lescot asked to represent Haiti at the 1941 Pan-American Conference in Washington, D.C. It may seem contradictory that the same president who backed the anti-Vodou *renons* campaign could be so supportive of Vodou folklore, but folklore was viewed as a modern, sanitized expression of heritage and local color, even while the contemporary *practice* of Vodou was considered archaic, barbaric, and threatening. To promote folklore (and presumably to siphon off the organizing efforts of "radicals"), President Lescot formed a state Bureau d'Ethnologie and recruited the exiled communist author Jacques Roumain to be its first director.

Later choirs on the model of Blanchet's group included the Choeur Michel Déjean, which was recorded for a joint Folkways release with folkloric singer and dancer Emerante de Pradines (daughter of the troubadour Kandjo) from Blanchet's group; the Choeur Simidor, directed by musicologist Férère Laguerre; and, of course, the Troupe Folklorique Nationale, led by Jean Léon Destiné, of which we will hear more later. Out of these folkloric troupes came many of the artists who would champion the nativist arts in the 1940s and 1950s; for example, Lumane Casimir, a talented singer of songs from her home in Gonaïves and the surrounding Artibonite Valley, was recruited by Lina Mathon Blanchet for her choir. Another powerful exponent of indigenous music, singer Martha Jean-Claude, first appeared in a series of folkloric concerts at the Rex Theater in 1942 accompanying singer Emerante de Pradines, later opting for a solo career.

Case Study: "Native Born and Truly National"—Jazz des Jeunes, Vodou-Jazz, and Estimé's Bicentennial

In 1942, in the middle-class district of Moren-à-Tuf, Pierre Riché and the brothers René and Ferdinand Dor formed the Trio des Jeunes (Yound People's Trio), which, with additional personnel, grew to a quartet, quintet, sextet, *conjunto,* and was finally called Jazz des Jeunes. By this time (late 1943), it also included future bandleader and saxophonist René St. Aude (fresh from a nine-year stint with the Gonaïves army *fanfa*), and pianist Félix Guignard.[54] St. Aude recruited composer, arranger, and trumpeter Antalcidas O. Murat (formerly with Baby Blue Jazz, Jazz Chancy, and the Orchestre Saïeh), whose work with the Saïeh ensemble had opened up the world of traditional music to the composer. Murat set about to learn all he could of *mizik vodou,* functioning as amateur ethnologist in a similar fashion to some of the *folklorique* art-music composers.

   Jazz des Jeunes developed a reputation for dance-band arrangements of "folkloric" music and for having responded to the call of *noirisme* by fashioning an indigenous popular music. Their music, dubbed Vodou-jazz, was characterized by *mereng*-like song forms, traditional folkloric rhythms, and big band arrangements which borrowed from American and Cuban examples. Songs were listed by the rhythms they employed: *ibo, petwo, rabòday, mereng, kongo.* Others were less traditional: *méringue-cha-cha-cha,* Afro-Haïtien (a clone of the rhythm—commercially dubbed Afro-Cubano—played by Cuban groups for the deity of iron and war, Ogun). The band also recruited the young *chanteur de charme,* Gérard Dupervil, who could handle French-style café songs such as "Fleur de Mai" as well as songs borrowed from Vodou temples and *rara* bands.

   Jazz des Jeunes was the first popular dance band to embody a *noiriste* ideology, and throughout their early career, they demeaned various competitors whom they saw as less authentic, less *natif natal* (native born). This distinction is cast dramatically in the song "Natif natal":

Nan ti peyi-nou-an, ti nèg ap fe tintin	**In our little country, guys are spouting nonsense**

Genyen k'ta vle bliye ke yo se ay-
    isyen
N ap mache fè chalbè kwè kaka
    poul se bè
Yo kwè yo se etranje sa se trist pou
    pale . . .
Moun ki natifnatal, ki vreman na-
    syonal
Yanvalou ak kongo, petwo, djouba,
    ibo

Some want to forget they're
    Haitian
Wanting braggards to think
    chicken shit is butter
They believe they're foreigners,
    sad to say . . .
People who are native born, truly
    national:
Yanvalou and *kongo, petwo,
    djouba, ibo*[55]

The first four lines are an invective against the mulatto elite for their antinationalist ideals, their identification with foreign culture, and the premium placed on light skin coloration (this is implied in the metaphor of chicken shit and butter). A second verse lists all of the national musics possessed by other countries and admonishes Haitians for not promoting their own traditional music. In a final chorus, Haitian authenticity is linked to the use of traditional sacred rhythms from Vodou.

Another song "Anciens jeunes" (Ancient youth) functions as a praise song for the group and as a distillation of their central message. Constructed on *kongo* and *ibo* rhythms, it opposed foreign influence, promoted Haitian folklore, linked folklore and Vodou to the triumph of the revolution of 1804, and established Africa as the source of Haitian authenticity. The lyrics compare the use of indigenous symbols in expressive culture to living off your own garden (a goal of Haitian peasants who seek food self-sufficiency).

Jazz des Jeunes, l'enfant chéri
Du peuple haïten
Son orgueil, sa fierté
C'est de manger son propre bien

Vivant de son jardin
Il aime bien être ancien
Prenant l'étranger
On ne fait que trahir les siens

Jazz des Jeunes, dear child
Of the Haitian people
Their pride and dignity
Is in eating from their own
    [home grown] food

Living from their garden
They love being ancient
Extolling the foreign
You only betray yourself[56]

According to the lyrics, the rhythms of Jazz des Jeunes were "ancient," "real," "Haitian," "African," and "authentic."

Yanvalou, rabòday	*Yanvalou, rabòday*
Petwo, ibo, kongo, djouba	*Petwo, ibo, kongo, djouba*
Sont des rythmes de nos ancêtres	**Are rhythms of our ancestors**
Nègres aradas	**Black Aradas**
De tous les Haïtiens authentiques	**Of all authentic Haitians**
Réels sans fard	**Real without pretense**[57]

The line *"réels sans fard,"* literally, "real without powder" (i.e., makeup), refers to the practice of lightening black women's skin with facial powders; in contrast, the lyrics suggest that the music of Jazz des Jeunes makes no pretense of "whitening" its blackness. Thus "Anciens jeunes" suggests that economic and political independence are linked to racial pride.

A competition developed between Jazz des Jeunes and Orchestre Saïeh, the two orchestras most devoted to Vodou-jazz. The Orchestre Saïeh was under the direction of Issah el Saïeh, scion of the family that owned La Belle Créole, a major department store in Port-au-Prince. The orchestra included *chanteur de charme* and clarinettist Guy Durosier, Raoul and Raymond Guillaume on saxophone, Nono Lamy on piano, and trumpeters Alphonse Simon and Serge Lebonde. Raoul Guillaume and Guy Durosier wrote a bolero-beguine called "Ma brune," which became an enormous hit, even before being recorded in 1949. Saïeh's group was known for its sophisticated jazz settings of traditional songs, for their inventive harmonies, and for their emulation of American big bands. From time to time, Saïeh would bring American jazz artists such as pianist Billy Taylor and tenor saxophonist Budd Johnson to Haiti to give workshops for the group in harmony and instrumental technique. Bobby Hicks, an American living in Puerto Rico, arranged the songs for the band.

In the song "Rele m" (Name me or What's my name?), the Orchestre Saïeh plays a *kont* (riddle game), an example of the kinds of traditional materials that were incorporated by the Vodou-jazz composers for their arrangements. The clues in this *kont* relate to a nativist sense of Haitian identity. The percussion is Haitian, and the vocalist aims for a rougher, rural style of delivery, but the refrain has swelling trumpet lines over lush jazz harmonies, adding up to a very cosmopolitan treatment of an indigenous piece.

Rele m rele m rele	**Name me, What's my name?**
Mande sa pou fè mwen	**Ask about this to identify me**
Manman mwen se manbo	**My mother is a Vodou priestess**

| Papa mwen se oungan | **My father is a Vodou priest** |
| Mande sa pou fè m | **Ask about this to identify me**[58] |

Although they played a similar mix of musics, these two orchestras and the competition between them encompassed conflicts of class, race, and authenticity. These differences were articulated in differences in style, especially apparent in horn intonation and articulation. Saïeh's orchestra drew on a group of musicians with higher-class backgrounds and achieved a more polished sound that was regarded as *stil blan* (a foreign style). For this reason, rather than for reasons of repertory, Orchestre Saïeh was considered less authentic than Jazz des Jeunes.

Jazz des Jeunes began to incorporate *rara* along with the single-note *vaksin*-s (bamboo trumpets found in *rara* groups) into urban dance music with a well-known peasant *rara* song they orchestrated called "Kote moun yo?" (Where are the people?). The arrangement begins with the ostinato produced by three hocketed *vaksin*-s, the sound of which is buried under the full orchestra until it emerges during a break later in the piece. The lyrics of "Kote moun yo?" are in the tradition of the adversary songs, in which the singer intimates that unspecified enemies (*neg-sa-yo*, or those guys) are gossiping (*zen* or *tripotay*), slandering (*pale mal*), plotting (*fè konplo*), or working magic against the singer and/or his or her group.[59] The song incorporates a Haitian proverb for the final line, a common characteristic of neotraditionalist compositions. In times of political tension, as with the rise of the *noiriste* movement or the campaign of François Duvalier for the presidency a decade later, these songs take on additional connotations directed at the mysterious machinations of one political group or another.

Kote moun yo, woy? Mwen pa we moun yo e	**Where are the people? I don't see the people**
Kote moun k ap pale moun mal?	**Where are the people slandering others?**
Mwen pa we moun k ap pale moun mal	**I don't see the people insulting others**
Woy . . . devan byen, deye mal o!	**Nice to your face, nasty behind your back!**[60]

Looking at these examples, we can see that Voudou-jazz movement composers incorporated proverbs, Vodou ceremonial songs, children's songs, *kont*, and *rara* songs into their repertory. Through their lyrics, arrangements, instrumental resources, vocal melodies, and rhythms, they strove to evoke peasant music and to signal a basic sympathy with *négritude* ideals. The reception of Jazz des Jeunes and the Vodou-jazz artists by the pro-*noiriste* press was characterized by a flowery rhetoric of the "soul" and "character" of Haiti. The following remark from a Jazz des Jeunes fortieth-anniversary concert review is typical of this discourse: "Jazz des Jeunes is the oldest authentically Haitian orchestra whose repertory is rich in Haitian colors and whose music is inspired by the soul and breath of Haiti. After all, when one speaks of Jazz des Jeunes, it is the Haitian soul that one causes to vibrate."[61]

But romantic *noirisme* has to be viewed in its political context. The *campagne antisuperstitieuse* of the Lescot government had created an indelible connection in middle-class consciousness between a *milat*-dominated government and the narrow-minded prosecution of traditional Afro-Haitian culture. The pro-*milat* racial policies of the government also left the *noiristes* bitter, hungry for retribution, and ready to make a concerted run for power. A student strike on January 7, 1946, convinced the army, led by Major Paul Magloire, to remove Elie Lescot and set up a temporary tribunal. The Carnival following the success of the popular demonstrations of 1946 allowed the masses to celebrate their victory, and the *bann apye* reflected this collective effervescence.

Later that year, the *noiriste*-dominated legislature voted middle-class schoolteacher Dumarsais Estimé as president. Estimés election was described by Rotberg as "the victory of the *folklorique* movement of black intellectuals . . . who had long sought political power."[62] Under Estimé, and later under Duvalier, the government promoted members of the black middle class to administrative positions, creating an emergent black *klas politik* (political class). The mulatto elite regarded Estimé with anything from reservation to horror, and many considered him a *manje-milat* (eater of mulattos, i.e., a fervent opponent). With the ascension of Estimé, businesses refused to participate in carnival, leaving only the acoustic music groups and the *bann apye*, energetic as they were, to entertain the mutitudes. The "official" component of the carnival, the floats and queens, didn't return until 1949.

The members of Jazz des Jeunes and most of the other musicians playing traditional music considered themselves part of (or at least allied with) the "Revolution of 1946," the "Revolution of January 7th," or "Generation of 1946," as they were sometimes called. The Vodou-jazz of Jazz des Jeunes was considered a weapon in this struggle: a condemnation of the Europhile elite and their antipopular ideology and a tribute to the cultural contributions of Haiti's black peasantry

. . . in short, an advertisement for black power. René Beaubrun, writing retrospectively in a *noiriste* journal, praised the combativeness of Jazz des Jeunes for their "irrefutable contribution to the development of Haitian music, their combativeness in the struggle against the 'disdainers' from a class of Haitians who reject folklore because of its lower class origins."[63]

The evolution of a Haitian indigenous school of music was paralleled by that of an indigenous school of painting. DeWitt Peters, a California artist, had arrived in Haiti during the war to teach English. Impressed by local artistic talent, he founded the Centre d'Art in 1944, which at first presented mainly artists from the elite as well as a sprinkling of foreign artists resident in Haiti. The success of the shows led to a search for Haitian artists, which turned up some who came from more humble origins and from the provincial cities, including Wilson Bigaud, Préfète Duffaut, Hector Hyppolite, and Philomé Obin, and who were to personify what art collectors started calling the Haitian "primitive" or "naive" movement. Peters and art collector/playwright Selden Rodman set about to promote the movement worldwide. As a result of their early efforts, Hector Hyppolite, an *ougan* form St. Marc, had a one-man show in Paris in 1947, but it was a 1946–47 tour of Haitian art throughout Europe and the United States organized by UNESCO that placed the "primitives" on the map. Although the styles of the various artists were actually distinct, art critics linked them within an aesthetic of primitive surrealism that reveals their intimate relationship to the Haitian landscape and people. The sprinkling of Vodou priests in his movement helped to establish its indigenous credentials.

The postwar years brought an economic boom to Haiti. With the devastation of Europe, the Caribbean "playgrounds" (especially Havana, Cuba; San Juan, Puerto Rico; and Port-au-Prince) became the foci of an invigorated Caribbean tourist market, and Haitian raw materials (especially sisal) fed booming postwar manufacturing industries. Radio, which was a marginal medium before the war, emerged as an important vehicle for communications and expressive culture after the war. By 1949 there were at leaset seven stations operating in the vicinity of Port-au-Prince.[64]

Estimé and his advisers planned an extravagant international exposition for 1949 to celebrate the 200th anniversary of the founding of Port-au-Prince. The exposition was also intended to build an infrastructure for tourism, showcase Haiti (and especially Haitian indigenous arts), further the modernization of Haiti, and create a lasting monument to Estimé's *noiriste* revolution. It was built on the site of a former waterfront slum, renamed Cité Dumarsais Estimé or Cité de l'Exposition, now simply called the Bizantnè (after the French *Bicentenaire,* or bicentennial, the informal name of the event). The construction of buildings and new roads along the waterfront was an exercise in urban renewal, or, as the propaganda director for the exposition said, "our waterfront, which is the site of first contact [with tourists]—and everyone knows that it's first impressions that count—will offer a less desolate spectacle."[65]

As is typical of world's fairs and exhibitions, the project was designed to produce "multiplier effects" in housing, food, transportation, and entertainment. Government records for the period are packed with laws authorizing "extraordinary credits" for projects such as the building of first-class hotels, the Delmas road, telephone cables, and so forth. Estimé's government supervised the building of a host of modern white buildings along the waterfront, including the Casino International, a gambling casino and nightclub that became a major dollar-earning enterprise and a principal venue for dance bands of the next few decades. The casino was leased as a concession to two American entrepreneurs, who were given a state-guaranteed monopoly over the gambling business in Haiti. The period from the outbreak of World War II until the end of the exposition saw the construction of luxury hotels Oloffson, royal Haytian Hotel (formerly Hotel Roosevelt), Beau Rivage, El Rancho, and the Montana (formerly Fairy Hill).

If one were to drive south along the new Boulevard Harry S. Truman during the exposition, one would pass through the shade of a stand of royal palm trees called the "palm forest," or "Les Palmistes," and then encounter an entertainment area containing the open-air Théâtre de Verdure. The theater was designed to present Haiti's arts for international consumption and to import "world renowned artists" to help Haitians (in the patronizing words of the exposition's publicist) "distinguish the good from the bad, the mediocre from the polished. And for those with a sociological sense, this is not a meager result."[66] Among the visiting artists who performed at the theater were the American singer Marian Anderson and the National Opera of New York (soloist Christina Caroll sang "Panama m tonbe" accompanied by drummer Ti-Roro).[67]

Near the Théâtre de Verdure, the government constructed a large *gagè* (cockfight arena). A gambling ship anchored off the coast, and an American variety act (and "freak" show), the Ross Manning Show, set up camp "fresh from the county fair circuit of the states."[68] Among

Manning's attractions were a hermaphrodite and a circus horse that danced the tango. The entertainment section (beaux arts, folklore, and amusements) opened on December 4, 1949, but the remainder of the exhibit opened on February 12, 1950. The week-long opening ceremonies featured performances of the folkloric show, cockfights, Vodou dances, and daily fireworks.

The exposition showcased Haiti's pictorial and performance arts. Seldan Rodman arranged for some of the artists, including Pétion Sylvain and Pierre Bourdelle, to receive commissions to paint murals for the pavillions of the exposition. The murals featured religious themes (the warrior *lwa* Ogun Feray), pastoral themes (peasant markets and dances), and political-historic themes such as a slave breaking his chains. Bishop Charles Voegli sponsored a massive mural by four of the "primitives" on the walls of the Cathédrale Ste. Trinité as the Episcopal church's contribution to the exposition. This was a daring step for the major Christian denominations, because the primitive movement was so closely associated with pratitioners of Vodou.

The Troupe Folklorique Nationale and other folkloric choirs and dance troupes were cultural centerpieces of the exposition. Choreographer Jean Léon Destiné, who got his start in the Legba Singers, had come back to Haiti from his job with the American Museum of Natural History to choreograph a concert in 1943 and then in 1946 at the Haitan-American Institute, and then returned to form the Troupe Folklorique Nationale for the exposition. He recruited dancers from all over the country for the new ensemble. His model was the stylized folkloric cultural show of the "national ballets" and *"grupos folklóricos"* that were premiering in the decolonizing Third World as part of "unity within diversity" cultural strategies. Destiné recruited drummers Ti-Marcel, the legendary Ti-Roro, and Alphonse Cimer to accompany the group, and Lumane Casimar came on board as lead singer. The combination of Ti-Roro, Lumane Casimir, and Jazz des Jeunes had their tryout run at the 1948 opening of the cinema Montparnasse. By 1949, Lumane Casimir had proven herself the most accomplished singer in the Legba Singers, and she was asked to solo at the exposition. Her renditions of traditional songs, especially the *mereng* "Panama m tonbe," "Se la rivyè mwen te ye," "Papa Gede bèl gason," and the *kongo* song "Carolina acao" are legendary in Haiti, and she, along with Martha Jean-Claude, was the model for many Haitian female folkloric singers to follow. Dance troupes such as Wanda Wiener's Troupe Macaya, Troupe Simbi, Max Denis's Lococia, and Siméon Benjamin's Troupe Aïda gained exposure at the exposition; in the years that followed, dance troupes along the lines of the Troupe Folklorique Nationale were led by such choreographers as Lavinia Williams-Yarbourough, Louinès Louinis, and Katherine Dunham.[69]

Jazz des Jeunes was contracted to perform at the Théâtre de Verdure along with the Troupe Folklorique Nationale and Lumane Casimir. This line up of *indigène* performers was immortalized in a Jazz des Jeunes song,

Comme Claudinette, la plus belles	Like Claudinette, the most beautiful
Des filles d'Haïti	Of the women of Haiti
Jazz des Jeunes en musique	Jazz des Jeunes in music
Est notre cathédrale	Is our cathedral
Claudinette, Jazz des Jeunes,	Claudinette, Jazz des Jeunes,
Et la Troupe Nationale	And the National Folkloric Troupe
La plus belle trilogie	The most beautiful trilogy
Tout l'art de nôtre beau pays	All the arts of our lovely country[70]

The former Cuban ambassodor to Haiti complimented the artistic presentations, "Last evening, at the Théâtre de Verdue, I admired the National Folkloric Troupe. No other country could present a more original and artistic spectacle within the space of the Palmistes, which is a dream."[71] The folkloric show (with the Troupe Folklorique, Jazz des Jeunes, and Casimir) continued on after the exhibition at the Théâtre de Verdure on Tuesday, Thursday, and Sunday evenings during the tourist season.

Despite a generally positive tone to the foreign coverage of the event, the exposition did little to firm up Estimé's political fortunes at home. The treasury had already been strained by Estimé's construction of a frontier town at Belladère near the Dominician Republic, and the Exposition's high cost exacerbated the concerns of Estimé's critics in the legislature and military. Having cost over $6 million, the exposition attracted no more than 4,000 extra tourists (for a total of a little over 9,000 that year); by any accounting, a spectacular financial failure. Yet, among its successes was its contribution to consolidating the indigenous arts movements and the crop of new hotels and nightclubs that served as venues for the orchestras of the period.

Reeling from a constitutional crisis, from attacks by his opponents, and from the consequences of his financial largesse, Estimé tried to energize his support among the masses with a tour of the capital.

Echoing the theme of jobs for the poor, a popular work-brigade song of 1950 encouraged Estimé to tighten his grip on power:

Se Bondyè nan syèl-la ki ba n pwèzidan-sila	God in heaven gave us this president
Kenbe peyi-a pa lage o	Keep hold of the country, don't let go
Pòtoprens o tounen Havann o	Port-au-Prince is becoming another Havana[72]

"Four Years of Partying": The Reign of General Magloire

On May 10, 1950, the army removed Estimé and installed a junta led by Colonel Paul Magloire. Magloire was known to be a great friend of the mulatto elite and a dedicated devotee of the *banbòch* (party); his six-year reign was called *"six ans de kermesse"* (six years of partying).[73] Magloire and the junta allowed the exposition to run its course.

The fall of Estimé didn't end government patronage of Jazz des Jeunes, largely because a display of *noiriste* pride proved useful to the new government and its *politique de doublure* (titular black presidents serving the interests of the elite). In 1951, President Magloire selected Jazz des Jeunes to represent Haiti in Canada, at an exposition in Washington, D.C. (where the orchestra won first prize for a band from the Americas), and at a stadium in Cuba. During their tour, Jazz des Jeunes, the Troupe Folklorique Nationale, and Lumane Caismir performed at New York's Ziegfield Theatre. A *New York Times* review of the performance praised the drummers and dancers, but had this to say about the rest of the music: "If Mlle. Casimir fares better in her native land with her songs, it is undoubtedly because there her language is familiar. On the negative side of the evening was a *pit band* [sic] *complete with saxophones.*"[74]

Voudou-jazz was adopted and popularized by a number of performers of the 1950s. Raoul Guillaume, a saxophonist for the Saïeh organization, formed his own group, releasing a version of the children's game song *balanse yaya* (even up the yaya).

Troubadour Rodolphe "Dodòf" Legros included indigenous-style tunes in his repertory, including his version of "Twa fèy," a Vodou ceremonial song for the puposes of divination by a *bòkò* (specialist in magical practices), directed to the deity Simbi, a guardian of springs for whom "Simbi twa fèy" and "Simbi twa rasin" are two avatars.

Twa fèy, twa rasin o	Three leaves, three roots
Jete bliye, ranmase sonje	Throw away to forget, pick up to remember
Mwen genyen basen mwen	I have my pool (or basin) of water
Twa fèy tonbe ladan	Three leaves fell into it
Jete bliye, ranmase sonje	Throw away to forget, pick up to remember[75]

The period from the mid-1940s until the mid-1950s was probably the most fecund period for nightlife in Haiti's history. Crowds packed the hotel ballrooms at Ibo Lélé and Hotel Riviera and partied through weekend evenings and nights in such clubs as Casino International, Cabane Choucoune, Simbi Nightclub, Ronde Point and Aux Caleb-asses. During the Magloire years, the exclusive club Cercle Bellevue moved to a palatial new complex above Pétion-Ville in Bourdon, and dance bands found constant employment in the many clubs and hotels. Other than Jazz des Jeunes, the most popular bands of the *bèl epòk* (the "beautiful period," i.e., the decade or so after World War II) included Orchestre Casino International, Ensemble Nérette, Aster Jazz, Jazz Atomique, Orchestre Citadelle, Orchestre Septentrional, Orchestre Saïeh, and the Ensemble du Riviera Hotel. These Haitian orchestras performed a mixed repertory, including Latin dance numbers, American jazz, Haitian *mereng*, and the new *indigène* compositions. The Orchestre Casino International was the most widely traveled Haitian dance band of the period, playing in Cuba, Brazil, the United States, France, and Italy. Like the Gais Troubadours, it was a training grounds for musicians who were to become influential in their own right including Wébert Sicot, Charles Déssalines, Nemours Jean-Baptiste, Ulrick Pierre-Louis (maestro of Septentrional for forty years), and the singer Joe Trouillot. The casino where they were based was built as part of the Cité de l'Exposition for the 1949 bicentennial and became a landmark on the Port-au-Prince waterfront. It was the most popular tourist destination in Haiti and a cash cow for its foreign managers and for the government, which sold the concession.

There was a strong presence of Cuban orchestras in Port-au-Prince in the era. Sonora Matancera visited Haiti with the Puerto Rican singer Daniel Santos (who had performed at the 1949 exposition) and learned some songs written or orchestrated by Guy Durosier, including "Ma brune" and the traditional "Panama m tonbe." In the late 1950s, Nono Lamy's band was playing at the Casino International, and the casino sent for Machito's Afro-Cuban big band for a series of joint concerts. The casino received word that Machito couldn't come, so they booked the Dominican radio orchestra of Papa Molino. Because of poor communications, all three bands showed up, and Port-au-Prince was treated to a week of the best in Cuban, Dominican, and Haitian dance music.[76]

In the early 1950s, radio station 4RVW (Radio d'Haïti) broadcast live programs from the nightclub Cabane Choucoune and the Sunday morning *radio-théâtres* from the Ciné Paramount.[77] Performers included Jazz des Jeunes, the Orchestre Saïeh, l'Ensemble Wébert Sicot, Aster-Jazz Latino, singer Guy Durosier solo, and Louis Lahens (a singer with Orchestre Citadelle who later left to join the Ensemble aux Calebasses led by Nemours Jean-Baptiste). Every Sunday morning for eleven years (spanning the terms of three different presidents), Jazz des Jeunes hosted the enormously popular "Radio Théâtre" on Radio d'Haïti from 11:30 until 2:00. A musician recalled his childhood memory of this program, "It doesn't matter where you go in the country, every house would be turned to Radio d'Haïti from 11:30 until 2:00. It was "Make sure you eat Sunday dinner while the program is on!" Everybody would be sitting down listening to Jazz des Jeunes on the radio."[78]

Magloire sponsored his own lavish celebration to compete with Estimé's bicentennial: the *tricinquantenaire* (sesquicentennial) of independence in January of 1954. Magloire brought the black American opera star Marian Anderson to Haiti to perform with a folkloric choir for 700 guests on the esplanade of Sans Souci, the early nineteenth-century palace bult by Emperor Henri Christophe. At a ball two days later, Magloire hosted 3,000 guests at the National Palace.[79]

Although Magloire was renowned as a supporter of the arts, he played a part in the exile of singer Martha Jean-Claude. Jean-Claude's Cuban husband had become embroiled in a construction scheme in which many perspective homeowners lost their downpayments. After Jean-Claude's husband fled, Magloire had her jailed to entice her husband to come back into the country. But, because she was pregnant at the time and required hospitalization, she was allowed to leave the country to join her husband, and she remained outside the country during the Duvalier years. Despite her exile, Jean-Claude's recordings remained treasured souvenirs for Haitian folkloric music enthusiasts, and she became a legend of sorts in her former country. Political singer Manno Charlemagne explained Jean-Claude's contribution and standing among Haitian artists, "Martha Jean-Claude *was* the *raisin* [roots] movement. She had to endure a lot. To be a woman singing in those days [1940s–50s] in Haiti—she was called a *puta*, a whore. But she is a monument."[80]

Not all Haitian classes participated equally in the "six years of *kermesse*" and the *"bèl epòk"* of Magloire's rule. To the contrary, while the elite and political class lived it up, social tensions were on the rise. The *authentiques* considered the Estimé reign to have been an unfinished revolution, and they longed to complete the transition to a black-led state. The growing urban underclass trapped in the *bidonvilles* (slums) circling Port-au-Prince was seething with anger and a potentially revolunary fervor. The corruption of the regime and the instability resulting from its decay opened up new possibilities for the *noiristes*.

As a product of European colonialism, Haiti has always been at a global crossroads. Nevertheless, the American occupation dramatically opened Haiti up to international influences and to currents in popular culture. It also helped to erode the status of the traditional ruling elite, at least in the eyes of the middle class. The doctrine of *noirisme*, a serious political force after World War II, marginalized the ruling class, tainting it politically and culturally because of the elite's historical, cultural, and racial ties to foreign dominance. The ascendant black middle class wielded the concept of authenticity to gain political capital in the struggle. Vodou-jazz was the manifestation in dance music of this middle-class ideology of an African cultural heritage. During the Estimé presidency, this ideology was promoted to national doctrine, largely fashioning Haiti's self-image in the world.

"Konpa-dirèk for Life"
François Duvalier's Dictatorship and *Konpa-dirèk*

Dr. François Duvalier's cultural politics were a center post of his regime's durability and its unprecedented degree of control over Haitian
social and cultural life. Through patronage (especially his system of
economic redistribution) and through his *koudyay* politics (the production of popular enthusiasm for political ends), large segments of
the population were implicated in at least tacit support of the regime.
Duvalier's government, the emerging political class, and Duvalier's militia patronized a new style of commercial dance music, the *konpa-
dirèk* of Nemours Jean-Baptiste (and its close relative, the *kadans-
ranpa* of Wébert Sicot). The competition between these two band-
leaders became a national fixation and dominated Carnival in the
Duvalier years.

Nevertheless, Duvalier never achieved total domination. Limits on
the totalitarian nature of the regime included Haiti's continued immer-
sion in a global political economy, a stubborn and dedicated (even if
small and fractious) opposition, and the emergence of the diaspora as
a "liberated territory" for Haitian expatriates. This chapter looks at the
evolution of Duvalierist cultural politics, at the genesis of an oppositional neotraditional music, and at the various music movements that
negotiated local and international influences and identities within the
framework of the dictatorship.

"God Nominates You for Six Years": Duvalier's *Noiriste* Triumph

The final Magloire years and the period just after Magloire's exile were
times of tremendous political strife, articulated to an unprecedented
extent along racial lines. Duvalier, the soft-spoken country doctor with

noiriste intellectual credentials, appropriated the mantle of former President Dumarsais Estimé and positioned himself as the candidate in 1956 to complete Estimé's truncated *noiriste* revolution. Duvalier championed the black middle class, which he considered to be the natural leadership of the peasants and urban proletariat by virtue of its "authentic" racial makeup and of its education and administrative competence. Lower-class urbanites, however, leaned decisively toward one of his rivals, the black populist Daniel Fignolé, another former Estimé minister, who was capable of mobilizing his supporters in the slums into huge, sometimes violent, throngs that he called his "steam-roller." Perfecting the tactics that Haitians had come to call *kansonfè-isme* ("iron pants politics," after a remark made by General Paul Magloire), Duvalier directed his militant supporters to intimidate his opponents in the election. Duvalier's militants were at first called *cagoulards,* from the masks, or *cagoules,* they wore over their faces, but as they became a permanent fixture on the political landscape and as Duvalier's opponents continued to disappear, Haitians gave the militants the nickname *tonton makout*-s (literally, "Uncle Side-bag," the name of a malevolent figure from Haitian folktales who steals little children by placing them in his bag).[1] Aggressive thuggery for political goals was by no means an invention of Duvalier; there were many antecedents in Haitian political history and in the recent history of European fascism that provided ample demonstration of its effectiveness. Signaling his cooperative intentions to the army and sectors of the elite, Duvalier was able to emerge as the compromise candidate, acceptable to the lower classes, but clearly more malleable than Fignolé. It is widely believed that the army helped to rig the election in Duvalier's favor.

Once elected in 1957, Duvalier set about ruthlessly to destroy his enemies and all potential bases of oppositional power. What was perceived at the outset as a blend of racial assertion, authoritarianism, and nationalism gave way to a paranoid totalitariansim more developed than perhaps anywhere else in the hemisphere, including that of his counterpart across the border, President Rafael Trujillo of the Dominican Republic. In the meantime, Duvalier's private militia evolved into one of Haiti's few national organizations, giving a taste of power and status to thousands of Duvalierists, including those from the middle class and from the lumpen proletariat.

One by-product of Duvalier's work as an ethnologist was his ability to coopt grass-roots peasant leadership (including a preponderance of *ougan*-s, or Vodou priests) into the leadership of the *tonton makout*-s.

Duvalier thoroughly incorporated Vodou into his system of domination, endowed his rule with authenticating symbols from both Christianity and Vodou, and mobilized a vast network of *sevitè*-s (Vodou practitioners) in support of his revolution. *Makout*-s were part of the system of redistribution of state resources intended to ensure a complacent population and a degree of popular consent. If direct redistribution proved insufficient, *makout*-s had nearly unlimited power to raise money (extortion, bribes, etc.) as they saw fit. Through coercion, constraint, aggressive patronage, and general terror, Duvalier shrank the available cultural space for criticism and creativity while managing to produce a measure of consent, cooperation, and accommodation from the majority of the population. With the reign of *makout* terror, with ruthless campaigns to subjugate all private and public organizations to the state (and the state to Duvalier), and with increasing control over communications and symbolic systems, Duvalier cannily maneuvered his tenuous presidency into a totalitarian dictatorship and dynastic presidency until his death in 1971.[2]

During Duvalier's earliest years, opposition to his policies emerged in the legislature among his rivals' supporters and among student activists (whose graffiti branded him "Kaka Doc," or Dr. Shit). Yet none of the attempts to invade Haiti to overthrow or assassinate him proved successful. The first major invasion attempt, led by Alix Pasquet, a partisan of former President Magloire, ended with a brutal slaughter of the invaders, including some Americans who had joined the eight-person group. The Ensemble Raphaël Nérette commemorated the failure of the July 29 invasion with a *méringue* entitled "Duvalier nan bataille" (Duvalier in battle). The song gives a blow-by-blow account of the unfolding drama, ending with the radio announcement that they had *"touye tout"* (killed them all).

Duvalier yap barou mitraille ou pas couri	Duvalier, under machine gun fire, you didn't run
Cé Bon Dieu qui voyer'ou ici comme Président	God sent you here as president
Duvalier yap barou canno ou pas mouri	Duvalier, they gave you cannon, you didn't die
Cé Bon Dieu qui voyer'ou ici	God sent you here
Comme gnou Sauveur	As a savior
Duvalier ou metter en militaire pou'r commande	Duvalier, you command the military[3]

Among Duvalier's earliest and most fervent supporters were many of the leading figures of the *noiriste* movement. Exactly one year after his election, supporters from the *noiriste* musical movement held a competition for songs to honor the president. Song texts were then compiled into a book in Duvalier's honor. The composers represented the cream of the Vodou-jazz movement: for example, Antalcidas O. Murat, Jean Legros, Gérard Dupervil, Joe Trouillot, Alfred Dorlette, and Luc Mondesir. Entitled *Chansons populaires composées en l'honneur du chef spirituel de la nation,* the book represented (in the words of its editors), "patriotic cries of a people thirsty for freedom and which is trying to express all the remarkable emotions aroused in them for a man worthy of directing their destinies. As you can ascertain through the songs, the People by no means had an exaggerated Passion for deifying their leader but instead a great concern with improving their condition."[4]

To the contrary, a religious passion for Duvalier was very much in evidence. A famous portrait of Duvalier showed him seated at a desk with Jesus standing behind him. The paternal use of praise names like *"Bon Papa"* (good father), "Messenger," "Savior," were also part of the effort to sacralize his reign. Religious imagery is rampant in songs from the volume in his praise. For example, Jean Legros (brother of Dodòf Legros) wrote:

Duvalier bon papa	**Duvalier, good Father**
Duvalier bon chef d'Etat	**Duvalier, good Chief of State**
Cé bon Dieu qui mété ou la	**It's God who puts you here**
Pou viné sauvé Haïti	**In order to save Haiti**
Haïti ap régénéré	**Haiti is regenerating**
Grâce à Docteur Duvalier	**Thanks to Doctor Duvalier**
Toute rue an asphaltée	**Every road will be paved in asphalt**
Toute travailleur au bien touché	**Every worker will be well paid**
Duvalier chef protocol	**Duvalier, chief of protocol**
Ca'p vine banou auréol	**Who comes to crown us in glory**
Bon Dieu nomme pou six an ou	**God nominates you for six years**
Cé pou ou rété pou fé temp ou	**You must remain to complete your term**[5]

In addition to their paternalism and deification, the songs give vent to the paranoid rhetoric often found in Vodou "adversary" songs. The songs plead for a forceful rule of the country, providing a glimpse into the political rhetoric and cultural strategies of the regime. Some of the songs hint at the recourse to the aforementioned "iron pants politics" and contain veiled warnings to opponents of Duvalier:

Pa touché Duvalier	Don't touch Duvalier
Pou Piquant Pa Piqué'ou	For the thorn not to prick [kill] you
Duvalier cé ou Poteau Planté	Duvalier is a planted post
Pa Proché	Don't come near
Min Si'n cé Haïtien	But if you are Haitian
Foc nou Pa Fè tintin	You shouldn't be making any nonsense
Bon Dieu qui Fè'n cadeau ou	God gave [Duvalier] to us as a gift
Papa ou Pi du	Papa, you're the most severe[6]

Some of the songs in the collection refer to the continuing divisions in the country and to the simmering resistance to Duvalier:

Président Duvalier ouay oh	President Duvalier, woy o
Pa couté chien ca'p japé ouay oh	Don't listen to the dogs who are barking, woy o[7]

Or:

Réactionnaire yo compren'n Doc ta'p dormi	The reactionareirs thought Doc was sleeping
L'armée et le Peuple té la ta'p veillé Doc	But the army and the people wanted Doc[8]

We find a well-developed rhetoric of strongman rule in the songs and slogans of the day. This historically emerges from the lower classes in Haiti, who arrive at the conclusion that only someone with dictatorial powers can successfully confront elite dominance. Duvalier was often greeted with the chant *"Divalye, peyi a se pou w"* (Duvalier, the country is all yours).[9] In "Bonjou Duvalier, Papa Moin" (Gooday, Duvalier, my father), the composer writes,

Pays ya nan main ou . . .	The country is in your hands . . .
Après bon Dieu li nan main ou	After God, it's in your hands[10]

A typical parting expression in Haiti is *"Kenbe, pa lage"* (literally, "Hold on, don't let go"), more or less equivalent to "hang in there" in English. The following song text, written by members of Jazz des Jeunes, employs this expression in relation to the nation:

François Duvalier ou connin gouvené	François Duvalier, you know how to govern
Oua quimbé Pays ya pa lagué'l oh	You'll hold on to the country—don't let go of it[11]

Duvalier typically portrayed himself as a selfless vessel for the aspirations of his people, a notion that also appears in some of the commemorative songs, such as in "Min président peuple là" (Here's the president of the people),

Tou't ambition'ou, Cé pou peuple là	All your ambition is for the people
Tout sa ou mandé, Cé pou peuple là	All that you ask for is for the people
Lor'ou pa dormi, Cé pou peuple là	When you don't sleep, it's for the people[12]

Because the rhetoric of *noiriste* dictatorship contained elements that were religious, paranoid, retaliatory, and paternalistic, it should not be surprising that it was also heavily gendered. In Creole, to *mete gason sou w* (literally, put the boy on you) is to get up your courage. A *gason kason* (boy with pants) describes a courageous person. Thus, one composer wrote of Duvalier:

Docteur Duvalier lideur de la Nation	Doctor Duvalier, leader of the Nation
Parcequé ou cé garçon	Because you're a real guy
Nou connin ou poté canson	We know you wear the pants[13]

Some of the more outrageous popular slogans of the period, especially those employing *betiz* (obscenity/vulgarity) equated sexual aggression with political power. Class relations, too, were often sexualized in this way, such that the concept of a *manje milat* (mulatto eater) became transposed to one who "screws" the elite.

Haitian scholars have debated the connection between *noirisme* and dictatorship in the years since the inception of Duvalierist rule. One camp holds that *noirisme* leads inevitably to dictatorship, while the other sees Duvalierism as a deformation (even a negation) of *noiriste* ideology. As I have implied, I believe that the essentialist, racialist, and romantic roots of *noirisime* have many things in common with the *volkgeist* underpinnings of fascism (including its admiration for total or ultimate solutions) and that it contains elements that can develop in dictatorial directions under the right (or wrong) historical circumstances. However, I have also endeavored to show that Duvalierism is an extreme form of a historical pattern of authoritarian solutions to Haiti's race-infused class struggle. While he ruthlessly employed the mechanisms of totalitarian governance in Haiti, Duvalier (an exponent of a particularly intolerant and paranoid *noirisme*) did not invent them.

Intellectual *noirisme* and *négritude* played a problematic role in Duvalier's cultural policies. Many *noiristes* hoped for an Estimé-style explosion of indigenous arts under Duvalier, but this project was never realized. Political success, rather, helped to blunt the edge and vigor of the *noiriste* cultural movement. Jazz des Jeunes continued their popular run on state radio, they were recorded for the first time, and they continued to headline the folkloric show at the Théâtre de Verdure, but they were never able to regenerate the public perception that there was something novel and of contemporary significance happening in their music.[14] In the Duvalier years, Jazz des Jeunes was increasingly relegated to a role of a quaint, safe, and "folklorized" representation of "national culture." The Jazz des Jeunes show at the Théâtre de Verdure may have represented a wholesome, patriotic, and educational experience, but urbanties were much more likely to go out dancing at night to the Super Ensemble Nemours Jean-Baptiste. It was Jean-Baptiste's type of new, popular dance that the *arrivistes* (the emergent black political class) were more likely to patronize. For defenders of the *noiriste* arts, the increasing irrelevance of Jazz des Jeunes was a lesson in the difference between a revolution-in-the-making and a revolution-in-power. It was also a lesson in the nature of Duvalierism, which veered quickly from an ideological *noirisme* toward the celebration of its own power.

"It's What Makes Us Original": Commercial *Konpa-dirèk*, 1954–57

The genre of dance music called *konpa* (originally, *konpa-dirèk*) arose in the same period as Duvalierism, and its trajectory was closely tied to that of the dictatorship. Although *konpa* emerged as the undisputed national dance music, cultural nationalists never forgave its origins as an adaption of the Dominican *merengue*. The *merengue* attained an unprecedented popularity in the Dominican Republic thanks to the advocacy of President Trujillo and was exported via records and band tours to Haiti.[15] Dominican radio, especially Trujillo's La Voz Dominicana, blanketed Haiti, and many Haitian musicians grew up listening to *perico ripiao* or Cibaeño-style *merengues* of Nico Lora and Angel Viloria or the big band *merengues* of Luis Alberti's orchestra, Lira des Yaqui (known in later years as Orquestra Generalissimo Trjillo). Lira des Yaqui visited Port-au-Prince in 1955 in the thick of *merengue* fever in Haiti, but it was Viloria's group, Tipico Cibaeño, that—more than any other—inspired Haitian musicians.[16] Their *merengue* consisted only of a *jaleo,* the last of three sections in the traditional *merengues*. One observer of the Haitian musical scene at the time told me, "In 1954, the Dominican group Típico Cibaeño led by Angel Viloria had a hit record in Haiti. That thing hit like a bomb. The Haitians loved the *merengue* because it had a lively beat for dancing. They were doing it in every nightclub, especially down by Carrefour. The Dominican girls [prostitutes] were there and would teach the Haitian guys how to dance."[17]

In the midst of the clamor for Dominican *merengue* in the summer of 1955, Nemours Jean-Baptiste launched his new Domincan-influenced dance at the Club aux Palmistes, where he directed the house ensemble. Raymond Gaspard, Nemours's guitarist, is credited with the term *konpa-dirèk,* which became the commercial label for the new sound. The term literally means direct or straight-ahead beat.

Nemours Jean-Baptiste was born into a middle-class family in Port-au-Prince on February 2, 1918, and studied guitar and banjo with Barrato Destinoble in the southern city of Les Cayes. Back in Port-au-Prince, he continued studies with M. Saint-Armand and with Victor Flambert, who taught Nemours to play the saxophone, an instrument that would bring the performer better pay than the guitar.[18] In the early 1940s he joined the Jazz Guignard and the Conjunto International, where he met his future partner and later rival Wébert Sicot. Nemours was a featured performer in the Trio (later Orchestre) Atomique, named after its lead singer, Djo Atomique (originally José Laveau), who was of mixed Dominican and Haitian parentage. The band had reputation for a Cuban and Dominican repertory. Around 1952, Nemours left the Orchestre Atomique and in 1953 founded his own orchestra at the club Aux Calebasses in Carrefour. Nemours's first composition at Aux Calebasses paid tribute to the club in the title, "Deux petites calebasses" (Two little gourds).

Nemours's *konpa-dirèk* was slower than the Dominican *merengue*, and its success can be partially credited to its choreographic simplicity. The Vodou-jazz rhythms of Jazz des Jeunes were more popular with trained folkloric dancers than they were with social dancers in clubs. The dance that was performed for *konpa* (at first called *kare*, meaning square) arrived in the dance halls of Carrefour and was patterned, as was the music, on the Dominican *merengue*. *Konpa* was the first Haitian music to evolve within a fully commercial milieu. There is a Haitian expression about the power of money in Haiti which puns on the word "back" in "greenback": *Devan grinbak, nanpwen fè bak* (In the face of the greenback, there is no going back). Historian Jean Fouchard bemoaned the role of mass markets and popular tastes, the power of greenbacks, and the foreign roots of *konpa*. He called for the return of the *mereng* after its

> long ordeal imposed by the popularity of records and imported music, with which Wébert Sicot and Nemours Jean-Baptiste . . . believed it useful to modernize our national dance. They attempted to adapt it to a foreign rhythm they baptized with the bewildering names *konpa-dirèk* and *kadans ranpa*, an extravagant addition to their reckless enterprise. Is this evolution? It is arguable when, under the easy pretext of adaptation to popular taste, the very structure of our *méringue* is gravely shaken, and its languorous grace, its essential characteristic, is replaced by jerky rhythms in a style foreign to our tradition. The *konpa* is seeking, with the complicity of ensembles qualified by "super," a commercial and worldly career . . . and in the name of art and respect for our culture some courageous orchestras and admirable trios continue to cling to the debris of our traditional heritage.[19]

Nemours Jean-Baptiste's extrovert personality is stamped on the profile of the popular music industry in Haiti. Concerned with the mobilization of broad patronage networks for commercial success, Nemours aimed squarely for a mass audience using a commercial formula. In his song "Rhythme commercial" (Commercial rhythm), Nemours boasts of his commercial success:

Konpa-dirèk komèsyal   **Commercial *konpa-dirèk***
Se sak rann nou orijinal   **Is what makes us original**
Se li tout djay ape jwe, se vwe **It's what all the groups are
                                 playing, it's true!**[20]

The Ensemble aux Calebasses under Nemours Jean-Baptiste was among the earliest groups to be commercially recorded. Their *konpa-dirèk* ushered in the era of such Creole neologisms as *cho biznès, fann klèb,* and *hit parèd* (show business, fan club, and hit parade). A Haitian journalist described Nemours's impact in these terms: "Nemours Jean-Baptiste was the first Haitian maestro to seize upon the significance of show-business. Producing a commercial music in the extreme, he succeeded in imposing his rhythm at the very outset by quantity, by repetition, by harassment [of his competitors], and by a constant and continually revived presence."[21]

Although the performers and their immediate audiences were most often from the urban middle class, Nemours strove to overcome class barriers to a mass market. In the late 1950s and early 1960s, Nemours and his band played on Friday nights for urban teenagers; on Saturday nights at soirees at Cabane Choucoune in Pétion-Ville for the elite; and on Sundays at Aux Calebasses or Sou les Palmistes for the middle classes. For a *fèt patwonal* and *fèt champèt,* Nemours bused the band to the provinces. Tickets for the rural dances were generally in the $1 range; concerts were advertised by word-of-mouth and inevitably crowded. A band member recounted how peasants sometimes lined the dirt roads leading into town to give the band the *bat bravo* (applause) traditionally reserved for dignitaries and heads of state.[22] Nemours, like Jazz des Jeunes, also appeared on weekly radio shows broadcast all over the island on Radio Haïti.

The mass popularity of *konpa-dirèk* and the access that Nemours and his band had to the radio opened the possibility for the first time of commercial sponsorhip of a band. A band member explained, "We had a lot of business people support us. Nemours used to make a song for them. They pay us every week to play that song one time in the nightclub. Like Claude Duvalle. We made a song for his business, "Mouen Gladé," so they pay us every week just to play that song in Cabane Choucoune. We make a song called "Stepover Carnival" Stepover Shoes pay us every week to play that song. They give us more money when we play it on radio. When we put that song on a record, they have to pay us more. We put Les Milkies on record for the milk company in Haiti."[23] In 1957, two years after introducing the *konpa-dirèk* and the same year as the election of François Duvalier, Nemours parted ways with his manager and renamed his group the Super Ensemble (sometimes Orchestre) Compas-Direct de Nemours Jean-Baptiste and took up residence at the Palladium, another club in Carrefour. By 1957, *konpa-dirèk* was considered the most popular style in

Haiti, and it imposed a dominant paradigm on Haitian popular music for thirty years. It became a natioinal urban obsession, replacing the *mereng* as the typical Haitan dance. Nemours Jean-Baptiste was reputed to have said, *"Depi ou konn make pa, ou toujou sou konpa"* (From when you can first take a step, you're always on *konpa* [in the groove]). Nemours also tried to crack an international market.

Case Study: "In a Musical Duel—Nemours Jean Baptiste and His Rivals

The tendency for Haitian commercial music, at any given time, to revolve around major dyadic competitions and rivalries is nowhere better illustrated than in the career trajectory of Nemours Jean-Baptiste. His public battles with his competitors provides insight into the tendency of Haitian society toward factionalism and divisiveness, into the combativeness of constituencies galvanized by charismatic leaders, and into the cultural effects of the totalitarian policies pursued by Duvalier.

Nemours's first taste of polemic was at the hands of Jazz des Jeunes. With their status as Haiti's premiere orchestra challenged by Nemours's *konpa-dirèk*, Jazz des Jeunes criticized the new fad and the orchestra responsible for it in a series of commercial *chan pwen*-s. As is typical with a *chan pwen*, the recipient is never named. In the song "Macaque salé" (The dirty monkey), Jazz des Jeunes provided an imaginary (and depreciatory) origin myth for the Super Ensemble Compas-Direct de Nemours Jean-Baptiste:

Makak sale ki te vle fè mizik	The dirty monkeys who wanted to play music
Te reyini sou yon pye kalbasik	Got together under a calabash tree
Fanmi makak te fòme yon ansanm	The monkey family formed an ensemble
Pou yap boule ansanm, ansanm, ansanm	To get along [burn] together, together, together
Yo kouri bri Ansanm Makak kanpe	They ran to the Monkey Ensemble's noise
Nan bouch tout moun sa sèvi yon chante	The songs were on everyone's lips

Kon pèp la byen renmen bagay komik	Because people really love something comic
Yo ale souke kò yo kou bèt ki gen chik	Shaking their bodies like animals with chiggers
Makak pa gen memwa	Monkeys don't have a memory
Nòm mo chantel l se twa	They can sing only three words
Li tankou Rossignol	They're like a nightingale [a toy instrument]
Toutan lan si bemòl . . .	All the time in A-flat . . .
Orang-outang rèt sou sa l di konpa l	Orangutang stays with his so-called *konpa*.[24]

This *pwen* is packed with coded insults and put-downs. Nemours's monkeys "have no memory," lacking appreciation for Haitian folklore and the respect due their elders. According to Jazz des Jeunes, Nemours's ensemble was musically and poetically unsophisticated ("three words," "toy instrument," and a paucity of key signatures), limited in their rhythmic repertoire ("stays with his so-called *konpa*"), and lacking in grace. The calabash tree refers to the club (Aux Calebasses, where the ensemble got its start), and the repetition of the world *ansanm* (ensemble, meaning alternately a musical organization or "together" in Creole as well as French) is a play on the name of the band. In another song with the chastening function of *chan pwen*, Jazz des Jeunes exposed the foreign roots of *konpa* by calling it a "neighbor beat" (i.e., from the Dominican Republic), while musical skill is again made into an issue:

Vous n'avez qu'un seul rhythm	You have only a single rhythm
Quelle honte, compas voisin	What a shame, neighbor beat (*konpa*)
A nous entendre, on croit	To hear you, one would think
N'ouir que de simples stagiaires	One was hearing training exercises[25]

Jazz des Jeunes employed some of the sternest religious imagery available in Vodou to chastise Nemours. In the song "Cafou" (labeled a *kongo*), Baron Samdi—a Gede deity, guardian of the cemeteries, and one of the most fearsome of the Vodou pantheon—is invoked to teach the insolent youngsters a lesson. The crossroads referred to in the song are certainly a musical crossroads, but also refer to the political crossroads of the late 1950s and to the band's belief in committing to the political restructuring of Haiti along *noiriste* lines. Baron Samdi and the Gedes were the deities with whom Papa Doc Duvalier was most closely associated throughout his long presidency, and Duvalier has been accused of intentionally mimicking popular images of Baron Samdi/Papa Gede in his dress, speech, and comportment, fusing his public image with the *lwa*. The song's plea for Baron to bring an opponent to the cemetery for a failure to commit has an eerie parallel in the reign of political terror under way in Haiti.

Baron! Baron woy!	**Baron! Baron oh!**
Piti moun fronte kape joure gran moun	**A nasty little guy is insulting his superior**
Kondwi l ale lan simityè, Kafou o o!	**Take him to the cemetery, crossroads oh!**
Pa wè angaje	**He's not committed to the struggle.**[26]

The period from 1957 until about 1968 is known in Haiti as the *epòk polemik Nemou ak Siko* (epoch of the controversy, or polemic, between Nemours and Sicot), a period in which the competition between the two performers occupied center stage in Haitian popular culture.[27] It is striking how well these events are recalled by urban Haitians who witnessed the period. Producer Fred Paul remembered his own childhood as being profoundly affected by the two bands:

I grew up at the time when Nemours Jean-Baptiste was at his best. That was a great time in Haiti—I loved it. It's a pity because I know that none of these kids now are having half the time I had. We didn't need money, there was no drugs. All we did was enjoy the music. Kids' idols were . . . well, most of the people were for Nemours Jean-Baptiste and the rest were for Wébert Sicot. People loved Sicot for his sax playing and for his accordian player, Toto Duval. Nemours wasn't as good a musician, but he was a great band leader, and they loved his singers, but the idol really was Richard Duroseau [accordionist for Nemours Jean-Baptiste]. I used to love him, and knew his solos before I knew my lessons. We were at school, and we used to memorize his solos and sing them and fantasize with them, and it was so great! Saturday night, always listening to the *konpa* shows. Nemours, and all the Nemours songs, and like big discussion, polemic, and things like that.[28]

Wébert Sicot, the self-proclaimed "Maestro Difficile," was Haiti's foremost saxophonist and a great showman. Nemours and Sicot had played together in the Conjunto International, and Nemours asked him to join his new group, Ensemble aux Calebasses. At the time, Sicot was playing in the Orchestre Atomique which Nemours had left the year before. After Nemours achieved success with the *konpa-dirèk*, Sicot left Nemours's organization and by 1956 was playing in the very popular Orchestre Casino International. In 1957–58, Sicot put together his own band and coined a new dance rhythm barely distinguishable from Nemours's *konpa-dirèk*, which he called *kadans ranpa*. *Kadans* means rhythm, and *ranpa* comes from "ramparts," signaling the fighting spirit that characterized their relationship from then on. As with the Super Ensemble Compas Direct de Nemours Jean-Baptiste, Sicot used the name of his rhythm as his ensemble's name: Super Ensemble Cadence Rampas de Wébert Sicot. Sicot's *kadans ranpa* was a competitive strategy designed to capture some of the limelight from Nemours.

Sicot was Nemours's main competitor for the Haitian market in the late 1950s and early 1960s. Although Nemours had aimed his first musical broadsides at Jazz des Jeunes, he quickly turned his competitive broadsides and his newfound skill with musical invective toward Sicot and the threat posed by the *kadans ranpa*. The two groups imitated each other, strove to outdo the other, and occasionally stole material. Wagner Lalanne, Nemours's former keyboardist, talked about musical piracy in the period: "If we hear Jazz des Jeunes make a good song, we always picked it up. If we hear Sicot make a good song, we picked it up. So when we hear on the radio the Sicot song "Cadence rampas numéro un," Nemours said, "By God, that's a very good song. We'll pick up the same song and ours will beat it." When we came out with the *konpa* "Compas cabane choucoune," it was the biggest song in the country. But if you listen, you'll see it was "Cadence rampas numéro un!"[29]

The polemic developed through a series of songs of derision which explored putative points of contrast between the two groups: Sicot's superior musicianship and Nemours's claim to originality. But both recognized that the polemic had become a mutually beneficial marketing strategy, raising the general level of fan identification and interest. Although dubbed a *polemik* (polemic, controversy) in Creole, the relationship between Nemours Jean-Baptiste and Wébert Sicot could more accurately be described as a rivalry. Nemours lauded the effects of competition in his song "Rythme commercial," which portrayed Nemours as a productive, fruit-bearing mango tree at which rocks are thrown. Nemours borrowed this image from a Haitian proverb meaning, "One only throws rocks at mango trees that are full." The song frames Sicot's motives as an attempt to imitate Nemours's musical creativity:

Se sou pyebwa ki gen fwi	The tree that's bearing fruit
Se sou li yap voye wòch	It's at him they're throwing rocks
Men sispann fè jalouzi, Se vwe	But let's halt all this jealousy, truly!
Nemou se yon pye mango	Nemours is a mango tree
Kontre tan donnen tout bon	Defying time, always yielding fruit
Voye wòch toutlajounnen, Sou li!	They're throwing rocks all the time, at him!
Konkirans se bèl bagay	Competition is a good thing
Se sak rann youn nonm travay	It's what makes us work
Pa chita fè tripotay, Se vwe!	Don't keep on spreading gossip, truly![30]

Sicot, widely considered the better musician, demeaned Nemours's musical talent in "Deux guidons" (Two standards):

Monchè vwazen se ave w m ape pale	My dear neighbor, I'm going to talk with you
Paske mwen vini pou m di w verite	Because I come to tell you the truth
Se pou w sispann kapab tronpe moun seryè	You have to stop trying to fool serious people
Paske tout Ayisyen konnen bon mizik	Because every Haitian knows good music
Depi ou koumanse son sèl kout sakstofòn	From when you start until you fnish
Jisk'ou fini! Men monchè	It's a single saxophone honk! But my friend
Fòk ou kapab fè tèt ou travay, se pa manti . . .	You have to make yourself work. No lie . . .
Ou pa onte! Ou pa kapab fè yon solo	You have no shame! You can't do a solo

Toutan se moun k ap fè l pou w	**All the time, other people are playing for you**
Men pa w, men pa . . .	**But not you, not you . . .**[31]

Nemours countered wth "Byen konte, mal kalkile" (Well counted, but badly calculated):

Byen konte wi, mal kalkile	**Well counted yes, but badly calculated**
Mayestwo Nemou tèt kare	**Maestro Nemours is a level-headed guy**
Nemou se yon gran misyonè	**Nemours is a great missionary**
Ke Bondyè voye sou latè	**That God sent to Earth**[32]

Aspects of the Nemours-Sicot rivalry elided with political (Duvalierist) discourse of the period. The characterization of Nemours as "a great missionary that God sent to Earth" was strikingly similar to the *poésie commandée* for Duvalier such as that at the beginning of this chapter; the term "missionary" was often used to describe Duvalier. Other examples of the "bleed through" of political and musical discourses will follow later in this section.

At Carnival, the two bands polarized audiences with their rivalry. Participants in Carnival by the new *konpa-dirèk* and *kadans ranpa* groups symbolized the rising importance of the middle class in the country's political affairs. In the procession, the commercial bands were mounted on floats pulled by trucks or on flatbed trucks with signs announcing their commercial sponsors. Nemours and Sicot used amplified instruments and sound systems capable of overwhelming acoustic bands-on-foot. They were the magnets around which the largest crowds at Carnival gathered to demonstrate their affiliation with their favorite group. After the parade, Nemours and Sicot were stationed in the area near the club Ronde Point on the Bizantnè for continuous dancing.

The commercially competitive spirit that Nemours and Sicot helped to generate in the polemic has a close parallel to the competition between *ekip futbols*-s (soccer teams) and to the highly fractionalized geographical competition between carnival bands (and *rara* bands) from different neighborhoods (which have decidedly martial or militaristic derivations). The sports and military metaphors discussed in the Introduction became a prominent feature of *konpa* in this period. Nemours helped to originate the use of colors and banners reminiscent of *futbol* teams. He took red and white as his colors, and when he died in 1982, he was buried in his red and white clothes, with the red and white flag of *konpa-dirèk* laid out on a bier resembling a carnival float.[33] During carnival, Sicot's and Nemours' fans would often clash. Partisans could be recognized by the colors they wore to identify with their favorite band. Even the *tonton makout*-s split down the middle at carnival, sporting one set of colors or the other in addition to their denim uniforms. Papa Doc's children also had conflicting fan loyalties: Jean-Claude favored Sicot's *kadans ranpa* and Denise the *konpa-dirèk*. Because Nemours was so well-liked by the *makout*-s and because they patronized his band so heavily, an impression developed that Nemours's group was the band of the political elite, while Sicot's group was more popular among the masses. The following lines from Sicot's song "Symbol de la cadence" discuss his set of four colors, the banner of *kadans,* and the quest for victory (over *konpa*):

Kat koulè byen chwasi	**Four well-chosen colors**
Vèt e blan, nwa e rouj	**Green, white, black, and red**
Ala youn bèl etandard	**Such a beautiful banner**
K ap simbolize kadans ranpa	**Symbolizing** *kadans ranpa* . . .
Avèk vèt, simbòl de lesperans	**With green, symbol of hope**
Se sak fè n toujou pi ot	**That's what always keeps us higher**
Avèk blan, simbol de lapirite	**With white, symbol of purity**
Nou toujou inosan	**We are always innocent**
Koulè nwa, simbol de nòt koulè	**The color black, symbol of our race**
Fanatik-yo byen chwazi	**The fans have chosen it well**
Koulè rouj, viktwa l ap kontinye	**The color red, victory is continuing**
Kadans l ap toujou an jwa	*Kadans* **will always bring joy**[34]

   The symbolism of red and black is discussed in such a way as to make a connection with the colors for the Duvalierist flag (red and black, not the red and blue of the traditional Haitian flag). The flags, colors, and talk of victory drive home the militaristic and sports metaphors. The Nemours and Sicot bands played a *futbol* match in 1964 in the Stade Sylvio Cator before 35,000 fans, a case of the sports and combat metaphors in commercial music becoming reality. Each group followed up on the tie game (score: one to one) by releasing its own account of the event in song form. Sicot offered "Pété filet" (Noise at the net):

Nou menm kadans ranpa	We in the cadence rampa
Metyè n se jwe mizik	Our profession is playing music
Nou tande afè foutbal	But we heard about the football affair
Nou blije pran pozisyon	And we had to take a position
Siko rèt deye kare	Sicot stayed behind the square
Li pase de aryè	He passed two defenders
Li chavire l sou kote	He upset it in place
Yo wè balon-an nan file	And they saw the ball in the net
Men mwen pa janm konprann	I never understood
Pou ou aprann jwe foubal	How you could learn to play soccer
Ala yon bèl fomasyon	What a great team!
Men vwazen ou gen chans	You were lucky, neighbor[35]

The version of the story from the Nemours Jean-Baptiste camp was called "Huit Avril" (April 8th). The "Atomic rhythm" is a reference to Nemours Jean-Baptiste's earlier musical evolution within the Dominican-influenced group, Trio Atomique, but it also reiterates the militaristic sensibilities engaged by the polemic (i.e., our rhythm is as effective as an atomic bomb).

Wit avril, nan Stad Silvyo Katò	Eighth of April in Sylvio Cator Stadium
Mezanmi, nan yon doul mizikal	My friends, in a musical duel
Ni graden ni tribin lateral	Bleachers and box seats
Tout chaje a tout kapasite	All of them full to capacity
Pèp-la te si telman ape jwi	People were enjoying themselves so much
Yo nome konpa-dirèk avi	They proclaimed *konpa-dirèk* for life!!
Rit-nou-an se rit ki Atomik	Our rhythm is an atomic rhythm[36]

Despite sporadic efforts to quiet the polemic, Nemours and Sicot waged war on each other throughout the 1960s.[37] At the 1967 Carnival, the Super Ensemble Nemours Jean-Baptiste sang, "*Siko se mawoule, nou pote fèy pou ba li medsin*" (Sicot is a goatherd, let's bring him leaves for medicine), casting Sicot as an ignorant peasant. In return, Sicot's group boasted of the band's effect on their carnival *fanatik* (fans), *"Depi Siko parèt, gason pa kanpe, fanm mare tete-yo sere"* (When Sicot appears, guys can't stand still, women have to tie their breasts down tight). The competition between Sicot's "Bon jan vant" (A good wind) and Nemours's "Pwen fè pa" (Merciless) was the centerpiece of the 1968 Carnival: "This year Wébert Sicot launched 'Bon jan vant' and Nemours Jean-Baptiste 'Pwen fè pa.' The two pieces with their captivating rhythms were quickly picked up by the partisans of the two groups which get the carnival rolling."[38]

The rivalry of course, was rooted not only in sports metaphors and commercial dictates, but also in the competitive habitus of Carnival (see below) and in the peculiarities of Haitian politics under Duvalier. Duvalierism, which attempted to monopolize political space, outlawed competing political parties and imposed the Partie Unité Nationale as the only political party in Haiti. By proclaiming an end to political struggle, Duvalier created a vacuum filled by various simulacra of political struggle (especially the musical polemic).

"Don't Touch Duvalier": Papa Doc's *Koudyay* Politics

Koudyay is a redistributive process deeply embedded in Haitian popular politics. Deriving from military celebrations, *koudyay*-s are "hosted" by those in power, who supply the drink, food, music, theme, and transportation, if necessary, for a popular and exuberant street party. The interaction provides the lower classes with a good party while they give the appearance of widespread popular support for the *koudyay*'s sponsor. *Koudyay* was a political tactic that Duvalier employed enthusiastically and often. Duvalier masterfully orchestrated Carnival and *koudyay* for political purposes, diverting popular attention from social and economic problems and harnessing the populist passions of the masses for pro-Duvalier, anti-elite displays. Duvalier's July festivals, called "Carnival des Fleurs," special carnivals, and impromptu *koudyay* all served as weapons in his politicocultural arsenal. As I mentioned previously, Duvalier, his lieutenants, and his militia patronized popular musicians and carnival organizations in such a way as to incorporate them into the system, using the musicians' appeal and sway with the people as a buttress of the regime. Musicians were expected to play at Carnival, at *koudyay*-like demonstrations, and for private parties of the political class.

For the first two Carnivals under Duvalier, the government was concerned that the economic crisis and the diminished funds available for carnival would reflect badly on the new president. Progovernment journalists argued that the public should not hold the government responsible for the sorry state of Carnival.[39] For Duvalier's first Carnival in 1958, the government experimented with a stationary event, a "Foire Carnavalesque" (carnival fair), on the waterfront grounds of the 1949 exposition.[40] This was perhaps the most ambitious effort to reconfigure Carnival's meaning since the ascendancy of bourgeois Carnival under the American occupation. Traditional carnival ambience requires moving through, taking over, transforming, and transgressing space, and thus carnival crowds typically resist map-like or tableau stagings.[41] The lack of public support for the experiment was evident on the first day, and the Carnival Committee reinstated the traditional parade for Monday and Tuesday.

Carnival bands were mobilized in support of Duvalier's revolution. In 1959, the carnival group Titato carried signs proclaiming "Long live Duvalier, the successor to Dessalines" and "Don't touch Duvalier."[42] In the next few years, carnival groups sported name such as 22d of May, New Haiti, In Danger of Dying,[43] and Thank You, Papa Doc, We Have No More Yaws.[44] Like the *tonton makout*-s, these neighborhood carnival bands were incorporated into the state redistributive network, and the support and financing that the government offered helped to insure their allegiance.

A prominent *makout* named Antoine Khouri (immortalized in Nemours's 1966 song "Ti Carole") led the Nemours ensemble on a motorcycle. His counterpart, another *makout* named Jean Fils-Aimé, also on motorcycle, led the Sicot band.[45] The final float in the carnival parade was reserved for the year's favorite band, but in one legendary instance, fourteen-year-old Jean-Claude Duvalier sent a group of *tonton makout*-s to intmidate the Nemours party, which had won the competition for best carnival méringue, into parading in front of Sicot's group.

The Nemours and Sicot bands were hired to play official and private parties of the political elite. A member of the Ensemble Nemours Jean-Baptiste discussed their relation to the Duvalier government: "That's the way it was with the government. They give us jobs to play, and they pay. That is our job, so we play. Sometme they give you what subject you have to do. You play the government's song on radio. Sometime the government member calls you, and he say, 'I give you that subject, so you have to make a song.' But we would never put that song on record! [Laughs] Sometime we could make a song for the president,

so when we have to put that song on the record, we get the same song and put other words on it."[46]
This quotation suggests that the band often practiced a subtle kind of *mawonaj* rather than commit presidential praise songs to vinyl. However, nearly all of the popular musicians of the era were recipients in one way or another of Duvalierist patronage. As one musician recounted, an invitation from the president was difficult to turn down:

> Do you know how many times I have to play in front of Duvalier? I had to play for Duvalier, because, let me tell you, my band was the number one band in Haiti at that time. . . . You don't [decide] to play for the government—they force you to play. . . . I sing for Duvalier. I was not a Duvalierist, but they come to your house talking to you like, "I got a contract for you. You have to sign it . . . some papers, a little money." They say, "Listen, tomorrow morning I want to see you at the palace at eight o'clock. That's it! You think there's any Haitian who says, "No, I'm not coming?" No way! Only if you want to kill yourself, because if you say, "No, I'm not coming," pow, that's it. Okay, who can say no to that guy who had such a lot of power? They'll kill you in a second. When you are a Haitian, you have to deal with those things every day. . . . But people want you to say no, when nobody else dare say no to those people at that time.[47]

The government made use of *konpa* bands for Carnival even in the provincial cities. A member of a 1960s band from the northern city of Cap-Haïtien told me: "Every time there was a political manifestation [demonstration], every time there was a Carnival, the mayor or police chief would come to us and give us orders to go out. . . . The last thing they did was to arrest a guy in our band who was going to Port-au-Prince in his truck with a load of lumber in order to make him stay in Cap-Haïtien and play at Carnival."[45] Duvalier's *koudyay*-s accompanied most political events of any importance. Duvalier's reelection in 1961 was greeted by a *koudyay* in which crowds were singing, "Papa Doc, dig your feet in deep."[49] After the shooting of his children's bodyguards in 1963 (later attributed to some of Duvalier's close aides), Duvalier launched one of the bloodiest massacres of his reign. With potential victims seeking asylum in the Dominican embassy, Duvalier decreed a special carnival. Bands, floats, and masques surrounded the embassy, intensifying a diplomatic impasse that almost brought the two countries to war. Not long after, on April 30, 1963, as an Organization of

American States investigative committee arrived in Haiti, Papa Doc trucked thousands of peasants into the capital and supplied them with rum and music in order to impress the committee with Duvalier's fanatic support from the people.[50]

The 1964 Carnival was organized around the theme "Papa Doc for life" in preparation for the upcoming plebiscite on the proposed presidency for life. Carnival songs became campaign theme songs, broadcast throughout Haiti in the period before the vote. The day of the plebiscite was organized as a *koudyay* with music and alcohol provided to potential voters. This was also the year in which the celebrated rivalry between Nemours and Sicot was played out on the field of combat. Recall the lyrics from a song by Nemours Jean-Baptiste commemorating the event. Here again, we see political rhetoric and context bleeding into popular songs that are not intended to be political in a strict sense:

Pèp-la te si telman ape jwi	**People were enjoying themselves so much**
Yo nome konpa-dirèk avi	**They proclaimed *konpa-dirèk* for life!**

With the further consolidation of his revolution, Papa Doc made his presence keenly felt at Carnival. For Carnival 1965, the mayor reminded the population to experience an "explosion of joy and a triumph of art under the sign of the order of the country of Duvalierists" and asked residents to decorate their houses and vehicles.[51] Wébert Sicot won for best carnival song in 1965 with his "Men jet-la" (Here comes the jet), encapsulating that year's carnival theme: "To pay homage to His Majestic Excellency President for Life, the Incomparable Leader Dr. François DUVALIER, the Inspired Constructor of New Haiti, who wrote, to the glory of the Fatherland, the most beautiful, the most dazzling page of National History after that of January 1, 1804 [independence]: the construction of the Mais Gate INTERNATIONAL AIRPORT."[52] The Nemours Jean-Baptiste entry that year was "Tout limen" (All lit up), in recognition of Duvalier's electricity program. Duvalier's grand carnival ball in honor of the airport took place at the nightclub Cabane Choucoune featuring Jazz des Jeunes in a folkloric show and l'Ensemble Nemours Jean-Baptiste playing for the dancers.

An incident at the Rumba Bar in Cap-Haïtien provoked a major crisis for Duvalier in 1965. The club was a popular *makout* hangout, and patrons regularly fired guns for fun. The director of a local band, who was a personal friend of Duvalier, made a trip to the capital to ask that he intercede to stop the shooting in nghtclubs. When a Cap-Haïtien army lieutenant who was also a *makout* found out about the request, he went into the club with a machine gun looking for the bandleader. Failing to find him, he opened fire and killed a prominent Cap-Haïtien citizen, Antoine Piquion, son of the former prefect of the city and brother-in-law of former President Magloire. The killer appeared before Duvalier to explain and was subsequently released without punishment. A similar shooting had occurred in a Port-au-Prince bar three months earlier, and a bandleader had been shot and killed at Carnival in the capitol the previous month. Tired of the escalating public violence of the *tonton makout*-s, over 8,000 people came out for the funeral of Piquion to send a message to the government.[53]

In 1967, the "Year Ten of the Duvalierist Revolution," carnival enthusiasm was dampened by the economic crisis (aggravated by a hurricane) and by a guerrilla war waged by the new United Communist Party of Haiti (PUCH). That year, Duvalier celebrated his sixtieth birthday with a second five-day April carnival called the "Carnival au Printemps" (Springtime carnival). Opponents (reputed to be either communists or his own close aides) set off a bomb at this carnival in a *frèsko* (shaved ice) cart under a float on which a band was playing a pro-Duvalier carnival *méringue*. 1968 was the year in which Duvalier "involved himself personally in the organization of Carnival by offering four floats symbolizing important projects of his government," including the Temple of Culture, and the new Red Cross building.[54] The theme for carnival was "Peligré in Action," commemorating a new hydroelectric plant, and represented by a float from the Department of Economic Affairs with a giant "V" for the victory of Papa Doc over the *blakawout* (blackout). The *tonton makout* float represented a planned housing project, Cité Simone Olvide Duvalier, named after Duvalier's wife; Public Transportation financed a float depicting the new airport; and Foreign Affairs sponsored a float on the theme of the writings of Papa Doc.[55] The success of the 1968 Carnival was ascribed to "the climate of peace and order installed in the country by the preeminent Man of State, his Excellency the President for Life of the Republic Doctor François Duvalier . . . who has been able to muzzle and exorcise the demon of political adventurism."[56]

Another *koudyay* was staged for Nelson Rockefeller's 1969 visit to Haiti. The celebratory crowd inspired Rockefeller to walk out onto the balcony of the palace with the now frail Duvalier on his arm to wave to the masses. The resulting "photo-op" for Duvalier, a smiling American envoy arm in arm with Duvalier, appeared in newscasts and in print stories around the world and undercut the calculated distance that U.S. administrations had put between the United States and the dis-comfortng ally in the Caribbean. Duvalier's mastery of *koudyay* politics was so well-tuned that he was able to use it to embarrass the United States while projecting his popularity on a world scale.

"The *Vaksin* Is Roaring": Communist Roots Music

While the regime polished its cultural armor, popular music was also put into the service of the anti-Duvalierist movement. Duvalier had a strategic relationship to communism, allowing communist organizing and propagandizing (and communist or former-communist advisers) early on in his regime if it served his purposes. The presence of com-munists was especially helpful as a card to be played with the Castro-fixated U.S. State Department. When it suited his purposes, Duvalier launched pogroms against the left to convince the United States that he was their ally in the fight against communism. For example, in 1960, after the National Students Union released a pro-Cuba message, Duvalier had twenty of its leaders arrested.[57] Students pressured the government to release those arrested and began a national student strike in November. Although the students were eventually released, the strike dragged on until March. By then, Duvalier had expelled the Catholic archbishop of Port-au-Prince, changed the name of the uni-versity to the Université de l'Etat, required noncommunist certification for all students, and fired many faculty members who supported the students. Author Jacques Alexis's Party of National Accord (one of two communist parties in Haiti at the time; the Haitian Communist Party, or PCH, disbanded in 1947) withdrew its support of the strike in a strategic retreat. With direct political action frustrated for the student activists, many turned to cultural agitation.

During their strike, the student activists found themselves politically isolated. They understood that broad-based anti-Duvalierist organiz-ing was called for, but a great social and cultural gulf separated the students from Haiti's large peasant majority, who were largely illiterate and thus had no access to the communist literary and propaganda efforts. The students resolved to incorporate cultural outreach to the peasants with literacy campaigns. In the spring of 1962, a group of leftist students in Port-au-Prince formed a cultural organization called

Karako Blè (blue peasant dress), which was followed that summer by another group, Vaksin (bamboo trumpet), and soon after by Lanbi (conch shell). These three groups launched a cultural struggle to develop a peasant-style music and poetry (in Creole, not French) with which to build bridges to Haiti's peasants. Karako Blè and the other groups fomented their cultural revolution while opposition continued in other channels, including the *kamoken* invasion of exiles in 1963, radio broadcasts by communist writer René Dépestre from Cuba, and continued labor and student organizing by the left.

As leftists and as members of the heavily Catholic middle class, the activists had an often uncomfortable relationship to Vodou, and disputes broke out among the groups over how to deal with peasant and working-class religious beliefs. Karako Blè, which was considered a more "polished" group with a greater tolerance for religion, peppered their songs with references to Bondyè (God) and the *lwa* (Haitian deities). Their 1962 song "Nwèl abitan" (Peasants' Christmas) contained the lyrics:

Nwèl abitan . . .
Sou tout latè ke Bondyè fe
Nwèl y ape chante

Peasants' Christmas . . .
All over the land that God made
They're singing songs of Christmas

In another song, they sang *"Ogou mande tout kè, tout tèt, tout bra"* (Ogou—deity of war—asks for every heart, every head, every arm). Vaksin, which considered religious beliefs exclusively a residue of bourgeois hegemony, responded "point for point" to each "politically incorrect" song of Karako Blè. Their response to the song about Ogou was a piece entitled "Kanmarad" (Comrade).

Kanmarad, souk kò-nou
Mete san nou sou nou, pran sa n bezwen
Mete n an wout, pa rete nan chimen
Ann ale ann ale, vaksin ape gwonde
N ap fè yon chèn ka vini yon gwo chèn
Se pou n travay pou peyi a ka bèl

Comrades, rouse yourselves
Get your blood going, take what you need
Take to the road, don't stop along the way
Let's go, let's go, the *vaksin* is roaring
We're making a chain that's growing longer
We'll work to make the country beautiful

Vaksin gwonde, ann ale se nou li   The *vaksin* is roaring, it's us that
    rele   it's calling[58]

Vaksin sang a song called "You jou konsa" (One of these days):

Peyizan, peyizan rele "Anmwe   Peasants are crying "help!"
    . . . o"
Bofrè vini keyi flè janden-mwen o   The "godfather" cuts flowers in
                                                         my garden
Travayè, travayè rele o "Anmwe   Workers are crying "help!"
    . . . o"
Chen frans chita rès kouray-   A French dog sits on my courage
    mwen o
Toutlanwit m pa sa domi o   All night long, I can't sleep
Toutlanwit je m pa fenmen o   All night long, my eyes are wide
                                                        open
Bèl banbilay fèt lan nòs bofrè   The "godfather" is having a grand
                                                        party
Bling youn jou konsa   But one day still
Vè va kraze sou tab bofrè o   The glass will break on the "god-
                                                        father's" table
Adye konpè ban mwen tan   Just give me a little time, my
    mwen o   brother[59]

The cultural organizations taught Creole literacy using their own educational materials, and they performed wherever they could in the urban areas and countryside. Some members worked in the official or governmental literacy organizations as well. Members took *noms de guerre* as a hedge against Duvalierist retribution, but most were able to operate at least covertly up until about 1968. In 1968, the two major communist factions united to form PUCH to wage armed struggle against Duvalierist rule. Duvalier resolved to step up his campaign against communist and leftist organizations, to wipe out the Creole culture movement (which he correctly understood as influenced by Marxists), and to expose leftist sympathizers. He ordered crackdowns on unions, schools, and universities, Haitians returning from abroad, and even the church. In 1969, on the advice of his ally Edouard C. Paul, the anticommunist director of the state literacy bureau (ONAAC, National organization for literacy and community action), Duvalier ordered Paul to disband his own organization because of reputed communist influence within the group.[60] With nearly all oppositional routes cut off, it became clear that the left had failed to build a significant popular base among the peasants; this achievement, unfortunately, was claimed instead by the Duvalierist movement which, with its *tonton makout*-s, bridged the city and countryside rather effectively for one of the first times in Haitian history.

Members of the leftist cultural organizations joined a burgeoning Haitian immigrant population in the United States and Canada and in the educational and medical missions to French-speaking Africa. At the same time, activists in the movement, whch came to call itself *kilti libète* (freedom culture), found sustenance and inspiration in the engagée cultural expressions of the 1968 Paris student rebellion, the *nueva cancion* (new song) movement of Latin America, and the "freedom song" component of the civil rights and black power movement in the United States.[61] These political refugees, intellectuals from middle-class backgrounds, constituted a new expatriate political movement, distinct from the conservative opposition to Duvalier, which was under the influence of former Haitian presidents Magloire and Fignolé. The refugees were the nucleus for new leftist cultural organizations in the diaspora during the 1970s (see Chapter 4).

"Everybody Was Somebody from Overseas": *Yeye* and *Mini-djaz*

The early 1960s in Haiti generally associated with the popularity of *konpa*, but it was also the period during which Haitian schoolchildren, mostly children of the elite or of the comfortable middle classes, first began playing rock and roll and small-group jazz. Many of the young from the elite and middle-class shared a cosmopolitan interest in jazz, rhythm and blues, rock-and-roll, *pachanga* (an outgrowth of the cha-cha), and later the twist. The following account from the daily newspaper *Le Nouvelliste* chronicled the 100th anniversary party for Barbancourt Rum in April 1962, at which a new Haitian composition in the style of a twist premiered: "The enthusiastic clamor that saluted the Barbancourt Twist made the Rex Theatre tremble, the audience was literally transported. The ovation seemed like it would never finish. . . . Twist and peppermint [peppermint twist] for the youth, *méringues* and *pachangas* for everybody."[62]

Hard-core Duvalierists saw the interest in foreign popular forms as a rejection of indigenous culture. After a performance of the pop-jazz vocal group the Starlettes in early 1960, a harsh critique was launched in *Le Nouvelliste*. The group was directed by vocalist and composer

Herby Widmaïer and was influenced by pop-jazz vocal combos of the
United State such as the Hi-Lo's and the Four Freshmen, although
their repertoire was weighted toward indigenous music. Georges Fidélia accused Widmaïer of neglecting to explain the bourgeois roots of
the song "Souvenir d'Haïti" (also known as "Haïti cherie"), which was
on the program, and of singing in such a way that his sonority *"n'avait
rien de terroire"* (lacked local flavor). Fidélia claimed that Widmaïer's
arrangements were an "emasculation of the Haitian soul . . . under the
pretext of modernism." He complained of the American and Cuban
influences in some songs:

> Herby offers us this American imitation of a Haitian melody which is
> itself only an imitation of an Afro-Cuban music, which is now an out-
> of-fashion genre even in its country of origin. It's for good reason that
> we complain of having received this fourth-hand junk. . . . Herby, in his
> new technique of harmonization, has the tendency to conserve only
> the melody whose insufficiency [in comparison to rhythm] has been
> recognized. Thus, we ask ourselves what remains of essence in the ex-
> pression of the Haitian soul that won't be diluted in the universality of
> the too-academic inspiration of this young innovator? He thinks that
> it is important to help Haitian popular music evolve. But he should
> worry about the capacity of the audience to follow him.[63]

There was much of the fervor of Duvalier's *négritude* in Fidélia's
stance. Widmaïer's program for that night included "Haïti cherie,"
"Papa Simbi," and "Papa bon Dieu," all local pieces by well-loved Haitian composers (Otello Bayard,Guy Durosier, Raoul Guillaume). Yet
his modern and jazzy treatment of these, combined with his light skin
and foreign heritage, left him vulnerable to the "inauthentic" charge.

Haiti was courted by the French music industry as a market for
rock and roll. Young boys formed rock-influenced combos that after
about 1962 were generically *yeye* (from the Beatle's refrain "She loves
you, yeah, yeah, yeah").[64] Some groups, like a quartet named Kaka
Poul (Chicken Shit), mixed Latin and jazz with a bit of rock-and-roll.
Kaka Poul played as early as 1958 at Horseback, a club in Furcy (in
the mountains above Port-au-Prince). Alix "Tit" Pascal, a member of
the *yeye* Les As de Pétion-Ville (The aces of Pétion-Ville) discussed
this period:

> This is the early sixties. We had the influence of the twist, Chubby
> Checker, Elvis Presley, and from France, Johnny Halladay. There was

also an effort by the promoters from this era in the United States and Europe to push these things in the Caribbean, so they organized the youth into fan clubs. The girls were part of these fan clubs, so the guys who were fourteen, fifteen, sixteen, wanted to emulate these guys. So what you have is the mushrooming of small groups [trying to be] Elvis Presley. Les Copains came in with a singer who was like Elvis. We had two types of singers in the bands: we had the *chanteurs de choque* ["shock" singers for the boisterous songs] and the *chanteurs de charme* ["charm" singers for the romantic songs]. Every Sunday, the concerts happened in all the movie theaters of Port-au-Prince. Then you had this twist kind of group. Some guy would pain [hurt] themselves in a leather jacket in the heat we have in Haiti. On the stage, throwing themselves on the floor; those guys were crazy. Everybody was [imitating] somebody from overseas.[65]

These groups took tough-sounding French names like Les Copains (The buddies), Les As de Pétion-ville, Les Jets, Les Vampires, Les Mordues (The bitten), Les Blousons Noirs (The black shirts, i.e., The Teddy Boys), Les Shelberts (The show-offs), Les Loups Noirs (The black wolves). Some *yeye* made it to the Rex Theater, considered the best performance venue in Haiti. An advertisement for a 1962 Rex concert lists the *yeye* quintet Blousons Noirs as the opening group for Nemours Jean-Baptiste.[66] In addition to the movie theater concerts, they played for school parties and for radio concerts at Radio d'Haïti. Radio d'Haïti became a hangout for the *yeye* generation of musicians, who absorbed jazz theory from Herby Widmaïer and mixed jazz tunes in with their French and American rock repertory.

The *yeye* movement, with its strong cosmopolitan component, was spearheaded by boys from families that could afford to send them to school. But there was an increasing pressure on young Haitian musicians not simply to copy foreign styles but to adapt them to Haitian circumstances, contexts, and ideology. In 1963, the relationship had deteriorated between the United States and Haiti. President Kennedy was pressuring Duvalier to step down at the end of his contitutional term even while Duvalier was orchestrating a campaign to have himself voted president for life. As a result, relations continued to deteriorate. American aid and tourism dried up. Anti-Americanism and aggressive nationalism contributed to the pressure for the young groups to Haitianize their repertoire, to avoid becoming culturally "contaminated" by foreign powers. Live audiences at dance concerts also contributed to the shift toward indigenous material (in this case *konpa*) in the repertories of the *yeye*. Rock and roll was popular for listening, but Haitian dancers never took to the improvisational or free-style dancing of the twist and watusi era, preferring the close-contact step of Nemours's *konpa-dirèk*. In order to play school graduation parties, the groups learned to translate *konpa* hits into a samll combo format by adding conga drums and a bell. the resulting formation was the seed for the ensemble called *mini-djaz.*

In 1963, the Hotel Ibo Lele put together a small combo using players from the *yeye* bands as well as from some of the older *mereng* orchestras. Initially called Ensemble Ibo Lélé, they later changed their name to emphasize their independence from the hotel. Their new name, Ibo Combo, was considered a very "Haitian" sounding name for a dance band. Ibo refers to a group of deities in Haitian Vodou associated with the Igbo people from what is now called Nigeria, and the term "combo" was added to demonstrate their affinity with small combo jazz and with bossa nova groups in Brazil. Under the tutelage of Herby Widmaïer, the band attempted to modernize the *konpa* with jazz settings, jazz solos, and with a studied sophistication reminiscent of bossa nova. They enjoyed a few years of success as a favorite band of Haiti's urban elite, playing steady gigs at the Ibo Lélé hotel on Fridays and for private parties. In the words of Widmaïer, "Ibo Combo was young guys willing to modernize. I say modernize—they were using the Nemours beat but with harmonies a little bit more elaborate, a little jazzier. I made an arrangement of 'The Song of Laura' from *Doctor Zhivago* which sat on a *konpa* beat like it was made for it. Everybody was dancing *konpa* to it, but there was a fellow who came up afterwards and said, 'That's nice boys, but why don't you play a little *konpa-dirèk* for me.' We had a big laugh, but to them it wasn't *konpa-dirèk* because it had more than two chords and it had a different kind of melody."[66]

Ibo Combo introduced these more complex chord progressions and improvised solos, and they introduced a new generation of Haitians to Brazilian bossa nova and American jazz. According to drummer José Tavernier, "We were the first professional small group that would perform for crowds and get paid for it. We paved the way for young Haitians to play music and be accepted by their parents as musicians. And I'm very proud that musicians respect Ibo Combo, because wherever we played, we tried to put a certain feeling in the music. We wanted to be the first ones satisfied. Because of that, we couldn't make money!"[67]

In 1965, some teenage students from the middle-class neighborhood Bas-Peu-de-Choses formed a small ensemble under the leadership of alto saxophonist Tony Moïse, soon taking the name Shleu-Shleu. The band once claimed that "the name is from an ancient tribe of mysterious Africa," but it is generally acknowledged that the name was a fabrication.[68] A few months later, Syrian-mulatto businessman Dada Jacaman heard them practicing and asked to take over as manager. His extensive contacts with the Port-au-Prince elite were indispensible in their rapid rise in popularity. The instrumentation of the group set the standard of nine musicians for the *mini-djaz* era.[69] The term *mini-djaz*, supposedly coined by Nemours Jean-Baptiste, linked the new smaller *djaz* to the image of stylistic novelty conveyed in the 1960s by the miniskirt.

Their audience was a middle-class and bourgeois one. Shleu-Shleu played regularly at the restaurant Ronde Point, at the Collège Saint-Pierre, and in the early days between Nemours's sets at Cabane Choucoune. They played for teenagers at the movie theater programs called *sine teyat* and at school *kèmès* (Sunday and early evening dances). This was a period when volleyball games were a major social function for school children, and Shleu-Shleu regulary played the volleyball circuit. The youthful nature of the music is conveyed by the liner notes for Shleu-Shleu's first album: "The youth of the land of the sun no longer say: 'Let's dance!' For two years, they've preferred to shout: 'Let's shleu-shleu!' They have since finished school: other young musicians have taken up the path of these nine young guys who, at barbecues and surprise parties, bring joy to all the youth."[70]

Shleu-Shleu was a purely recreational group at first, but with their first record and with graduation from school after their baccalaureate exams, the group took up the pursuit of music full-time. With their success, a career in the *mini-djaz* emerged as an option for middle-class boys to earn respect among their peers while eking out a living. Shleu-Shleu–like groups proliferated in the Port-au-Prince area, resulting in a vast increase in the number of musicians with commercial pretensions, many of whom were musically untrained. Georges Loubert Chancy, who later joined Shleu-Shleu, spoke of his first experience with the band: "Ten days after I started playing my first C scale on the saxophone, I was chosen to be a part of one of the block bands called the Consuls. The band didn't have a horn—we had to rent it from school. I would go rent it for twenty American cents to practice. Until I became a part of another band called Les Gars de Ste. Cecile, and that band had their own horn, but not a very good one. I was always using rubber bands and things to hold it together."[71]

Why did so many young future professionals cast their lot permanently with the *mini-djaz*? The first reason was the popularity of *mini-djaz* and the expanding commercial potential of music. The growing Haitian communities in the diaspora were hungry for a taste of *mini-djaz*; a few tours by groups like Shleu-Shleu were all it took to convince musicians that there was money to be made playing for the comparatively wealthy Haitians in New York. A second factor was the diminishing opportunities for professionals in Haiti. In the 1960s, as a result of economic decline, repression, and political cronyism, a generation of Haitian teachers, professionals, and civil servants left Haiti for work in French-speaking Africa (especially Zaire), at the UN, in the United States, and in Canada. Haitian schools continued to turn out well-educated children of the middle and upper classes who had little future as professionals in Haiti.

"Doing Nothing Serious": Ideological Content of *Mini-djaz Konpa*

Band names, song titles, and song texts speak volumes about the class origins and ideological content of the *mini-djaz* movement. The early *mini-djaz* era was the time in which every neighborhood—in some cases every block—had its own band. Youth in the surrounding neighborhood formed the immediate support network (patrons, fans, and replacement players) for the bands. Coming from the same neighborhoods, the audiences tended to reproduce the subtle distinctions in class and racial backgrounds of the performers. The most common naming strategy was to employ a laudatory French noun with geographic qualifier signaling the band's immediate neighborhood: Los Incognitos de Pétion-Ville, Les Difficiles de Pétion-Ville, Les Gars de Ste. Cecille. Les Fantaisistes de Carrefour, Les Shelberts du Canapé-Vert, Frères Dejean de Pétion-Ville, Les Virtuoses du St. Marc, Super Star du Cap, Les As du Pétion-Ville, Les Pachas du Canapé-Vert, Les Légendaires de Delmas, Les Lionceaux des Cayes.

There were at least two other prominent naming strategies among *mini-djaz*. Following Ibo Combo, a number of other bands chose the "combo" designation, including Tabou Combo, Bossa Combo, and Shoogar Combo. This choice was meant to have a particularly modern and international feel. Shleu-Shleu also had an effect on *mini-djaz* naming, and the repeated nonsense sound (or something akin to it) was used by many bands: Shoupa Shoupa, Shibo Shibo, Skah Shah, Sham Sham, and Volo Volo, for example. One Haitian musician connected the vogue for nonsense names to the political climate, which placed a premium on staying out of trouble. In the 1970s, the English word "band" became more popular, especially for groups based in the United States and Canada (e.g., Magnum Band, System Band, Dixie Band, Macho Band, Thamad Band). There was also a small number of groups that imitated the name of D. P. Express (which formed from the break-up of the *Difficiles de Pétion-Ville*): Gamma Express, Delta Express, G. P. Express. "Express" was meant to suggest a (locomotive) train. Modernist, mechanical transportation contributed many later names to Haitian *mini-djaz*, for example, Djet-X, Astros, Missile 727.

Pétion-Ville, an upper-class suburb of the capital, produced many of the leading groups of the period, and fans of such groups as Les Fantaisistes de Carrefour and Les Loups Noirs from Port-au-Prince criticized the Pétion-Ville bands for what they perceived as snobbery. Alfred Michel, the percussionist for Bossa Combo, discussed their origins, "It's a group that was formed on the 14th of August, 1968, in the neighborhood of Wané, Carrefour. It was like a school team in that epoch. We played music to bring a little gaiety to the neighborhood."[72]

Mini-djaz specialized in light-hearted, teenage dance music, in part because the increasing terror of Papa Doc's rule made music with a serious content or ideological focus suspect and dangerous. Song texts, especially between 1967 and 1978, painted an untroubled portrait of a very troubled country, as in the songs "Valleyball" (Volleyball) by Shleu-Shleu, "Téléphone" by Les Difficiles, "Ti fi a" (Little girl) by Les Ambassadeurs, "Elève l'ecole" (School student)', or "Bébé paramount" (an ode to a groupie at the Paramount Cinema) by Tabou Combo. Many album covers from the period emphasized the quest for middle-class success and respectability. Invasions, repression, persecution, the flight of the intelligentsia, the worsening environmental crisis, press censorship, the plight of Haitian *braceros* (cane cutters) in the Dominican Republic, international isolation, corruption, the *tonton makout*-s, torture and assassination, and the rest of the dark side of Haitian politics under the dictatorship formed an invisible backdrop to this music of teenage pleasures, a music that still resonated with youthful, middle-class optimism.

This was the first generation to have grown up under the dictatorship, and for many, the situation in Haiti was as normal as any they had experienced. In Haiti, even in the worst of times, the great majority goes about its business within the comforting structures of day-to-day life, adjusting to difficulties with flexibility and some resignation. One *mini-djaz* musician who later joined the leftist cultural organizations looked on the situation in this manner, "*Mini-djaz* came about in

1964 or '65. By that time, there was no way you could get together
with anybody and do anything serious. Everything was politics with
Duvalier . . . young guys getting together in the club even. So *mini-djaz*
was a way of avoiding political persecution . . . doing nothing serious.
They couldn't do anything else."[73]

In part to balance the modernist, internationalist, and consumerist
orientation of *mini-djaz,* the first album of each of the major *mini-djaz*
groups had a patriotic song with titles such as "Haïti" or "Haïti, mon
pays" (Haiti, my country). These songs tended to be slower that the
regular fare (some were *boleros*) and borrowed from the kind of nostalgic rhetoric that characterized the turn-of-the-century *mereng* "Souvenir d'Haïti" ("Haïti cherie"). During the nineteenth and early twentieth
centuries, this type of poetry was penned by nationalist writers who
celebrated the landscape, flora, people, and indigenous culture of Haiti
while rejecting European classical literary forms. In the *mini-djaz* era,
the "pastoral" tradition was recycled as an expression of patriotic sentiment while strengthening the "local character" and authenticity of
the movement's creative output. This kind of transposable nostalgic
and idyllic imagery of tropical life has been called *doudouisme* (sweet-
sweetism or sweetheartism), "a postcard image of the Antilles: tourist
Antilles, paradisiacal with sun, sea and sex."[74] These kinds of representations are formed in the overlapping spaces of tourist fantasies and
local nostalgia. On their first album, Shleu-Shleu sang (in French)
"Haïti mon pays," with the chorus,

Haïti mon pays	**Haiti my country**
La perle des Antillais	**The pearl of the Antilles**
Belle cherie, ma patrie	**Beautiful darling, my fatherhood**
Comme je ne puis pas t'oublier	**I will never be able to forget you**[75]

Les Fantaisistes de Carrefour followed with "Haïti," including the
verse,

O Ayiti, se vreman yon paradi	**O Haiti, it's truly a paradise**
Yo gen rezon pou rele w "la perle des Antilles"	**They should call you "the pearl of the Antilles"**
Ou jwèn ladan de bèl ti Kreyòl, bèl ti nègrès	**You'll find lovely Creole women and negresses**
O Ayiti, pa bliye mwen renmen ou anpil	**O Haiti, don't forget I love you so much**

Menm si m pati yon jou	Even if I leave one day
Fòk mwen tounnen	I'll have to come back[76]

Similar songs (also called "Haïti") are to be found in the initial recordings by Les Ambassadeurs and Tabou Combo. The pastoral mode encompassed songs of peasant life. Shleu-Shleu recorded a number of these, notably a song about a Vodou ceremony called "Seremoni lwa" (Ceremony for the saints):

Map mande mwen ki lwa pou sove mwen	I'm wondering which deity will serve me
Depi nèf mwa map laboure	For nine months I've been working
Kòve sou kòve mwen pa rekolte	One work brigade after another, I harvest nothing
M pral bay lwa manje	I'm going to give the deity some food
Se sa k pou sove mwen	I have to do this in order to save myself[77]

Les Difficiles de Pétion-Ville recorded a song called "Musiciens temps longtemps" (Musicians long ago) with a well-known Vodou chorus ("*Ki lè wa vini wè m ankò, wayo?*" When are you going to come see me again?), recorded in a different version by Boukman Eksperyans in 1991. In "Machan yo" (The market women), Shleu-Shleu sketched a market scene that served as a platform for sexual double entendres concerning the produce sold by peasant women merchants,

Machan rapadou, vini vann rapadou	Candy seller, sell your hard brown sugar
Machan doukounou, vini vann doukounou	Cornbread seller, sell your sweet corn pudding
Machan labapen, vini vann labapen	Breadfruit merchant, sell your seedy breadfruit
A wi, machan koko-ye-ye-ye-ye	Ah yes, sellers of coconut [koko = vagina]
A wi, machan kaka-o-o-o-o	Ah yes, sellers of cocoa [kaka = shit]
A wi, machan laba-pen-pen-pen-pen	Ah yes, sellers of breadfruit
Machan yo, machan yo	The merchants[78]

Despite the middle-class aspirations of most commercial musicians and despite their largely apolitical stance, they were occasionally touched by violence and repression. Guitarist "Tit" Pascal of Ibo Combo was shot in 1967 by a *makout*, reputedly in a dispute over a woman. Pascal sustained serious injury to his spinal cord, paralyzing his lower body, and he required an operation in the United States. Duvalier, embarrassed by the incident, published a confession purportedly by Pascal in the daily paper, stating that he had secretly joined the *makout*-s only to be wounded in a training exercise.[79] A fundraiser for Pascal's medical bills attracted much of Haiti's musical talent to the Ibo Lélé Hotel. In another notorious incident, the internationally celebrated bandleader Raoul Guillaume, who had played for the Orchestre Saïeh and who had recorded many albums with his own group, was thrown in jail by the *makout*-s in 1968, an experience that convinced him to leave the country. The violence musicians experienced was the product of a system where perhaps 170,000 *makout*-s were given a free rein (and where an estimated 10,000–40,000 of them carried firearms) and where terror was employed by the state as a weapon against many of its own people.

During Papa Doc's last year, he appointed his teenage son, Jean-Claude ("Baby Doc"), to succeed him, and François planned a carnival to herald the future president for life. A $1,000 prize was offered at the 1971 carnival for the best carnival *méringue* composed in Jean-Claude's honor. The Duvalierist state went to some lengths in this period to transfer the dynasty smoothly. Jean-Claude was pictured seated with a stern expression on his face, his father standing behind him, hand on his shoulder, passing on the sacred power (even as François had been pictured with Jesus Christ many years earlier). Many of Papa Doc's opponents assumed that the Duvalierist system could not sustain itself after his death. Few expected his designated heir, the portly, irresponsible Jean-Claude, to manage a coherent transition and long-lasting rule.

Papa Doc died on April 21, 1971, and Jean-Claude was installed on the twenty-second. Singer Guy Durosier sang the hymm to his memory to the tune of the "Ode to Joy" from Beethoven's Ninth Symphony with the newly composed lyrics: "François, we thank thee for loving us so much. Thy star will be shining in the firmament."[80] After some years in exile, Durosier had returned to Haiti to visit his mother and was decorated with the order of *Honneur et Mérite* by Papa Doc. He became a music teacher to the teenage Jean-Claude and counseled Jean-Claude's favorite orchestra, Bossa Combo.[81]

Papa Doc Duvalier manipulated the entire national cultural inventory for one overarching goal: to achieve and maintain total power. It is one of the small ironies of Haitian musical history that the coming to power of a "revolutionary," *noiriste* regime helped to eclipse the popularity of Vodou-jazz in favor of an imported and assiduously apolitical *konpa-dirék*. The new *klas politik* embraced commercial popular culture with gusto and heavily patronized the new groups, incorporating them, along with carnival and *rara* bands, into what Michel-Rolph Trouillot calls the "unofficial network of redistribution," by which a part of the state coffers (filled through taxation of peasant export produce, graft, extortion, and theft) was redistributed to secure the consent of broad segments of the population.[82] The chilling effect of Duvalierist terror helped to constrain most expressive culture within a restricted political space defined by the dictatorship.

Duvalier's carnival and *koudyay* politics co-opted the exuberance and the antistructural impulse of carnivalesque celebration to support an emergent political force (Duvalierism) against the residual economic and political status quo (i.e., the mulatto elite). Duvalier's revolution transformed Carnival into an event that was saturated with the state apparatus, a "government on parade," with each Carnival devoted to the achievements of the state. Carnival and the many *koudyay*-s, in turn, conferred prestige on Duvalier and his revolution, and the money spent by the government assured ordinary Haitians that Duvalier took their simple pleasures seriously.

However, the thirteen years of Papa Doc's rule also marked the emergence of an effort to wrest the symbolics of traditional culture away from a strictly *noiriste* paradigm and render them productive of leftist *mawonaj* (guerrilla struggle). It is also important to note that despite the extreme nationalism (even xenophobia) of the period and despite the increasing political isolation of the country, Haitian popular music (*konpa-dirèk, yeye,* and *mini-djaz*) continued to develop within a local-global dialectic.

"Musicians Are a Single Family"
Critical Discourse in Music under Baby Doc Duvalier

Jean-Claude "Baby Doc" Duvalier was a devoted fan of *konpa* and of *mini-djaz*. He earned his reputation early on as a "party animal" whose lack of interest in affairs of state was matched by his passions for motorbikes, sports, hunting, parties, and popular music. A popular history of the Duvaliers portrayed a teenaged Jean-Claude fighting with his father over how loud he could play his stereo in the palace, with Papa Doc finally yanking the power cord to Jean-Claude's stereo.[1] Tutored in viola, Jean-Claude also dabbled in guitar. He hired (or commanded) *mini-djaz* for parties at the palace and at his country estate in Croix-des-Bouquets and frequented Pétion-Ville nightclubs, even sitting in with bands on occasion.

Jean-Claude's patronage fell most generously on the *mini-djaz* Bossa Combo, a group he befriended before he assumed the presidency. Bossa, financed by Jean-Claude, became what could best be described as the "house orchestra" of the president, and Duvalier financed their first recording on Dato Records: "A band like Bossa Combo used to be Jean-Claude Duvalier's property, right? He used to be the bandleader, and he would play with them too, with his big stomach [laughs]. Anytime he want those people to play for him, to enjoy himself or for his friends, he said, 'Go call my band for me.'"[2] Alfred Michel, the group's director, explained the band's relationship with the Duvaliers (from the perspective of the band many years later):

The manager was the person responsible for the orchestra. In this period, we had a man from the neighborhood who managed us named Lemaire Prospère. Lemaire Prospère was a guy who had connections in the National Palace. He had a brother-in-law who was named Ghilaise Joseph. We went to his house, and Lemaire explained that he was forming a *djaz*. This guy had two cars, and he sold one. With the money, Lemaire bought instruments, and we started to play a lot. This guy was good friends with Duvalier, the father, with François Duvalier. But Jean-Claude Duvalier . . . when the guy came and said he starting a band and was selling his car because the band lacked instruments . . . Jean-Claude gave him money to buy keyboards, a guitar, and a drum set. He made a gift of it. And we started to play lots [for Duvalier] in order to become a great band. That's why they call Bossa Combo the "orchestra of the president," but it's not true. We had to accept this because we couldn't say no in that period, but it was always Lemaire Prospère who was our owner, the president of the band, not Jean-Claude![3]

Contrary to most expectations, Jean-Claude (with the help of his mother, Simone, and some of his father's close advisers) consolidated power and was able to hang on to the presidency longer than his father had. Although Jean-Claude's policies weren't called *jeanclaudisme* until the late 1970s, this term signaled the liberalizing trends, rapprochement with the bourgeoisie, restraint in use of his father's *tonton makout*-s, and concern with public relations and foreign opinion that began with Jean-Claude's assumption of power, "Duvalierism with a human face" it was sometimes called by his apologists. These policies fostered a conducive climate for commercial music and the country's nightlife. Recording engineer Robert Denis recalled, "For us, it was a fast period, a wealthy period, because there was a flowering of *mini-djaz* orchestras in Port-au-Prince. Why? Because there was a lot more money circulating in Haiti; there had been a massive injection of money into Haiti."[4]

These were years of enormous contradictions for Haiti and Haitian music. The increased investments of foreign capital and the acceleration of factory construction around Port-au-Prince coincided with—some would say precipitated—a severe decline in living standards in the countryside. As tourist boats resumed their visits to Port-au-Prince, Haitian "boat people" were fleeing the country in rickety fishing boats. The *mini-djaz* movement flourished in Port-au-Prince and in the diaspora (and made inroads into French West Indian markets), while in the diaspora the left-wing cultural movement trained a generation of cultural activists who helped inspire the revolutionary movement of the 1980s that ousted the Duvaliers from Haiti. In this chapter, I will examine the impact of the diaspora, chart the course of many musical/ideological developments that emerged in the period of liberalization

(1978–81), and portray the decline of Duvalierist domination through musical texts at carnivals from 1981 to 1985. Along the way, I will also digress with a case study of "boat people" songs.

Haiti's Brooklyn Bridge: The Politics of Exile

Dictatorships feed on the kind of isolation that leaves their mythologies unchallenged and that limits the social space for resistance and rebellion. The new Duvalier regime sought continued domination of the instruments of ideological reproduction: media, schools, and expressive culture, and—as always—the threat of terror lurked behind the normative instruments of social control. Anti-Duvalierist activists had long used metaphors of darkness such as the *blakawout* (electrical blackout) or an eclipse of the sun to capture this sense of living under conditions of isolation and domination. The figure of the zombie, a human who has lost his or her will and soul, was another common metaphor.

The development of a diaspora (nearly a million Haitians living abroad) and its various transnational practices produced a real crisis in Haitian totalitarianism. The transnational circulation of ideas—from Marxism, to liberal internationalism (as in Carter's human rights doctrine), to Catholic liberation theology—and the availability of the diaspora as a free space for political, cultural, and intellectual activities, proved over the long run to be a powerful antidote to Duvalierism.[5] The diaspora's existence and its growth have arguably been the most significant developments in Haiti's political economy in the second half of the century.

The transnational exportation of labor became, under Baby Doc, one of Haiti's most efficient industries.[6] Although the export of labor functioned on a macroeconomic level as an industry, the motivations of the migrants themselves were more complex, often resulting from a general despair that the political system produced among the masses. Large-scale emigration from Haiti commenced with the exodus of political refugees (including former presidents and presidential candidates Magloire, Fignolé, and Déjoie) and of members of the traditional mulatto elite in the period surrounding Papa Doc Duvalier's election in 1957. They were joined by middle-class educators, merchants, professionals, civil servants, and students as economic opportunities for the middle class dried up and as state-sponsored terrorism spiraled between 1965 and 1970. With environmental and economic conditions in the countryside worsening, Haiti's middle-level peasants and marginalized urbanites began to pool savings and sell their belongings to buy passage for family members on boats sailing illegally to the United States.[7] Approximately 40,000 of these "boat people" migrated in the 1970s, with another 12,500 arriving in 1980.[8] Higher estimates allow for up to 80,000 boat people arriving in Florida in just the five-year period between 1976 and 1981. In the thirty years after the election of François Duvalier, perhaps a million Haitians—approximately 15% of the island nation's population—fled Haiti. Nearly half (more than 400,000) appear to have settled in New York City.

Prominent musicians and bands started migrating about 1970, settling among concentrations of Haitians immigrants, where they would find access to weekend club and party engagements. Few musicians left Haiti for strictly political reasons, as they were seldom direct targets of political repression in Haiti. However, many chafed under the arbitrary restrictions on freedom of expression, interference from *tonton makout*-s in economic matters (e.g., skimming profits from concerts), command performances for Duvalierists, and the periods of terror when few people went out at night to hear music.

Musicians and bands (such as Shleu-Shleu, Tabou Combo, and Skah Shah), their fame having spread to the diaspora through record sales and tours, arrived in their new communities with patronage networks already in place and with promoters willing to help them with residency permits and relocation. As it became increasingly difficult for Haitians to get U.S. travel visas, some music producers engaged in a profitable side business of forming bogus bands, recording and promoting a single, and then arranging a tour and securing visas so that the entire group could "jump ship" and try to establish residency.

The legendary Jazz des Jeunes stayed in New York after a tour when they discovered that Jean-Claude Duvalier, who considered them outdated, had replaced them in the lineup of artists performing weekly at the Théâtre de Verdure, where they had been ensconced for some thirty-five years. Their replacement was the group Super Choucoune, composed of musicians formerly with Jean-Claude's favorite band from his youth, the Ensemble Wébert Sicot. Out of favor with the new guard, Jazz des Jeunes never returned home.

Early Haitian immigrants commonly used the word *koloni* (colony) to describe the immigrant community. In contrast to the word *kominote* (community), *koloni* implied transience, a lack of integration into the host society, and a lack of internal community cohesion.[9] First-wave immigrants were deeply concerned with the political situation in

Haiti; most viewed themselves as temporary migrants in the United States and planned to return to Haiti after the overthrow of Duvalier. They saw little reason to ally themselves with more recent immigrants, who were generally of an inferior social standing in Haiti. Repeatedly, the social prejudices rooted in insular Haiti guided behavior in the new environment. Brooklyn came to be seen as the borough of lower-class Haitians, and as a result, those with bourgeois backgrounds (or aspirations) moved, if they could, out of the Bedford Stuyvesant and Flatbush areas of Brooklyn to Queens or to Rockland County.

Concerts and dances in the early immigrant community were segregated by class, and high ticket prices and invitational mailing lists kept out *moun dezòd* (unruly people or troublemakers), which made it more likely to attract *moun byennelve* ("proper" people). Because of class divisions, fear of the Immigration and Naturalization Service (INS), and political differences among Haitian immigrants, much of the early political activity as well as the socializing took place in comparatively private contexts such as at Friday night church socials or in rented ballrooms and clubs. A member of a new Ibo Combo that formed in New York in 1968 told me: "We had our own club in New York in a Chinese restaurant, and we called it Club Camaraderie. That's the name of a famous private club in Haiti at that time where families took their kids for special parties in the afternoon, and at nighttime, they return their families home and they go out by themselves".[10]

Many immigrants sought a taste of the life they had known in Haiti by participating in nightlife and cultural events. Nightclubs, restaurants, and dancehalls catering to Haitian audiences took the names of well-known clubs in Haiti, such as Club Camaraderie, Canne à Sucre, Cabane Créole, La Bacoulou, Djoumbala, and Château Royale, relying on the symbolic capital of reputation to transport into the diaspora residual merchant-client networks and patronage systems. Haitian bands in the United States and Canada often named themselves after bands in Haiti, whether they were connected to the original or not: Gypsies de Queens, Gypsies de New York, Les Fantaisistes de New York, and Les Fantaisistes de Montréal. Anthropologist Michel Laguerre observed similar patterns in New York Haitian businesses in general.[11] For record producer Fred Paul, immigrant nostalgia sparked his career choice: "I said to myself, 'It's funny that every Haitian in America is still eating like they were in Haiti. . . . They have to get their rice and beans every day, they have to get their plantains every day, and they still buy either Haitian music or they buy . . . all those Spanish acts that they always knew. It's funny.' So I said, 'That's the business I'm going to go into.'"[12]

The nostalgia that helped to determine Fred Paul's choice of career found its way into many Haitian immigrant songs of the era. The band Skah Shah produced a classic song of alienation, loneliness, and nostalgia in 1971. On the recording, sirens can be heard blaring in the background, emphasizing the inhospitality of the new environment. The line "Ayiti cheri!" (Dear Haiti) is sung to the melody of the classic *méringue* of the same name that lamented exile from Haiti.[13]

Matin an, mwen leve je m louvri	In the morning I get up and open my eyes
Gen youn doulé chita sou ké mwen	There's a sadness that sits on my heart
Mwen sonje peyi mwen, Ayiti cheri! . . .	I miss my country, Dear Haiti! . . .
Moun lakay pense m eréz	Folks at home think I'm happy
Lé m pa ekri yo kritike	When I don't write, they criticize me
San yo pa konnen se ké m	Without realizing that my heart
K ap rache nan Nouyók . . .	Is breaking in New York . . . My friends,
Mezanmi, nou pa ban m nouvel, o!	You don't give me any news of you!
Mezanmi, kouman nou ye?	My friends, how are you?[14]

In all of this early diasporic activity, we find that, in general, the immigrants were highly politicized, nostalgic, and intent on eventually returning to Haiti. In addition, many were highly educated professionals and intellectuals. All of this constituted a growing headache for Baby Doc and his regime.

"On the Edge of a Machete": Freedom Culture in the Diaspora

Left-wing Haitian activists, many of them veterans of groups such as Karako Blè and Vaksin (see Chapter 3), organized cultural troupes in the diaspora. The best known of these were three New York groups: Atis Endepandan (Independent artists), Soléy Leve (Rising sun), and Tanbou Libéte (Drum of freedom). Other groups included Ayiti Kiltirél

(Cultural Haiti, Boston), Gwoup Kiltirél Vaksin (Vaksin cultural group, Montreal), Kiskeya (an Indian name for the island of Hispañola), Grenn Banbou (Bamboo seeds), Kouto Digo (Blue knife), Sosyete Koukouy (Boston), and Troupe Kwidor (New York/Montreal). These groups were quite distinct from the less-political folkloric troupes (along the model of the Troupe Folklorique Nationale)—such as Paulette St. Lot's Ibo Dancers or the Twoup Louinés Louinis—which were also performing in the diaspora. According to musicologist Gerdès Fleurant (who was a member of Ayiti Kiltirél), at least three of the groups (Solè Leve, Ayiti Kiltirèl, and Vaksin) were associated with the Patriotic Action Movement, "the Marxist political wing of the opposition to Duvalier."[15] Their musical practice drew from or evoked *twoubadou* music, peasant *konbit* (work brigade), *rara*, and Vodou music. In the liner notes to their 1975 album, the group Atis Endepandan wrote: "We believe that a strong Haitian people's music exists, beginning with voodoo, rara, troubadours and other musical forms which had origins in slavery times. . . . We try always to popularize the struggles of the masses, to make revolutionary propaganda and political education, but also to pay particular attention to the music itself."[16]

Although many of these militants had pioneered a peasant outreach strategy as early as 1962, their approach was boosted by the then-popular Maoist critique of Soviet revisionism and emphasis on the revolutionary potential of the peasantry. In many cases, the groups rewrote and radicalized peasant songs, transforming them into weapons to use against the dictatorship. The tune "Dodinen" (Rocking) on Atis Endepandan's record was a traditional lullaby whose lyrics were transformed in order to focus on the exploitation of Haiti's impoverished workers and peasants and their potential as a revolutionary force. The song features a *rara* rhythm and a whistle (an important ritual instrument in *rara* groups and in Petwo ceremonies) in the introduction to alert the listener to the simulated *rara* environment; the acoustic guitar imitates the *vaksin* ostinato parts. The pronounced *rara* feeling appears only in the introduction, interlude, and coda, framing the verses. Group leader Max Antoine, a lawyer with a radio show on WKCR in New York, collaborated with guitarist "Tit" Pascal (the guitarist from Ibo Combo in Haiti who was shot by a *makout* in 1967) on the arrangements for guitars and traditional instruments. The second line paraphrases a Haitian proverb, *Fèzetnat-la fè mat men se li ki domi atè* (The mat-maker makes the bed, but it's he who sleeps on the ground), and the fourth line below paraphrases another proverb,

Granmesi chyen se kout baton deye tèt li (The big thanks given a dog is
a blow from a stick on the back of the head).

Se nou ki boulanje a, se nou k boule nan fè	We're the bakers, but we bake in the fire
Se nou ki fèzetnat-la, se nou k domi atè	We make the mats, but we sleep on ground
Bagay sila pa kapab dire, travayè di yon mo	This can't go on, workers are complaining
Gran mesi pa nou se kout baton li ye	The big thanks we get is a blow from a stick
Men zòt chita sou do n yap dodinen	But others are sitting on our backs rocking,
Dodinen mon konpè, wa dodinen	Rocking, my friend, you're rocking
Na rale chèz la, wava kase ren ou	We'll yank the chair, you'll break your butt[17]

As is typical in traditional songs of censure, the enemy is identified
by reference to "others"; the protagonist also uses the *konpè* form of
address (it literally means godfather to one's child) to address his oppressors. The songs of Atis Endepandan translated the group's Marxist
and anti-imperialist analysis by employing popular rhetoric. Note the
vivid sense of danger associated with migration in the following song
verse:

Kounye a menm lan tout peyi w ale	Today, in any country to which you go
Ou jwenn yon bann Ayisyen an egzil . . .	You'll find a lot of Haitians in exile . . .
Kèlkeswa kote n ye	No matter where we are
Se klè nou lan manchèt	It's clear we're on the edge of a machete[18]

Producer Fred Paul released three Solèy Leve albums (anonymously, not under his Mini Records label), and an American left-wing
label (Paredon Records) produced a single Atis Endepandan recording, but, in general, the *kilti libète* groups operated outside the commercial market. With the availability of cassette technology, movement
activists experimented in the early 1970s with cassettes as an inexpen-
sive means of disseminating their material (to Haiti as well as through-

out the diaspora) while evading the censorship of the dictatorship. Cheap, small, and reproducible, cassettes were used to spread oppositional music and messages, and they began to alter the political as well as the cultural landscape.

The *kilti libète* groups were multimedia performance troupes, combining poetry, music, dance, and theater in their performances. Like much didactic revolutionary music and poetry, the expressive output of these groups depended on conventional metaphors: shadows, darkness, and dusk = dictatorship and despair = wind = revolutionary change; rising red sun = hope for a socialist future; flowers and birds = happiness and joy, and so on. These images reappeared frequently in the political music of the following twenty years, where they were used to supply persuasive power to otherwise drab or cerebral notions.

The lead singer on the last two of Solèy Leve's albums was a young Haitian singer named Farah Juste. Farah came from Carrefour Feuilles near Saint Gerard, where she sang in the choir as a girl. As a teenager, she traveled to Montreal to study drama, but ended up in New York singing and acting with Solèy Leve in the early 1970s. The two albums she recorded as a soloist with Solèy Leve included the song, "Ayiti demen" (Haiti tomorrow), also known as "Lè la libere Ayiti va bèl" (When Haiti is liberated, it will be beautiful), that later became Farah's signature tune (although it was originally sung by another soloist for the group). The text for "Ayiti demen" was composed by Koralen, the pen name of poet Jean-Claude Martineau, and it was arranged by Gerdès Fleurant (musical coordinator for Ayiti Kiltirèl), who set it to a traditional Vodou song for the *lwa* Ogou Feray (St. Jacques Majeur).[19]

Another cultural organization, Tanbou Libète, sang "Alyenkat" (Alien card), documenting the history of invasions and occupations of Haiti by foreigners and contrasting this history to the rejection of Haitians everywhere they had fled. Often forced to live as illegal immigrants in their host countries, the Haitian migrants remained under the threat of deportation if found, for example, by the INS or by Bahamian immigration without an alien card (see the case study later in this chapter for an explanation of the politics of nautical emigration). This inherent inequality was condemned in the lyrics written by poet Jean-Claude Martineau (Koralen). This song was reprised separately over a decade later by two of Haiti's most famous *angaje* singers, Manno Charlemagne and Farah Juste. The rhythm of the song is in *yanvalou,* an important Vodou rhythm. Note the proverb near the end of the excerpt below:

Emmigrasyon tenten met men nan kolèt mwen	This immigration jerk grabbed my collar
Li d'i "M pa sitizenn"	He said, "I'm not a citizen"
"Wè iz . . . ?" Mwen di li, "What?"	He said, "Where is . . . ?" I said, "What?"
Li di m: "Vòt Alyenkat" . . .	He said, "Your Alien Card?" . . .
Pandan lokipasyon	During the occupation
Lè blan yo touye Peralt	When the Americans killed Peralte
Eske Meriken yo ten gen alyenkat? . . .	Did the Americans have alien cards? . . .
	At home we "break our bones"
Lakay nou kraze zo nou	"It's not we who ride the cattle
"Se pa nou k sou do bèf la	It's the cattle who ride us"[20]
Se bèf la ki se do nou"	

The *kilti libète* groups refined the use of Vodou, *rara,* and *twoubadou* music as resistant elements of the cultural repertory. They helped to craft a rhetoric linking traditional peasant culture to antidictatorial, egalitarian, nonsexist, progressive cultural forms. To a large extent, this meant reclaiming symbols previously appropriated by Duvalierist *noirisme.* The notion of *mawonaj* as resistance to the dictatorship had to be reclaimed from Duvalier. Duvalier had erected a statue across from the palace called Le Marron Inconnu (The unknown maroon), featuring an escaped slave sounding a conch shell, and the conch shell appeared on Duvalier's personal flag. Thus, the opposition had to revalorize it as a symbol of the call to resistance. The *konbit* (work brigade), a symbol of the peasant work ethic and selfless collectivism, had been the subject of Duvalier's famous 1963 call for discipline and sacrifice in the spirit of a *konbit nasyonal* (national work brigade). With Duvalier's sophisticated incorporation and manipulation of Vodou temples, *rara* bands, peasant secret societies, and *konbit*-s, the whole of rural life seemed to be implicated (to many among Haiti's middle-class intelligentsia) in the Duvalierist project. The task that *kilti libète* activists faced was to show that traditional culture and dictatorship were linked by Duvalierist assertion and strategic manipulation and not by a logical relationship. They needed to demonstrate that there was another face to Vodou, a progressive and liberatory impulse in traditional peasant culture and social organization.

Most of the *kilti libète* organizations did not survive the 1970s, and they were never popular enough to compete with commercial musicians. In many ways, however, they were quite successful. They helped to define *mizik angaje* (engaged music) and the *chanson patriyotik ayisyen* (Haitian patriotic song) for a generation of Haitian exiles. They were, according to Gerdès Fleurant, "visionaries who saw a day when the message of the Freedom Culture would become the *common denominator* of Haitian culture, and dominate the musical productions of the 1980s and beyond."[21] These organizations helped to develop the talents of a number of young cultural activists, such as singer Farah Juste, poet Jean-Claude Martineau, pianist Nikol Levy, and guitarist "Tit" Pascal, all of whom continued their advocacy for political and roots-oriented materials through other vehicles. The early New York roots bands of the 1980s (Ayizan and Sakad) grew directly out of this movement. Other artists, notably Ti-Manno and Manno Charlemagne, who would become central in the more broad-based opposition movement of the 1980s, were influenced by the *kilti libète* groups at one stage or another of their careers. In addition, many songs of the movement, such as "Ayiti demen" and Tanbou Libète's "Alyenkat," entered into the *angaje* repertory. By exploiting their location in the so-called liberated territory of the diaspora and by smuggling cassettes in to Haiti, however few, they contributed to a breakdown in the cordon sanitaire around Haiti and to a transnational exchange of information and ideas that later rocked the dictatorship.

"There Is No Reason for Us to Argue"

In Haiti, during the mid-1970s, a powerful rivalry between D. P. Express and Gypsies (later Scorpio) enlivened the Carnivals of the period, but the intensity (even viciousness) of the competition led some to brand it the era of *konpa vyolans* (*konpa* violence). However, from about 1978 to 1985, many *mini-djaz* and commercial musicians went through a remarkable shift in their attitudes about—and their relationship to—the dictatorship. This was not a sea change, but rather a drawn-out awakening of conscience, or to use a rather awkward Creolized French word popular among Haitian activists, a *konsyentizasyon* (literally, conscience-ization). The first indication that this process was under way was in a new sense of purpose among musicians: They began to take their own musical history seriously, they fervently experimented with musical style, and they began to understand the political effect they had as cultural "leaders."

Paradoxically, Bossa Combo, the "orchestra of the president," played a leading role in the changes. They had more leeway than other bands to offer up amiable reprimands to the government or to explore social crises as they had in their 1974 carnival winning entry, "Plante pa koupe bwa" (Plant, don't cut, trees). In 1978, Bossa Combo launched a counteroffensive to *konpa vyolans* that became known as *l'accolade* (the acclaim). This was an effort to carve out a more serious role for the *mini-djaz*. Bossa Combo wanted to encourage Haitians to take pride in their popular music and musical history, especially because Martinicans and Guadeloupeans were successfully marketing a musical style, *kadans,* closely related to *konpa,* raising issues of the ownership of musical style.[22] In this context, the nostalgia movement was partly a defense of the cultural heritage of Haiti. According to Ralph Boncy, "A feeling of power and solidarity now united the Haitian groups who became conscious of their impact. Bossa Combo sounded the call, aided by the suggestions of Lionel Benjamin, singer, radio announcer, and producer. The word *konpa* came back into fashion."[23]

Bossa Combo dedicated their album *Accolade* to their competitors, with the following English: "Peace and love to D. P. Express, Scorpio, Loups Noir, Les Frères Dejean, Skah Shah, Coupé Cloué, Tabou Combo, Shleu-Shleu, Ambassadeurs, etc." Their title cut contained a medley of tunes from other bands, including Coupé Cloué's "Fanm kolokinte" and Skah Shah's "Haïti." The lyrics that introduced the medley predicted that the Haitian public would one day appreciate the bands who made them dance and that they would triumph over divisiveness.

Sonje ya sonje djaz-sila-yo	**They'll remember these bands**
Genyen lontan se yo k ape fè moun danse . . .	**For a long time they've made people dance . . .**
Ayisyen prefere tou sa ki etranje	**Haitians prefer anything that's foreign**
Yo refuse apresye sa frè yo fabrike . . .	**They refuse to appreciate their brothers' work . . .**
Tande mesaj: Respekte! Se frè nou ye!	**Hear the message: Respect! We're all brothers**[24]

Later, Bossa Combo songs "Ti pwason, se sa lavi pote" (Little fish, that's what life brings you) and "Message" helped to demonstrate that a political opening was indeed under way. The sentiment for unity among musicians was echoed by Ti-Manno and D. P. Express in "Ansanm ansanm" (Together/unity), a hit from their seminal 1980 album *David*.

Mizisyen son sèl kòd fanmi	**Musicians are a single family line**
Kelkeswa nasyonalite . . .	**Whatever their nationality . . .**
Pa gen rezòn pou nou fè polemik	**There is no reason for us to argue**
Polemik pap fè n avanse	**The polemic doesn't help us advance**
Ann sere kole fè sa ki pi bon	**Let's come together to make something better**
Egois kap fè n gade deye . . .	**Egotism keeps us looking behind . . .**
Fè konpa mache	**Make the *konpa* work**[25]

The message to take the music seriously had an effect on the originators of *konpa* and *kadans,* Nemours Jean-Baptiste and Wébert Sicot. The pair had fallen on hard times and into relative obscurity by the late 1970s. Musicians began to speak up for a neglected generation of musicians. In 1980, Tabou Combo released "Hommage à Nemours Jean-Baptiste":

Li pa ban nou travay	**He didn't give us work**
Li pa ban nou lajan	**He didn't give us money**
Men li ban nou konpa	**But he gave us the *konpa***
Ala bèl eritay-sa . . .	**What a beautiful heritage . . .**
Fòk nou pakab mete tèt ansanm	**We have to put our heads together**
Pou nou kab vevene ou	**To venerate him**
Tankou Lewòp te venere Moza	**The way Europe venerates Mozart**[26]

In the same year, a soiree was held in New York to celebrate the twenty-fifth anniversary of *konpa-dirèk,* and the organizers brought Nemours up from Haiti to play with a group of Skah Shah veterans. At the dance, a collection was taken up to buy Nemours a new saxophone, and there was talk of having him lead a new orchestra. The plight of many of Haiti's elder musicians became the subject of public debate and outrage. Guitarist Ricardo "Ti-Plume" Franck had this to say: "When Nemours died, he was very, very poor. He died like a dog.

It revolted me. When he passed away, he was blind and begging for money. "Pa gen moun ki ban m anyen, non. M pa gen anyen, non."[Nobody give me nothing. I don't have nothing.] It was very sad." [27]

Producer Fred Paul, with his Mini Records label and his studio orchestra, Mini All Stars, contributed to the revival of interest in early *konpa*. He released a Wébert Sicot album called *Gina* in 1977 and a retrospective in 1980 from José Tavernier, the original Ibo Combo drummer, called "My 25 Years of Music." Mini All Stars featured compositions of Nemours on a triple album in 1980–81 entitled *Pure Gold: 15 Titres de Nemours Jean-Baptiste*. Paul also produced a 1979 album featuring the singer from Jazz des Jeunes, Gérard Dupervil, with a collection of Dodòf Legros songs entitled *Vous en souvenez-vous?* (Do you remember?). Jean Yves Volcy, a singer formerly with Bossa Combo, issued a nostalgic album in 1982 called *Chansons d'hier et d'aujourdhui* (Songs of yesterday and today), which featured songs composed by the early *mini-djaz* group Les Ambassadeurs. All of this fascination with musical history was new for Haiti. [28]

The growing social conscience evident in Haitian popular music was concurrent with a fervent period of stylistic experimentation, much of which was inspired by international musical trends. D. P. Express, Scorpio, and others in Haiti had beefed up their horn sections to compete with Exile One, Grammacks, and other Antillean bands. Tabou Combo and Skah Shah in New York were doing the same, remodeling themselves in the image of such American funk bands as the Commodores, Tower of Power, Parliament-Funkadelic, and Earth, Wind, and Fire. Tabou, Magnum Band, and Skah Shah all added American musicians on trumpet and trombone.

Tabou Combo's former lead guitarist, André "Dadou" Pasquet, left the band in 1975, and in the summer of 1976 he launched a new group with his brother, drummer Claude "Tico" Pasquet (formerly with Les Gypsies), calling the group Magnum Band and eventually settling in Miami. Dadou Pasquet looked to invigorate *konpa* with innovations inspired by George Benson–style jazz-fusion and with elements from Haitian traditional music. As an example of the latter, Pasquet revived a song written by his maternal uncle, Dodòf Legros, called "Congo nan Vodou" (Kongo in vodou) on the album *Expérience*. Both Magnum Band and Tabou Combo were among Haitian bands strongly influenced by the philosophy of Freemasonry, which is extremely popular among Haiti's middle class and its political elite. Masonic symbols grace many of the albums by these bands, and paeans to discipline and hard work are infused with a Masonic spiritualism.

Caribbean Sextet was formed by former members of the second in-carnation of Ibo Combo who had moved back to Haiti from the United States. In the words of pianist Réginald Policard, Caribbean Sextet was "the lead group to stray from traditional style . . . in terms of a musical plan. . . . [We] were always in the forefront of our genera-tion."[29] The interest in jazz and bossa nova, clearly evident even in the early days of Ibo Combo, was audible as well in the work of Caribbean Sextet. There was also an appreciation for American jazz-fusionists such as Chick Corea, Keith Jarrett, George Benson, Gary Burton, and Herbie Hancock. The sextet sound was a hybridized jazz-fusion with an infectious *konpa* rhythm. The chord progressions grew more com-plex, and the solos were exploratory in nature. "The audience that re-sponds to the Caribbean Sextet style is perhaps better educated. It's certainly an audience that listens to imported music a bit more than local music. This audience sees in Caribbean Sextet a music that's bet-ter constructed, that's capable of being danced or listened to. We listen a lot to jazz and Brazilian music, but we don't play imported music. Moreover, we don't neglect our roots, because certain of our songs are influenced by our folklore, but with a more studied approach to harmony."[30]

Composer Gérard Merceron attempted to craft a new popular music for Haiti with his album *L'Energie mysterieuse,* the result of a sound-track he wrote for French filmmaker Bob Lemoine.[31] A follow-up al-bum entitled *Tèt san kò* was released in 1981 with four members of Caribbean Sextet. Merceron envisioned a "new popular Haitian music which would adapt the Creole language to the needs of modernity."[32] The intergenerational core group, called Haïti 2000, comprised Mer-ceron, Herby Widmaïer, and novelist and playwright Franck Etienne, along with vocalists Boulo Valcourt and Lionel Benjamin. Etienne was one of the founders in the 1960s of the *spiralisme* movement in Haitian literature, which was perhaps best explained by Philocète in 1963: "We refuse to do like others, to imprison ourselves in a narrow poetic re-gionalism, to write according to imposed norms. . . . Out with deter-minism. We want Haitian literature to take its place among other liter-atures."[33]

Merceron's musicians were—or would later be—associated with groups (Caribbean Sextet, Zèklè, etc.) that similarly rejected locally "determinist" conventions. All were in the forefront of what was con-sidered a less essentialist and more universalist tendency in Haitian music, with the goal of producing a refined, complex, and cosmopoli-tan popular music. Merceron's chord progressions, frequent modulations, and use of instruments such as the cello and flute and even a chamber ensemble mark these two albums as truly idiosyncratic. This wasn't a purely cosmopolitan effort however; Merceron was consumed with transcending local/global and modern/traditional dichotomies. Although his variation on the *konpa* rhythm, *shanpa*, never caught on, he helped to sharpen the debate among commercial musicians about the future of Haitian music. The involvement of a number of people with anti-Duvalierist leanings (Valcourt, Etienne, and Merceron himself) lent this project a vaguely oppositional feel, although there was no direct political content to the musical texts.

The group Zèklè (Lightning) formed in 1982 and recorded their first album, *Cé Ou Minm'!* the next year.[34] Zèklè and its jazz-combo alterego Lakansyèl (Rainbow) were projects of the Widmaïer brothers (Joël and Mushi) and a group of musicians that included at different times keyboardist Raoul Denis Jr., lyricist Ralph Boncy, bassist Joe Charles, and Caribbean Sextet guitarist Claude Marcelin. In performance, the band shared percussion and wind players from Caribbean Sextet. Zèklè wanted to bridge the gap between dance and concert engagements. Mushi Widmaïer explained, "We opened a new world as far as concerts for bands were concerned. Because before, the only people who did concerts were Ansy Dérose [a romantic singer] and people like that. For a dance band to do that had never been possible. We had a light show and everything. A new era was starting."[35]

Zèklè blended *konpa* with funk and American jazz-rock in the tradition of Wayne Shorter's Weather Report (to whom they were often compared in the Haitian and French press). They used the bass as a more prominent instrument and integrated duel synthesizers, an innovation also being tried at the time by the French Antillean group Kassav'. Zèklè had a strong reception in France and caused quite a sensation among young urbanites in Haiti, but they found it difficult to break free of a narrow audience bounded by class and geography. Owing to the lack of concert halls other than the Rex Theater and because of the limited audience for concert music, the group was unable to establish a concert career in the country: "We started doing the *bal*-s [dances] because we couldn't beat the system. After three or four concerts in Rex Theater, we have already taken five thousand people. That's the minority who can afford to buy LPs. You can't go anywhere in Haiti beyond the 5,000. If you sell 6,000 records in Haiti, that's big. And the extra thousand is from people who like the band and buy the LP to give it as a gift. With the number of phonographs that exist still in the country, you can't go far."[36]

As a Haitian group dedicated to succeeding in international markets, honest about its cosmopolitan style, and aiming for a concert career, Zèklè provoked charges of elitism. An article in *Haïti-Observateur* criticized the class-restricted nature of their appeal and, with reference to "social composition," raised the issues of race and class: "An appreciable dose of snobbery explains in part the craze for Zèklè among the petite bourgeoisie of Port-au-Prince, on account of the social composition of the members of the group and of the more sophisticated character of their music. Many city kids recognize themselves in this cosmopolitan, fast-changing music, which reflects the social malaise and the uncertainty of the youth."[37]

Their bold second album, *Stop*, showcased a tribute to the influential deejay Rico Jean-Baptiste (who had committed suicide) against a nostalgic backdrop of the early *mini-djaz* period.[38] Rico's radio show, Tambou Battant (Beating drum), was used as the title of the song:

C'était le temps des Difficiles	It was the time of Difficiles de Pétion-Ville
On était tous d'accord!	We were all in agreement
Port-au-Prince bouge à 10h pile	Port-au-Prince shook at 10:00 sharp
Tambour Battant très fort!	The "Drum Beating" loudly
Fort comme le compas qui résonne	Strong like the *konpa* sounding
Dans nos coeurs, dans nos corps . . .	In our hearts, in our bodies . . .
Tu faisait chanter nos amours	You had our loves sung
Et tu disais toujours	And you would always say
"On est jeune: il faut que ça bouge"	"We're young, this has to work"
Haïti tout entière	Haiti all together
Les Combos dansent sur les ondes	The Combos dancing on the airwaves[39]

The nostalgia that the song evokes is a testament not only to Rico and his contributions to the music but also the importance of the music in defining the ambience of middle-class life in the period under the dictatorship and to the intense identification of Haiti's youth with the *mini-djaz*. It was also a part of the valorization of commercial music and its history that I have discussed in relation to *l'accolade*.

The new musical currents came together in a number of highly visible events, including the festival at Ibo Beach in 1983 that matched the fusion *konpa* of Zèklè with the funk *konpa* of Tabou Combo. Tabou's diasporic dalliance in rap and funk startled audiences in Haiti. Throughout the 1980s, urban Haitians experienced a sense of accelerating social change accompanying the collapse of Duvalierism. The musical experimentalism of Zèklè, Magnum Band, Caribbean Sextet, Yawfah Band, Mystik, and others demonstrated the rising interest among popular musicians in a music that wasn't tied slavishly to the dance floor. The new generation showed abundant signs of collaboration and mutual support, a far cry from the incessant rivalries of the earlier Duvalier years. The "new generation," an urban middle-class phenomenon, was clearly less patient with the boorishness, narrow-mindedness, and restrictiveness of the dictatorship. It was also clearly more cosmopolitan in orientation, and for this reason, many of its exponents would permanently suffer the "bourgeois" label.

"You Have to Correct This": Musicians Take a Stand

By the late 1970s, Jean-Claude had formed an alliance with the mulatto elite, and the country's businesses were basking in their spoils from *jeanclaudiste* economic policies. Jimmy Carter was elected American president, and Carter's explicit human rights program put aid-receiving nations on notice that future foreign aid would be linked to progress on human rights. All of this helped usher in a period in which dissident voices were allowed to emerge in Haiti. The nongovernmental press began to report more independently (and occasionally critically). Franck Etienne, the prominent author and poet, wrote his *angaje* Creole play *Tèt pelen*. A few politicians took advantage of the thaw to organize political parties; in 1979, Grégoire Eugène and Protestant minister Sylvio Claude founded competing Christian Democrat parties.

Into the opening marched a few hardy troubadours who used the opportunity to reestablish an *angaje* role for singer-songwriters in the tradition of Kandjo de Pradines, Dodòf Legros, (Robert) Moulin, and Ti-Paris (Achille Paris). As I have made clear, the *twoubadou* tradition is associated in Haiti with wry and caustic commentary on social life and class relations, a penchant for off-color humor (*betiz*), especially about gender relations, and an appreciation for the sensuous aspects of life (including drink, carousing, and the pursuit of relaxation). Rodrigue Milien and Jules Similien (later caled Toto Necessité) started off as a *twoubadou* duet, and after a very public split, each pursued a solo career. Together and apart, they helped revialize the *twoubadou* tradition. Milien's song "Rejettez," for example, listed a series of constrasting behaviors between *lelit-la* and *mas-la* (the elite and the masses). Coupé Cloué, with his feel for lower-class life and his ribald humor, would have to be classed in the same *twoubadou* category, as would the singer who wrote much of Coupé's material, Assad Francoeur. But the singers who had the greatest political impact were another *twoubadou* duo called Manno and Marco.

Born in 1948, Manno Charlemagne was raised among the lumpen proletariat in Port-au-Prince and Carrefour, and this environment helped to cultivate Manno's sensitivity to political and social injustice, as well as his expressive sensibility. Manno began singing and playing the guitar at the age of sixteen, and in 1968, at the age of twenty, he joined up with some neighborhood friends to form a *mini-djaz* called Les Remarquables. His second group, les Trouvères (The troubadours), moved in the direction of traditional *twoubadou* music and was a direct precursor to his alliance with Marco Jeanty. Charlemagne began to express a deep anguish about the poverty and degradation he saw around him. Charlemagne's neighborhood in Carrefour was a rundown area surrounding a commercial strip along Route 2 west of Port-au-Prince known for daily traffic jams, concrete shop fronts, houses piled on the hills, the *lavalas*, or deluges, that wash garbage down from the hills, and for its nightclubs and prostitution. Charlemagne talked of his upbringing,

> I was raised by my aunt, not my mother. And both of them are singers. I didn't know who my father was until I was thirty-seven years old, and it turns out that when I knew my father's family, they're all musicians, too. And I feel I had some psychological problems because of not knowing my father, some "child problems." If you listen to my songs, you can feel it. . . . Anyway, I lived in an "urban *lakou*" in Port-au-Prince. That means you have the Abel family, the Odé family, the Charlemagne family, etc. When Odé had a problem with my mother, I could hear them arguing. I could hear the dirty words they used. And I also learned from the workers, street workers, those macho guys who came from the countryside to Port-au-Prince. They are the ones who built the roads in Haiti. When they are digging they are singing songs, dirty songs. So I was a specialist in dirty songs. I was the one who brought those songs to my school, helping rich kids who were raised behind

high walls to know what was happening outside. I was their teacher. I
was also singing church songs. I went to Catholic schools, I was raised
by the priests, so you might hear that Gregorian thing when I'm singing. Eight years old, six years, learning things from Jesus, from my
school, and from the street. I always prefer the street. . . . Since I was
young, just sitting around in the neighborhood put me in some very
subversive company. When I was eight years old, I saw the overthrow
of Magloire [1956]. People fleeing bullets would come and hide in my
yard. I come from the lumpen proletariat, right in the center of Port-
au-Prince. And I spent my adolescence in Carrefour and the other
"popular" zones. I would walk around and see guys making homemade
bombs. Sometimes they would give me those bombs. I was nine, ten
years old. They'd call me over and say, "Hey Manno, walk slow and give
this to that man over there." I didn't know what it was for, but it made
me feel important. You know, a man from the area asks you to help
him and you're just a kid, that's really cool. I went to jail for the first
time in 1963. I was 15 years old.[40]

After Charlemagne teamed up with singer Marco Jeanty, they began
to play their *angaje* songs in Carrefour and later in the capital city. In
May of 1978, the duo came to the city for a session on Radio Haïti-
Inter, and, according to Ralph Boncy, they were "adopted" by the station and their politically conscious deejay, Richard Brisson. Before
that, "they had already attracted attention in presenting their caustic
tales in small nocturnal gatherings where some students, progressive
professors and intellectuals would empty bottles of Barbancourt
[rum]."[41] They impressed many among the musical "elite" (e.g., well-
educated professors and composers of classical music), including composer Gérard Merceron, who wrote liner notes for their album, and
music store owner (and husband of Haiti's premier concert pianist)
Raoul Denis, who recorded their album. The album, entitled *Manno et
Marco*, was released in 1978 by Marc Duveger's Marc Records label.
Based in New York and Montreal, Marc Records had a shop in Port-
au-Prince and was able to ensure domestic distribution. With radio
play and with concerts at the Institut Français, they began to take
shots at the power structure.

Their song lyrics, written primarily by Charlemagne, were typically
indirect and allusive in their political message, but they clearly sang
of the lives of Haiti's poor and unemployed. "Jebede" (To blather fool-
ishly) portrays "a character that providence has smiled upon, who
knows he can become an exploiter":

Gade kijan yon vanipye
Konprann ke li byen chita sou yon
    pyedestal
Gade kijan yon vakabon kanpe li
    deklere
Li di li ka achte yon kapital . . .
Pretensyon, anbisyon
Mwen konn se sa k enfliyanse
    w . . .
Kanmenm fòk sa chanje

Look how the conceited one
Believes he's solidly perched on
    his pedestal
Look at how the scoundrel stands
    there declaring
That he can buy a capital . . .
Pretensions, ambitions
I know that's what influences
    you . . .
Just so, this has to change[42]

Manno and Marco asked a series of simple questions in the song
"Pouki?" (Why) that reveal much about the condition of Haiti's poor
and their relation to the powerful:

Pouki lavi pa separe
Egalego fifti fifti
Pouki reken kraze brize

Gwo mak dan sou do ti pwason

Why doesn't life separate things
Equally, fifty-fifty?
Why does the shark bring such
    destruction
Large tooth marks on the back of
    the little fish?[43]

In "Zanj" (Spirits/angels), they sought after the nature and causes of
lower-class alienation from the political process:

La politique c'est pour les anges
C'est pour les gens qui ont un nom

Et c'est pour la grande société

Politics is for the angels/spirits
It's for people who have a [well-
    known] name
And it's for high society[44]

In "Nwèl" (Christmas), they sang that "Christmas comes and goes,
nothing changes." Christmas is a bittersweet indulgence that can't
erase bleak social conditions:

Son tradisyon, son bagay ki bèl

Se lavalas ki pase avèk gravwa

Ka apre sa se lèwa

It's a tradition, it's a beautiful
    thing
It's a deluge that washes away
    the garbage
After that is the Epiphany

| Si joudlan pat pot bon mesaj | **If New Year's Day doesn't bring good news** |
| Si mennenjit anvahi lespwa | **If menningitis invades hope** |

The songs on this album touched many listeners in ways that popular (especially recorded) music had not previously. At the same time that Manno and Marco were building an *angaje* song movement in Haiti, Farah Juste was doing the same in the diaspora, releasing her first solo recording in 1976. The Haitian press in New York nicknamed her the *symbole de la chanson patriotique haïtienne* (the symbol of the Haitian patriotic song). Farah embodied a tradition of female singers dating from Lumane Casimir in the 1940s and 1950s and includes Emerante de Pradines, Martha Jean-Claude, Carole Demismen, Maryse Coulanges, Myriam Dorismé, and others. That tradition has embraced romantic, folkloric, and patriotic songs and has been one of the few avenues of popular music available to women.

Opponents of Jean-Claude regularly excorporated *konpa* songs during this period for the purposes of *mawonaj*. A member of Atis Endepandan recounted in 1979 how groups of young kids in the north of Haiti got into trouble with the *makout*-s by singing the verse from a Skah Shah hit, "Zanmi" (Friends), that went: "*Vès de pyès pa alamòd ankò, Talon kikit retounnen pi rèd*" (Two-piece shirt-jackets aren't in style any more, spiked heels are coming back even harder). Apparently, ths was intended, and perceived to be, a slander of the *tonton makout*-s and their reliance on violence and repression in the face of popular resistance.[45]

In 1979, D. P. Express recruited a charismatic young lead singer from Gonaïves, Ti-Manno (Antoine Rossini Jean-Baptiste), who had recently returned from a number of years with the Boston-based bands Shupa Shupa, Astros, and Volo Volo. Ti-Manno's years in the diaspora were formative ones in his coming of age as a political artist. There was no escaping the anti-Duvalier movement in the diaspora, where Haitians overwhelmingly opposed the dictatorship and where *mini-djaz* frequently shared concert billings with political cultural troupes. D. P was already one of the two most popular bands in Haiti, and Ti-Manno's strong, clear voice, French-accented Creole and distinctive vibrato won hordes of fans and made D. P. the clear *konpa* champions during the time Ti-Manno was with the band. At carnival in 1979, they exploded with their exuberantly-titled "E!E!E!E!E!" The lyrics say that "*eseye fè yon bagay kap sevi timoun kap grandi*" (we have to try to do something for the children) and that the rich should *"pa rete pran va-kans"* (don't stay on vacation), which refers to a proverb, *Malere toujou bouke, rich yo toujou nan vakans* (The poor are always tired, the rich are always on vacation).

On tour in Dominica when Hurricane David tore through the Caribbean, the group found a patriotic message in their longing to be with loved ones in danger:

Nan ti peyi m sa, se la si m gran- gou m manje	In my litle country, if I'm hungry, I eat
Nan ti peyi m sa, se la si m malad y a trete	In my little country, if I'm sick, they treat me[46]

Their most pointed political critique was the song called "Corije" (Rectify). One of Haiti's first feminist popular songs, it exposed a common fact of life for women workers: sexual exploitation on the job.

Se pou nou korije . . . mesyè!	You have to rectify this . . . Sir!
Moun-sa-yo telman mechan	These guys are so evil
Avan yo bay fanm travay	Before they'll give a woman a job
Yo mande fè "overoll"	They ask them to make a "roll- over"
Overoll mennen "overtime"	The "roll-over" gets them overtime
Msyè pa vin pou tate m	Mister, don't come to touch me
Si w tate m ma rele, ma rele!	If you touch me, I'll yell out!
Gade mizè fanm ap pase pou travay	Look at the anguish women suffer for work[47]

The album cover showed the band dwarfed on a large stage surrounding a shirtless Ti-Manno with his left fist raised in the air. Below him, the album title *David* evoked the biblical David and Goliath, although it referred more immediately to the hurricane. The extensive use of reverberation for Ti-Manno's voice on "David" conveyed authority and injected a contemporary studio sound into the recording. Musical references to Jamaican reggae, the backbeat feeling of *kadans-lipso* (from the island of Dominica—a blend of Haitian *kadans/konpa* and calypso), and salsa (on "Corigé"), gave it an internationalist feel. This album's extraordinary success was due in part to the diversity of images and messages (provocative visual images, sexual wordplay, social criticism, carnival exuberance, patriotism, calls for unity, biblical references, and love of family) combined into a compelling image for a new Haiti.

Ti-Manno was the first among his peers in the *mini-djaz* movement to assert that music should play a role in advancing the country politically. He saw himself linked in a progressive international community of musicians united in the fight against injustice, challenging the system and influencing the political debates in their respective countries. Ti-Manno's "Hommage à Bob Marley" on a later album was an example of his growing internationalist consciousness and his awareness of the power of commercial music.[48] D. P. Express invigorated *angaje* music and encouraged others to folow in the *prise de conscience*.

"We Won't Forget": Urban *Sanba*-s and Their New Vodou Subculture

As the crisis of Haitian identity intensified as a result of the growth of the diaspora and the weakening of the dictatorship, roots music experiments were launched from a number of places. The New York–based arranger Dernst Emile experimented with roots sounds on a song he called "Rara" with his band Mystik (1980). He continued to push for a new Haitian music based on *rara* with a string of arrangements he did for System Band, Ti-Manno, and Skah Shah among others. Producer Fred Paul (Mini Records) wrote a neo-*rara* called "Raraman" for his studio band Mini All Stars that was recorded in 1985. In this song, *rara* becomes a metaphor for African cultural survival despite the hardships imposed by the system of slavery:

Jouk nan kè Lafrik bato yo vin chaje	From the heart of Africa, the boats came full
Sou do Karayib la èsklav yo debake	Slaves disembarked on the back of the Caribbean
Yo pat gen anyen pou yo te pote	They couldn't carry anything with them
Sèlman ti mizik yo pou yo te chante	Only songs for them to sing
Woy, yo se raraman	Oh, they're *rara* men[49]

Guitarist "Tit" Pascal had played with the original Ibo Combo before being shot by a *makout*. In New York, he arranged and played with the *kilti libète* group Atis Endepandan and served briefly as music teacher to Tabou Combo. In the mid-1970s, he urged Tabou to release a *rara* song, but with no success. Determined to carry through his vision of a fusion of jazz and *rara,* he founded Ayizan (named after the *lwa* who guards the marketplace) in 1983–84. Pascal connected the performance and compositional praxis of *rara* to the jazz avant-garde and specifically to John Coltrane. *Rara,* Pascal implied, is a complex music with its own dense aesthetic language: "I have been looking at *rara* the way we say *an kan* [on edge]; you look at it sideways and just let it go by. . . . I have never thought that I'm going to modernize *rara*. It is far more modern than anything modern we have. It is avant-garde. They used to think that the peasant doesn't know anything, but they carry with them thousands of years of African culture. So I said to myself, 'This is no ignorance, this is complex stuff. This is heavy stuff going down. Like when I heard Coltrane. . . .'"[50]

Ayizan was a remarkable ensemble for the time, musically most similar to the band Foula a few years later in Port-au-Prince. However, Ayizan's self-produced album, *Dilijans* (Diligence), never achieved mass distribution, and the group, like Mystik before it, failed to capture a significant audience for *rara*-jazz (despite being widely admired by other musicians).

Like Pascal, keyboardist Nikol Levy also started out with a *mini-djaz* (in the north of Haiti) and performed for a *kilti libète* group, Solèy Leve. He hoped to fashion a politically engaged roots music that remained true to traditional Afro-Haitian musical aesthetics: "The melodies we compose . . . we're trying to get them as close as possible to popular [traditional] music. Even in the form, the call-and-response, there's something very African, very Vodou . . . a dialogue between the lead vocalist and the chorus. Even between the instruments, between the guitar, keyboards, and the bass. We're trying to do that, trying to dialogue all the time . . . polyrhythm, different lines at the same time."[51]

The roots-music fusions up until the late 1970s had been inspired by various ideological projects somewhat distant from Vodou beliefs and practice (*indigènisme, noirisme,* Duvalierism, patriotism, pan-Africanism, communism). In addition, some in the early folkloric movement argued from a purely aesthetic basis that Haitian peasants had created expressive culture of stunning beauty that deserved to be staged for broader consumption. The attraction to Vodou by Pascal and Levy was still primarily political, nationalistic, and aesthetic, and not one of religious advocacy or proselytization. Based on their association with the lower classes (against the upper classes), with Africa

(against Europe), and with the nation (against the colonial and im-
perial powers), Vodou-influenced musics were natural vehicles with
which to articulate some form of political resistance or as a platform
for antihegemonic narratives and discourses of resistant traditionalism. In all of this, Vodou was the means to an end: Few of the musicians were initiates in Vodou, and none evangelized for Vodou through
their music. In other words, Vodou was a symbol standing for something else—a means to promote Haitian nationalism and African identity, or as a point of contact with which to educate and organize the
peasantry.

In contrast, in the late 1970s and early 1980s, there emerged a new
Afrocentric roots-oriented music linked to a participatory interest in
Vodou among middle-class musicians. Just as African identity had
emerged as a problematic through decades of black struggles around
decolonization, civil rights, apartheid, and cultural self-determination,
some young musicians began to see African diasporic religions as a
spiritual answer to their predicament. It was not solely a product of
local political and aesthetic conditions but was deeply embedded in a
diasporic discourse on African identity. The popularity of Jamaican
reggae, Rastafarianism, and Bob Marley in particular carried a number of messages for musicians in Haiti interested in roots musics, musicians who typically called each other "*sanba.*"[52] The "*sanba* movement" was first profiled abroad in an article in the French magazine
Liberation in January 1983 with the head, "Serge Samba, Dupont
Samba, Aboudia Samba. Enter into a trance. For these Rastas, para-
dise isn't a lost dream: 75% of the population lives on the margin in a
Vodou harmony."[53]

World markets were indeed opening up to Afro-Caribbean dance
musics defined (more or less) on their own terms. But it was Marley's
charismatic synthesis of defiant politics and Rastafarianism that
opened creative passages for the young Haitian musicians. The fusion
of Rastafarian spiritual messages, politics, and popular music in roots-
rock reggae was a crystallizing influence in the emergence of Haitian
roots music, authorizing a new appreciation for Afro-Haitian religion
and culture. Theodore "Lolo" Beaubrun of Boukman Eksperyans said,
"You know, growing up in Haiti, I had the chance to listen to Jimi
Hendrix and Santana . . . but it was above all Bob Marley who made
me think. When I heard Bob Marley sometime around 1976, I decided
that if he could do something like that in Jamaica, we could do that
with Vodou in Haiti."[54]

Drummer "Aboudja" Derenoncourt also commented on the rela-

tionship of the *sanba* movement to Rastafarianism, especially in relationship to choices over appearance: "Zawo [a leading roots musician]
had his personal philosophy—they had a way of dressing, they had
dreadlocks, and at that time they did not want to become Rasta, because they were not Rasta, because in Haiti you do have dreadlocks,
but we call them [*chève*] Simbi."[55]

The reference to *chève Simbi* (Simbi hair—Simbi is a Haitian *lwa*
of freshwater springs whose devotees often had long locks of hair)
highlights the role that the early roots exponents played in pioneering
a new, countercultural appearance for Haitian performers (and their
audiences). Dress often included elements from peasant garb (e.g.,
straw hats, *djakout*-s or straw bags, sandals, or rolled-up jeans, all in
the style of Kouzen Zaka, an agricultural deity). Thus, the *sanba*-s
semiotically linked themselves to two Afro-Haitian deities of special
importance to Haitian peasants. Later fashions tended toward a general African-identity look, with colorful dashikis and a layering of neo-
African fabrics. These decisions were not made without consequences:
Severe ostracism and sometimes even arrest awaited those caught vio-
lating urban dress and life-style norms.

The young men and women who formed these groups were from
the urban middle class, from a social stratum similar to that of most
mini-djaz musicians, but they were searching for a more "authentically
Haitian" musical experience than that afforded by *konpa*. Almost all
had been raised Christian (Catholic or evangelical Protestant), and like
almost all children of the middle class, they had been taught to revile
or fear Vodou and to avoid *rara* bands at all costs. Their accounts of
the period refer to epiphanies of encounter, discovery, and acceptance.
For example, drummer "Aboudja" related the story of his "coming of
age" in Vodou,

In 1981, I went to Souvenance [a Vodou ceremonial center in the Artibonite Valley] for the first time. I heard the drumming, and I was really
fascinated by the drumming. I started to learn how to drum, and I was
practicing something like twelve, sixteen hours every day. When I first
started to play in Groupe Sa, I didn't know anything about drumming;
it was just raw feelings. My first test was to go to a very big ceremony
to play with the big guys of Souvenance! I remember, it was Easter
Sunday 1984, and they were playing with close to a 1,000 people inside
the *peristil* [temple] and 700 *ounsis* [initiates] dancing—and I told the
guy, "I'd like to play the *manman*" [mother drum]. The guy looked at

me and said, "Well, if you cannot play, I'm going to have to take the
stick from you." And I remember, I played for one hour, so I passed the
test! It was the happiest time of my life. Bienaimé [the paterfamilias of
the *lakou*], who told me that I was never going to be able to play the
drum, came to pick me up, and he blessed my hands, washed my head,
and say, "Now, you are a drummer of the house."[56]

Similarly, in a passage from their song "Nou pap sa bliye" (We won't
forget this), the members of Boukman Eksperyans recall how they
overcame their alienation from peasant culture, beginning with their
first experience of Vodou:

Nou sonje, nou pap sa bliye	We remember, we won't forget
Jou ke nou di nou pral jwe	The day we said we were going to play
Mizik peyi an nou	Our country's music
Jwe mizik Vodou	To play the music of Vodou
Nou tout te santi nou fè younn	We felt that we became one
Ak tout lòt frè n kap viv kilti n	With all our other brothers who live the culture
Nou te santi nou Ayisyen	We truly felt we were Haitian[57]

The groups who launched the *mizik rasin* revolution in Haiti grew
out of a few groups of friends who began studying traditional music
around 1977–78. One of these groups was led by Fanfan Alexis and
included the future musicians of such groups as Group Sa, Foula, and
Rara Machine, Yves "Chiko" Boyer. Its lead singer was Theodore "Lolo"
Beaubrun (later of Boukman Eksperyans), and this early incarnation
briefly sported the Boukman Eksperyans name. In 1978, Denis Emile
(brother of arranger Dernst) left the *mini-djaz* Bossa Combo to research Vodou music along with the singer-composer known as Sanba
Zawo. Ronald Derenoncourt, now known simply as Aboudja, came
back to Haiti from the states in 1980. A talented trap-set drummer
named Piquion started playing with them but left, so a replacement
drummer named Jean Robert joined Aboudja, guitarist Wilfred "Tido"
Laveaud, bassist Yves "Chiko" Boyer, Jean-Raymond Giglio, saxophonist Doudou Chancy (brother of Georges Loubert Chancy, the saxophonist for Skah Shah), and others to form the band Group Sa (This
group).[58] The informal nature of the process was emphasized by Aboudja:

It was a get-together. It wasn't something like, "I'm going to create a movement to do this and that." We had our first concert at the Rex Theater [summer of 1982], and it was very interesting, although none of us had a good understanding of roots music at that time. None of us had mastered the drum, none of us, but it was a feeling. We wanted to show the people that we can do that. What I can tell you is that Groupe Sa was the first *rasin* band who performed commercially, where people paid to come to the concerts, the first band who performed commercially. And at that time Jean-Raymond was living with me. I turned my house into a center where everybody was coming, like Evans and Gary Seney, [later] from Boukman Eksperyans, Myrtho Exavier "Matisou," [later] from Boukan Ginen. All these guys were coming to my house, and we were learning how to play together.[59]

Group Sa broke up in 1984, and Tido, Giglio, Chiko, Aboudja and others formed the Vodou-jazz band Foula, inspired in part by fusion-jazz musicians Stanley Clarke, Jaco Pastorius, Wes Montgomery, and John McLaughlin. Then, in 1985, Aboudja left to form—along with Sanba Zawo, percussionist Gaston "Bonga" Jean-Baptiste, and the Sanon brothers (Harry "Ayizan" and Gregory "Azouke")—Sanba-yo (the Sanbas), a more traditionalist counterpart to Foula's avant-garde Vodou-jazz.

At the same time that Zawo and Denis Emile were first investigating Vodou music (1978), "Lolo" Beaubrun and Lolo's wife, Mimrose, influenced by unification theology (which seeks common ground among the world's leading religions), attempted to reconcile Christianity (and Buddhism, Islam, etc.) with Haitian Vodou. This led them ultimately to some of the more famous Vodou *lakou*-s, especially those in the Artibonite Valley—Soukri Danach, Souvenance Mystique, Badjo, and others. It was there that they met singers, drummers, and officiants steeped in traditions of Haiti's various *nanchon*-s (nations, various African ethnic groups) that reach back hundreds of years to the associations formed by slaves from the same homeland: for example, Ibo, Kongo, Dayome (Dahomey), Nago (Yoruba), and Mahi. The Beaubruns formed a group to study Vodou music called Moun Ife (roughly "people of the abode of Vodou deities").

Moun Ife grew from a loose-knit interest group into a performing ensemble in the mid-1980s, recruiting Vodou drummers from Port-au-Paix and expanding the group's electric instrumentation, including the addition of two guitar and bass players, Eddy François (vocalist also) and guitarist-bassist Daniel "Dady" Beaubrun, Lolo's brother (who became the chief arranger for the band). In 1985, the group changed their name to Boukman Eksperyans, the name of Fanfan Alexis's former band. The name is a tribute to the Jamaican-born slave leader (Boukman Jetty) who launched the Haitian slave rebellion at a Vodou ceremony in Bwa Kayiman (Cayman Woods) on August 14 and 15, 1791. "Eksperyans" suggested the influence of the progressive rock guitar playing of Jimi Hendrix (the Jimi Hendrix Experience). Boukman Eksperyans pioneered the mix of rock guitar and bass with synthesizer and a battery of traditional Afro-Haitian percussion that one finds in many later roots groups.

All three groups (Boukman Eksperyans, Sanba-yo, and Foula) engaged in lay ethnology, playing and studying with Vodou drummers and recording ceremonies and songs. Along with radio deejay Konpè Filo and other interested media personnel, the musicians in these three bands constituted some of the most ardent documenters of Haitian traditional musics in the 1980s. Before *dechoukaj*, there were few performance venues open to the bands and little media exposure available, yet in its slow maturation under Duvalier (1978–85), the roots-music movement grew not only musically but philosophically and spiritually as well.

The groups were facing a deeply entrenched Haitian middle-class prejudice that relegated Voudou and *rara* to the category of the satanic or demonic. Middle-class parents typically tell children that the *longa-wou,* or werewolves, in the *rara* bands will carry them off. In the words of a Boukman Eksperyans song,

Gen anpil moun ki wont pou nou	**There are many who were ashamed for us**
Yo tap di se mizik lougawou	**They were saying that it's werewolf music**[60]

The media ignored the movement during the dictatorship because, according to Lolo Beaubrun, "They used to say, (1) 'You play music of Satan,' (2) 'It's not commercial music. You're not going anywhere with it,' and (3) 'The message is not for relaxing people,' they said, 'You say too much in the music.'"[61] Anti-Vodou sentiments were perhaps even stronger in the diaspora, where Haitian immigrants were sensitive to the stigmatization of Haitians as "ignorant practitioners of voodoo." Nikol Levy lost a number of band members to pressure from their families. He explained, "I know some very good Haitian musicians who don't want to play this kind of music. They say 'That's voodoo!'

because of their religious beliefs. They'll play Brazilian music, without realizing that it comes from Brazilian cult music! But they won't play their own music."[62]

Max Lyncée, leader of a later-era Boston roots band, Batwèl Rada, spoke of Vodou as something akin to a dirty family secret best not discussed in front of strangers, "I am not the best qualified person to talk about Vodou because it was really kept from me. My father is a judge, my mother is a shopkeeper. They would go crazy if they heard me talk about this. For them, this is a bit shameful. . . . Some [diaspora residents] said we were embarrassing them before the rest of society, that this was not something we should be bringing out here."[63] Boukman Eksperyans targeted anti-Vodou prejudice in their African identity manifesto "Se Kreyòl nou ye" ("We're Creole"), which advocates understanding (and refashioning) Haitian identity as inscribed within an African diaspora:

Ayisyen yo, pito pale Fwanse	**Haitians prefer to speak French**
Olye yo pale Kreyòl! . . .	**It's better if they speak Creole!**
Nèg Kongo nou ye, fò n pa wont sa	**We're Kongo people, don't be ashamed**
Kote w sòti? Lafrik!	**Where have you come from? Africa!**
Kote w pwale?	**Where are you going?**
Kilès ki manman w? Lafrik!	**Who is your mother? Africa!**[64]

Mizik rasin, along with its Afrocentric counterparts in Jamaica, Brazil, and elsewhere, has constructed a discourse about history and identity that places African identity, black cultural unity, and the common historical experience of slavery at the center of the struggle for cultural survival. "Lolo" Beaubrun referred to the importance that the concept of slavery holds among proponents of *mizik rasin:* "After many years of mental slavery, as Bob Marley said, you must emancipate yourself from that servitude. Mental slavery is much worse than physical slavery. That's why we always say that Déssalines [a leader of the Haitian revolution] took away the physical slavery, but the slavery inside has not yet left us. We are slaves still."[65]

Because of their leading role in the movement, Boukman Eksperyans has had a strong voice in articulating an ideology for the movement. Their reading of Vodou differentiates Vodou *lakou* (courtyard Vodou, i.e., a collective or congregational practice) from Vodou *ougan* (priestly Vodou, i.e., charismatic Vodou based on the figure of the *ou-*

gan). The *lakou* (called a "yard" in the English-speaking Antilles) is viewed by these musicians as an ideal of communal living. In the songs of Boukman Eksperyans and many other roots groups, the *lakou* is an index of deep family roots and traditions, a tie to land and place, and a sense of commitment and community. Boukman Eksperyans also links their practice of Vodou to the concept of Ginen. Ginen is derived from the name for a region of West Africa (Guinée) and is considered an African homeland, a spiritual realm where the Vodou deities live, and a state of spiritual development and awareness among those who practice a "truer" form of Vodou. Members of Boukman Eksperyans often emphasize an idiosyncratic aspect of their philosophy, the "three words: love, truth, and justice" and the importance of having what you are "saying, thinking, and doing" be in harmony, as in the following song excerpt:

Jou a rive pou n kite Babilon	**The day has arrived for us to leave Babylon**
Moman rive pou n viv an twa pawòl	**The moment has arrived to live by three words**
Se pa yon mistè	**It is not a mystery**
Pou youn moun viv Ginen o	**For someone to live as a Ginen, oh**
Se sa wap di, sa w panse, sa wap fè	**It's putting into harmony**
Ki pou an amoni	**What you're saying, thinking, and doing**[66]

This ideological activity directed at reinventing Vodou should be viewed as an attempt to recoup Vodou from various practices (spells and charms, numerological consultations for the purposes of playing the lottery, unreliable healing practices, etc.) that are considreed by these musicians to be more properly sorcery than world religion, and from the shadows of Duvalierist manipulation of Vodou. A spiritual unification message is evident in many song texts and interviews, as in the following quote from "Lolo" Beaubrun: "I am waiting for a godly government where everyone shares without selfishness, without prejudice. Christ will walk with Buddha in the way of nonviolence that Gandhi has opened, like the civil disobedience that brought down Duvalier."[67]

Perhaps the most striking difference between this roots movement and its predecessors was in the ontological status of the performance.

The *mizik rasin* bands didn't see their work as folklore or as something conceptually distinct from Vodou-as-religion, but as an extension of Vodou spirituality into other realms.[68] Boukman Eksperyans labeled their music "Vodou *adjaye*," a term used for the dances at a *peristil* (temple) that follow ceremonies. Trance plays a critical role in authenticating roots music performances. Each of the *mizik rasin* bands has accumulated anecdotes about audience members, whether *ounsi kanzo* (initiated practitioners) or not, falling into trance possession at concerts. Trance possession serves as a vote of approval by the *lwa*-s for the music. I accompanied some of these bands as they tried their music out for the first time at Vodou ceremonies. Playing after the ceremonies proper were over at *perestil*-s such as Mystik Souvenans, Sanba-yo and Boukman Eksperyans hooked into portable generators and played well into the night. It was very much a point of pride that *ounsi* recognized the rhythms and performed the correct dances to each.

"Smash and Destroy": Jean-Claude Cracks Down

In 1980, Baby Doc married Michèle Bennet, a divorcee and daughter of a disreputable mulatto import-export businessman reportedly involved in smuggling. The marriage went against the wishes of Jean-Claude's family—including his powerful mother, Simone (Mama Doc), and grandmother—as well as the advice of all his political advisers. The "dinosaurs" (old-guard Duvalierist ministers) and *tonton makout*-s looked on the wedding as an affront to *noiriste* tenets, and the lavish marriage alienated many, especially the poor.

Under pressure from a vocal opposition and from his own family and regime, Baby Doc understood that he was courting political disaster. On November 2, 1980, Ronald Reagan defeated Jimmy Carter in the American presidential race, and Baby Doc and his advisers celebrated with a champagne party in Haiti's presidential palace. The dictatorship correctly perceived that "human rights" would no longer be a determining factor in American foreign policy and that they were free to respond to their political problems as they saw fit. By the end of November, the crackdown was on. The "opening" of the polity to criticism and debate (which helped to give birth to musical movements of roots, cosmopolitan, and political consciousness) was short-lived, as the dictatorship sought to break the back of the independent press and stifle dissent. Radio Haïti was ransacked; opposition political fig-

ures that weren't arrested sought refuge in foreign embassies; records
and cassettes of Frères Parent, Manno Charlemagne, and others were
removed from stores; and newspapers critical of the regime were con-
fiscated. Almost all of the better-known progressive artists left Haiti.
The family *mini-djaz* called Les Frères Parent that had been singing
religiously inspired *angaje* songs, took refuge in the Mexican embassy
in early 1981 and asked for asylum. In the subsequent five years, most
developments in *angaje* song took place in the diaspora; once again the
diaspora assumed its role as a "liberated territory" and as a base for
antidictatorial organizing and cultural work.

Manno Charlemagne slipped out from a performance at a cinema
in Carrefour and fled the country. He ended up in Boston, where he
released a series of albums, including *Konviksyon* (1984) and *Fini les
colonies* (1985, in French). These albums reflected Manno's increased
awareness of his role as a movement singer. One of his more didactic
titles was "Leta, laboujwazi, lepèp" (The state, the bourgeoisie, the
people):

Leta pa janm sèvi	The state never serves
Lepèp ki toutouni	The people who are barely clothed
Malere kap peri	Or the poor who are dying
Sa k pa ka jwi lavi	Those who cannot enjoy life
Men leta byen plase	But the state is well situated
Pou l kraze brize lè l vle	To sow destruction whenever it wants
Entere pi piti	To bury the smallest
Pou li fè laboujwazi plezi	For the pleasure of the bourgeoisie[69]

In 1984, Manno also critized international and nongovernmental
organizations (NGOs) in Haiti, linking them closely to the interests
of the Haitian bourgeoisie. His song "Oganizasyon Mondyal" (World
System) contained a stinging anti-imperialist critique:

Oganizasyon mondyal yo pa pou nou yo ye	International organizations aren't for us
Se la pou ede volè yo piye, devore . . .	They exist to help thieves plunder and steal . . .
Reyaksonè sou develope yo sa pi danjere	Third World reactionaries are the most dangerous

Lè enterese yo menase, se yo ki toujou rele	When their interests are threatened, they always
Tout fòs entèvansyonis yo pou pèp ki souleve	Scream for intervention to keep the people down

This critique was wedded to a sober class analysis of Haiti, especially of the class interests of those he called "Third World reactionaries":

Klas dominan entelijan ke li ye	The dominant class is very smart
An prensip konnen ke l an minorite	In principle they know they're the minority
Li konnen kijan pou l jwe	They know how to play the game
Posisyon de klas li se sa li konte	Their class status is what counts
La fè lenposib, l a kraze, l a brize	They'll do the unimaginable, smash and destroy
Pou l elimine timoun ki nan ze	To murder the child in the womb[70]

Farah Juste's song "Diaspò" (diaspora) characterized the scattering of Haitians throughout the world as a tragedy for the Haitian people, and connected the emergence of a diaspora to the machinations of foreign countries and NGOs that controlled development and humanitarian aid in Haiti.[71]

Yo bay Meriken yo zòn nò a	They give the Americans the north zone
Yo bay Kanadyen yo zòn sid la	They give the Canadians the south zone
Yo bay blan Fwanse yo tout plaj	They give the French whites the beaches
Yo pap gade sa Desalin te kite pou pèp-la	They're not protecting Dessalines's legacy
Ou jwenn Ayisyen nan Bahamas	You find Haitians in the Bahamas
Ou jwenn Ayisyen nan Sen Domeng . . .	You find Haitians in the Dominican Republic . . .
Ayiti fin tonbe yon diaspò	Haiti ends up becoming a diaspora[72]

Haitian leaders in the diaspora increasingly used the term *dyaspò* or *dyaspora* (rather than *koloni* or even *kominote,* or community) to promote a political agenda focused on Haitian politics in the United States.[73] Efforts to organize the population along ethnic lines stressed a new conern for local conditions, urban U.S. politics, and their doubly oppressed minority status (marginalized as blacks and as foreigners).

Political singer Ti-Manno, in exile in the United States, formed a new band, Gemini Express de Ti-Manno, and produced a series of *angaje* albums before this death in 1985 that outspokenly bridged insular and diasporic Haitian struggles. These albums were among the most popular Haitian albums in the diaspora and were ensured strong covert distribution in Haiti because of Ti-Manno's lingering superstar status there. Unlike the music of Manno Charlemagne, Ti-Manno's songs were consistently in the vein of dance-band *konpa*. As an *angaje* dance band, Gemini Express de Ti-Manno had no peers in its day. Composer Gérard Merceron spoke of the crowds who stood motionless to hear the words of Ti-Manno's songs even while others danced nearby, in part because "he underlined the content of his texts, the messages of protest against the defects of a Haitian society crushed by insatiable greed of a category of profiteers often coming from the same class as their victims. The powerless have made Ti-Manno the spokesman for their claims. Every generation has need of its heroes."[74]

In the song "Nèg kont nèg" (Black against black), Ti-Manno mourned the class and racial stratification that plagued Haitians and other African diasporic peoples. The first section of this song was sung in a *rara* rhythm with the cracking of whips and blowing of whistles. In this same section, Ti-Manno's text mimiced those of rural *sanba*-s (song leaders) with interjections about "Vyèj Mirak" (Holy Virgin) and with nonsemantic particles at the end of lines (often *wo* or *woy*). The introductory text is full of "adversary" references to Vodou texts ("I'm nearly dead, oh, they're carrying a rope to tie up the *sanba*"), and the section ended on the praise formula in Vodou, "Ayibobo." The *rara* rhythm and *sanba* vocal style amplify the "out of Africa" theme of the song, that "Africa's children" have been divided and manipulated by the colonists:

Lafrik o, nanpwen linyon nan pitit
   ou yo wo
	**Africa, there is no unity among
	   your children**

Nou kite moun ap jwe nan sèvo
   nou wo
	**We let people play with our
	   minds**

Youn pa vle wè lòt, wo	**We don't want to see each other**
Depwi yo deyò e	**Since we've been out [of Africa]**

Sitou nè nan Karayib la wo	Caribbean people, especially,
Yo youn vle pou l sipèyè lòt wo	They each think they're superior to the others
Youn ap meprize lòt . . .	Each one puts the others down . . .
Se mesye kolon blan yo	It was the white colonialist
Ki mete sa nan sèvo nou wo	Who put this in our heads
Pou nèg toujou nan divisyon wo	For blacks always to be divided
Yo menm pou yo renye	So that they can rule over us[75]

Like Manno Charlemagne, Ti-Manno continued to deepen the political analysis he presented in song texts, although his anti-imperialism, anti-Duvalierism, and cultural nationalism constituted a liberal, rather than a Marxist, critique of Haitian society. With a nod to the writings of Frantz Fanon, Ti-Manno's "Sort Tiers Monde" (Out of the Third World) looks at the psychological legacy of imperialism and underdevelopment for oppressed people of color in the Third World, finding in it many of the root causes of division and cultural insecurity:

N abandone pwòp kilti pa nou	We abandoned our own culture
Pou n adopte tout sak ki sot deyò	To adopt everything that came from overseas
N ap viv avèk yon konplèks denferiyorite	We are living with an inferiority complex
Patipwi "susudur" kinsepsyon san zobjèktivite	Prejudice linked to a lack objectivity
Sèk fenmen, klib pwive	A closed circle, a privileged club
San dizan distenksyon de klas	110 years of class distinction
Anpeche inite egalite fwatenite	Preventing unity, equality, fraternity
Tout moun konplekse, tout moun sou manti	Everybody feels inferior, living a lie
Pale fwanse vin tounnen metye	Speaking French becomes a habit/trade
Yon konfonn fakilite ak invesite	They confuse getting a degree with ability[76]

In an article on Ti-Manno's music, Nina Glick Schiller and Georges Fouron characterize Ti-Manno's political engagement with issues both in Haiti and in the diaspora as an example of the emergence of transnational identity among Haitians.[77] They note that after Ti-Manno died, leaders in the diaspora attempted to organize a movement called Operasyon Men Kontre (Operation "Clasped Hands," from a song title by Ti-Manno) to promote Haitian unity around the theme of Ti-Manno's "message." The movement capitalized on Ti-Manno's status as a charismatic culture hero, but it quickly became bogged down in struggles over direction and goals, with some leaders stressing building an ethnic community in the United States and others emphasizing the struggle in Haiti against Duvalierism. In any case, the leading role of a musician's message in building a political movement (however short-lived) can be interpreted as a precursor to the centrality of musicians in the years following the overthrow of the Duvaliers.

A number of other mainstream *mini-djaz* in the diaspora weighed in, however gingerly, in the movement for social change. In 1981, Farah Juste recorded an album (*Lespwa*) with an offshoot from the *mini-djaz* Skah Shah called Skah Shah d'Haïti. Tabou Combo's 1982–83 album, *Ce konsa ce konsa*, contained two *angaje* songs, "Préjugé" (Prejudice) and "Partagé" (Share), which were critical of the prejudice and greed of the wealthy and powerful. "Préjugé" asked: "Is there a law of nature that says that if you are black, you have to live in poverty?" and "Partagé" included the chorus:

Se pa nesèsè pou w genyen, pou w genyen	It's not necessary to own so much
Si sa yo genyen, yo pa fe debyen avèk li	If they have it, they don't do any good with it
Se pou w pataje, annou pataje	You have to share, let's share[78]

In the final years of Duvalier's rule, the diaspora became more polarized than ever before, and the lines between those cooperating with the regime and those steadfastly opposed to it were drawn more starkly. Although Bossa Combo, the "orchestra of the president," had distanced themselves from Jean-Claude, they never shook their Duvalierist reputation in the diaspora. After they lost a number of their musicians on a 1979 visit to the states (where the ex-Bossa musicians formed the group Accolade de New York), Bossa Combo organized a tour to the United States and Canada in May of 1982. Some Haitian weeklies refused to handle their publicity unless the band toured under another name. Under the name "Accolade d'Haïti," the tour sponsor booked engagements in New York and Montreal. Nonetheless, the conservative opposition weekly *Haïti-Observateur* editorialized: "They are what they are thanks to Jean-Claude Duvalier, creator and patron of the ensemble. Undoubtedly, they have a debt of recognition toward him, to the detriment of those who forget. . . . It's a fraud, because an orchestra doesn't exist under the name 'Accolade d'Haïti.' The Haitian community in New York and Montreal should never support these ambassadors of *jeanclaudisme* by spending dollars on them, which are scarce in Haiti. The musical ensemble Bossa Combo doesn't undertake an American tour in the name of Haitian culture, but rather to polish the star of *jeanclaudisme* in the eyes of diasporic Haitians." [79]

The opposition to Duvalier was aided by a series of crises that helped to turn public opinion decisively against Jean-Claude, and in the five-year period from the crackdown until Jean-Claude's exile, the government stumbled from crisis to crisis. In 1981, in order to stem the tide of nautical refugees, the Reagan administration persuaded Duvalier to sign an interdiction treaty that allowed the United States to return all Haitians seized at sea. Jean-Claude was widely vilified in 1982 and 1983 for allowing the United States to eradicate all of Haiti's "creole" pigs in response to U.S. fears that Haitian pigs would transmit African swine fever to American pigs. With pigs representing a large chunk of the worldly possessions of many peasants, the economic repercussions of this act for the peasantry were disastrous (as was the attempt to introduce American pig farming to Haiti). Perhaps the single most important moment in the growth of the opposition was the visit to Haiti by Pope John Paul II to Haiti in 1993. The pope's visit had been sought by the Duvaliers as a sign of papal support for the regime, and his visit was at first considered a coup by Jean-Claude and his advisers. However, the pope had set restrictions on the visit, such as refusing to leave the airport. On his arrival, the pope kissed the ground and then delivered a scathing indictment of Duvalierism that contained the memorable line in a French-accented Creole: "For you to achieve a better life in this country, something has to change!" Progressive and radical Catholics were energized by this strong stand. Grass-roots organizing by partisans of the *ti-legliz* (little church) movement, a Haitian branch of liberation theology, spearheaded the revolt against Duvalier. Finally, the tourism industry, a large component of the Haitian economy, was undermined in the following year by the decision of the U.S. Centers for Disease Control to label Haitians a population at risk for carrying HIV.

Case Study: "Misery Left and Right"—Musical Discourse on the "Boat People"

One of the most politically charged issues of the Baby Doc years was the plight of Haitian *bot pipèl* (Creolized from the English "boat people").[80] They became the subject of heated debates carried out in musical discourse and in press coverage and commentaries. Partly as a result of the ideological activity by the press and by artists (musicians, poets, painters, dramatists), the boat people captured the attention—and roused the sentiments—of Haitians of all classes.

The expressive material on this subject from artists and journalist alike—in other words, the discourse on boat people—was profoundly conditioned by Haitian historical experiences of the sea. The legacy of the slave trade, especially the notorious middle passage (the passage of enslaved Africans on ships bound for the Western hemisphere, characterized by mass suicides; deaths due to scurvy, rickets, and starvation; beatings; and the humiliation of a people in chains), has helped to establish the sea as a site of dangerous journeys. The sea has contributed directly to Haiti's political and cultural isolation, reflected in the use of the phrase *lòt bò dlo* (on the other side of the water), but the medium of separation is also the medium of contact and of connection. Even after Haiti's defeat of their overseas French colonial masters, Haiti was still at the mercy of powerful navies. From the time when Haiti was forced to pay tribute to German gunboats to the granting to the United States of the right to patrol Haiti's territorial waters (in order to interdict and repatriate boat people), Haiti has never been fully in control of its own waters.

Certain metaphysical associations of the sea also come into play in the songs about the boat people. Haitian *sèvitè*-s (practitioners of Vodou) believe in a spiritual homeland, called Ginen, pictured as *anba dlo* (under the waters).[81] A number of deities have a special relationship to the sea, including Mèt Agwe, also called Agwe Woyo, represented by the figure of a boat, and Lasirenn, pictured as a siren or mermaid with trumpet.[82] The sea is also interwoven into the discourse of death, especially in sayings such as *Li te pran yon bato pou peyi san chapeau a* (He has taken a boat to the country without hats, i.e., where hats are no longer necessary). Thus, the legacy of forced migration, the dangerous and humiliating middle passage, slavery, insularity, religious beliefs, risky maritime practices, and foreign colonialism and domination enacted over the sea have left deep traces in a Haitian outlook on the sea.

Let's look at the mechanics of nautical migration. Fishermen and a new class of entrepreneurs sold would-be migrants passage on small boats (called *bak, kannòt, kante,* or *bato*) for anywhere from $500 up to $2,000.[83] The ships were not designed as oceangoing human transports, but were intended for local fishing or for coastal transportation of goods such as *chabon* (charcoal). Out of the windward passage, they headed for the Bahamas (Inagua is the closest Bahamanian island) or took direct aim for Miami. The journey was dangerous and dramatic. The boats often leaked, they were nearly always overcrowded, few could withstand serious storms, few were stocked with adequate supplies of fresh water and food, and seldom were steps taken to shield passengers from the direct sun. If they were discovered by the U.S. Coast Guard during or after arrival, the INS lodged the migrants at Miami's Krome Detention Center, a prison-like building where some spent years waiting for decisions, court cases, appeals, and possible repatriation.[84]

The interdiction treaty signed by the United States and Haiti in 1981 was responsible for a decline in the numbers attempting passage to the United States.[85] The Bahamas, however, also repatriated Haitians in the 1970s. The Haitians were generally poorly received in the United States, the Bahamas, and in other destination countries. Although the United States welcomed expatriate Cubans and later Nicaraguans and Salvadorans, the INS classified Haitians as economic refugees, justifying their policy of refusing political asylum. Haitians in the diaspora and at home interpreted the American reaction as evidence of racism. With high-profile coverage in the Haitian press in the Untied States and with extensive treatment in expressive culture, the boat people provided the subtext for the first serious confrontation of the Haitian diaspora with the host society.

The exodus and its reception overseas activated Haitian sensitivities toward oppression and slavery by supplying images that resonated with those of the middle passage: Haitians starving and dying on board ships, or led away as prisoners after arriving in the United States or the Bahamas. The Haitian press detailed nautical disasters in which bodies washed up on shore. Most terrifying of all was the implication that dead Haitians were being consumed by animals, that they had been reduced to less-than-human status, a horrifying debasement reminiscent of an era when their African ancestors were considered chattel or beasts of burden to the Europeans. This drama produced a crisis of conscience for many middle- and upper-class Haitians, resulting in a corpus of expressive culture—poetry, graphic arts, literature, and music—that chronicled the situation, although it diverged ideologically according to the political persuasions of the artist.

The *kilti libète* group Atis Endepandan was perhaps the first group to detail the migratory dilemma in their song "Papa m monte yon bato" (Papa took a boat), recorded in 1975. The arts collective blamed the migration of boat people on spiraling poverty and Duvalierist terror, especially the appropriation of lands in the countryside by the *chefs de section* and the *tonton makout*-s. This song was based on a traditional tune, and the arrangement used the guitar-based *twoubadou* style, although there were also strong influences from jazz and bossa nova. The musical setting changed to an unaccompanied, dirge-like choral section describing the loss of both parents and then moved into a quicker traditional Vodou rhythm called *yanvalou* for the section encouraging Haitians to confront the agents of oppression:

Papa m monte yon bato	Papa took a boat
Yo di nou li ale Naso	They say he went to Nassau
L al chèche lavi pou nou ki dèye	To look for a better life for those left behind
Pa genyen ni manje ni lajan	There is no food nor money
Manman te oblije chire yon vye wòb	Mama had to cut up an old dress
Pou l te fè yon kazak pou Ti-wouj	To make a shift for Little Red (malnourished)
Makout sezi tè-l . . .	*Makout-s* took the land . . .
Manman te blije	Mama had to send Little Red away
Lè Ti-wouj chape	As soon as he was big enough
Voye l rete avèk yon gran nèg lavil	To be a slave for a big shot in the city
Pèsonn pa janm konnen sa papa-nou deveni	No one knows what happened to papa
Manman-menm sòti mouri anba yon move tous	Mama herself died from tuberculosis
La mizè blayi ko-li sou nou tout lan peyi-a	Misery stretches itself over us all in the country
Fòs kouray-nou pi gwo nèg	But our courage is a bigger "big shot"
Pase dlo ki sot nan je-n	Than the tears in our eyes[86]

The song "Rackêt," by Rodrigue Milien, a *twoubadou*-style singer, chronicles the dangers of the voyage, with the last two lines of the song providing an ironic twist on the well-known Haitian proverb *Lamizè pa dous o* (Poverty isn't sweet), signaling that the alternative to poverty, emigration, is also bitter and that Haitians are trapped between a rock and a hard place. Milien's protagonist prays to various Vodou *lwa*-s: Danbala Wedo, the serpent deity associated with waterfalls; Ezili Freda, a goddess of love; and finally Mèt Agwe, the sea deity. But on this trip to a foreign land, the Vodou *lwa*-s are silent. The Haitian migrants are truly alone, deserted even by their gods. The word *racket*, means both a type of prickly cactus used as a barrier planting between properties and a big racket or noisy fuss, and the album cover art by Joseph Thony Moïse details a foundering ship with passengers in the water threatened by sharks.

Nou kotize ak de twa zanmi	We collect a few friends
Pou n ale nou Mayami	To go to Miami
Devan la kout tan nou pa jwenn fòs	In the face of the storm we find no strength
Manje nou prale fini	Our food is nearly exhausted
Fanmi Nouyòk konnen nou rive	Our families in New York expect us
O Mondyè ki sa pou n fè	Oh my God, what are we to do?
Rele Danbala Wedo—Yo pa vini	Call out to Danballah Wedo—they don't come
Rele Ezili Freda—Yo pa reponn	Call out to Erzulie Freda—they don't answer
Yo rele Mèt Agwe—Yo pa tande	They call out to Master Agwe—they don't hear
Ki sa pou n fè mezanmi? . . .	What can we do my friends? . . .
Se nan mitan lanmè—Nou pral peri	In the middle of the sea we're going to perish
Enmigrasyon nan peyi blan sa pa dous o!	American immigration isn't any fun![87]

Kiki Wainwright was a well-known troubadour and cultural activist based in the United States in the early 1980s. His song "Lan Inagwa" (In Inagua) detailed the horrors of the journey to Inagua (the closest of the Bahamas) with pointed criticisms of the government of the Bahamas for sending the Haitians away to their deaths. Note that the Bahamanians send the Haitians "into Ginen," that is, to their deaths under the sea. The image of rejection is made visceral by the reference to *zantray* (literally, "entrails"), implying that the Bahamanians don't consider Haitians a kindred people, a people they would consider as close to them as their entrails. Wainwright's musical setting for this song combined a *twoubadou* approach with elements drawn from the Latin American new song movement (including a Latin American harp).

150 zanfan neye lan inagwa, lan inagwa . . .	150 children died in Inagua . . .
Vivan lan peyi sa yo voye y ale lan Ginen	People in that country sent them into Guinée
Yo di nèg Dayiti pa zantray yo . . .	They say that Haitians are not their comrades . . .
Mizè agòch, mizè adwat	Misery left and right
Tribilasyon tribòbabò . . .	Tribulation everywhere . . .
Piti ap rele amwe	Children are calling for help
Pou manman ka sove yo	For their mothers to save them
Vag yo anraje, manman an ap naje	The seas are angry, the mother is swimming
Lè li rive, se kadav piti li l jwenn	When she arrives, she'll find her child's corpse[88]

Kiki Wainwright's "23 nèg vanyan" (23 heroic Haitians) positioned the boat people as transnational Haitian heroes because of the adversity they faced in their odyssey. As for their socioeconomic status in Haiti, *"lakay yap manje mizè"* (at home they were eating misery). The song recounts their tearful goodbye in Haiti, their rejection by the Bahamas, and then, in the excerpt below, their deaths at sea and the organizing activities of Haitians who raised money to give the dead a proper burial. The rhythm is a Cuban bolero, which, having been borrowed from Cuban music and domesticated for romantic songs, evokes a mood of sadness. The use of a proverb in the final lines emphasizes the composer's sympathy for the lower classes.

Yo peche kadav 14 granmoun	They fished out the corpses of fourteen adults
Avèk nèf timoun	With those of nine children
Konsil Ayisyen lan Bahamas	The Haitian Consul in Bahamas
Di l pa responsab	Said they weren't responsible
Ayisyen deyò met tèt ansanm	Haitians elsewhere got together

Yo fè lanteman	To bury the dead
Paske "woch lan dlo pa konn mizè	Because "rocks in the sea don't understand
Woch ki lan solèy"	The misery of rocks in the sun"[89]

In "Nan danje" (We're in danger), written in 1982, political singer Ti-Manno protested the mistreatment of Haitians at the hands of foreigners and provided a historical context for their rejection of Haitians. To represent the horrifying spetacle of Haitian bodies washed ashore in Miami, Ti-Manno doesn't say "foreign dogs were devouring them," but that "foreigners were having their dogs devour them," implying malicious intent on the part of the foreigners.

Kote n pase nou gen pwoblèm	Where ever we go, we encounter problems
Kote n pase nan danje . . .	Wherever we pass, we're in danger . . .
26 desanm 81 sa m wè m pa sa pale	I can't express what I saw on December 26, 1981
Lan lakou Miyami tout moun te gen dlo nan je	In the Miami community, we all cried
Nap gade Ayisyen parèy nou	Watching Haitians like us
Blan ap fè chen devore	Foreigners had their dogs devour them . . . [90]

"Libète" (Liberty), by Dadou Pasquet of Miami's Magnum Band, contrasts Pasquet's own more privileged situation to that of the boat people. Written in 1982, the lyrics plead with God for help and with Haitians to organize and confront the American government over the refugee situation. The last couplet, included in the excerpt below, treats the issue of Haitians being reduced to food for animals. Although the bulk of the song is arranged as a *konpa*, Pasquet employs a traditional Vodou rhythm called *kongo* at the song's start:

Chans pou mwen m pati depi lè m te toupiti	I was lucky to leave when I was very young
M pa janm gen nesesite pou m te pwan kante	I never had to take a small boat
Kwak se lè m gade sa frè m yo ap pase	When I see what's happening to my brothers

Se zantray mwen fè mwen mal jistan m kriye . . .	My insides ache until I cry . . .
Libète nou mande pou frè n yo	We're asking for liberty for our brothers
Yo vann tout sa yo genyen lakay	They sold everything they had at home
Pou yo vin chèche yo meyè vi	To look for a better life
Lè yo rive se nan pwizon yo mete yo	When they arrive, they're put in prison
Genyen nan yo ki pa menm rive	Some never arrived
Rekin manje yo depi wout	Sharks ate them en route
Move tan bare yo sou dlo	They sank in terrible weather[91]

Many of these albums focusing on the boat people sported paintings by Haitian artists on their covers. The six songs I include in this section protest the indignities suffered by the boat people, raise public consciousness about their situation, and rally the public to organize on their behalf. Protest, conciousness raising, and rallying the public are, of course, standard functions for political songs all over the globe. Haitian songwriters addressing this subject brought into play a deeply historical Haitian experience of the sea that lent a particular potency to the issue and helped the boat people to emerge as affectively charged symbols around which diasporic and insular Haitian sentiment coalesced.

To many diaspora residents, the rejection of Haitian immigrants epitomized an anti-Haitian bias that they perceived daily, and musicians and artists responded with what Frederick Buell calls the "dystopian strain of American immigrant literature/film. Immigrants . . . come to the United States, inspired by its promises of freedom and prosperity, go through great hardships, and encounter tragedy rather than success in the end. The United States does not live up to its rhetoric; it proves to be a land, not of freedom and opportunity, but of discrimination and exploitation."[92]

Angaje composers portrayed migrants as examples of Duvalierist oppression and of Haiti's disadvantaged position within a system of global capital, penning songs to be used in building an antidictatorial and anti-imperialist movement. In their analysis, the boat people fled poverty and repression at home, risked death en route (in a second middle passage, just as full of danger and degradation as the first), only to encounter racism, rejection, and exploitative labor practices in their host countries. *Angaje* songwriters characterized Haiti as suffering from multiple oppressions: external (imperialist and neocolonial-ist), internal (totalitarian oppression and racial/class prejudice), and diasporic (minority marginalization in the United States, Canada, the Bahamas, etc.).

A strong illustration of this ideological construction of the boat people appears on the cover art for an album by Farah Juste, *La Voix des sans voix* (The voice of those without a voice). Painted by Haitian artist Jude Thegenus, the cover juxtaposes Farah against a backdrop of the migratory drama. Duvalierist repression is pictured on the left, as soldiers fire their guns under the Duvalierist flag in front of the notorious prison, Fort Dimanche. Boats load up with Haitians on the center left and arrive at right after they have crashed on the rocks, their phantom-like passengers listless in the hot sun, with a blood-red liquid dripping from the sail. At the far right, Krome Detention Center waits for Haitians beneath an American flag. Fort Dimanche on the left, Krome on the right . . . a journey between two flags, two horrors, two prisons.

"Let Us Pass!": Carnival and the Fall of Baby Doc

Carnival is the most important crossroads of music and power in Haiti. The *koudyay* ambience of carnival, the tradition of *chan pwen* in car-nival songs, the powerful impression made by tens of thousands of lower-class Haitians in control of the streets, and carnivalesque (Gede-esque) exuberance (obscenity, exaggeration, verbal play, parody, excessive consumption, the grotesque, debasement, sexuality, license, transgression, masking, conflict, and Signifying on hierarchies) all contribute to an event that is potentially threatening to the state and to the elite. The state is thus at pains to co-opt, incorporate, regulate, and control Carnival's "critique." I have argued elsewhere that Carnival takes place in spaces permeated with power relations, and it is not, as often suggested, "outside" those relations.[93] On one level, Carnival resembles a *koudyay* writ large and hosted by the state, at which the bands play their *ochan*-s to the mayor and to the president. If the mood at Carnival is good, it reflects well on the authorities.

François Duvalier was able to make use of carnival's exuberance and anti-elite sentiment. The totalitarian nature of the dictatorship as well as its popularity among certain sectors of the poor allowed for very few carnival songs critical of the regime, even under Baby Doc, before 1980. With the closing of the independent press and the exile of political artists, however, Carnival began to take on increased significance as a locus for the developing political critique of Baby Doc, his wife, and his govenment. The superstar popularity of the *mini-djaz* (and the fact that many of them were from the diaspora) helped to insulate them from the crackdown, as did the allusive, metaphorical, or allegorical nature of the *pwen*-s themselves. Full of strategic ambivalence and indirect signification, the *mereng kanaval*-s served as encoded political messages that could be understood only if one were cognizant of the nicknames, rumors, jokes, and insults making the rounds of the *teledjòl* (rumor mill or grapevine). In this way, the *mini-djaz* groups were able to clear a certain privileged social space for political criticism even in the midst of a repressive crackdown. With the gradual collapse of Duvalierism, businesses withdrew their patronage of Carnival, leaving only the dictatorship and the mayoralty of Port-au-Prince, run by *makout* Franck Romain, as sponsors. Although many of the Carnival songs of the period were never recorded, they were collected by Yves Robert Louis and printed by journalist Jean Fragat in an article in *Haïti-Observateur*.[94] (The carnival songs in this section, unless otherwise noted, are drawn from that article.)

At the 1981 Carnival, Bossa Combo, the former "orchestra of the president," ridiculed the power of Michèle Bennet Duvalier, singing about a woman named Janine driving a car without a license. Most of the songs in this section will follow the *chan pwen* convention of disguising the name of the intended recipient. Note that Bossa Combo used French, not Creole, to name the five fingers, poking fun at Michèle's bourgeois mannerisms (with a pun on the finger gesture).

Janin, kote lisan-ou?	**Janine, where is your driver's license?**
Janin, ou pa respèkte m	**You don't respect me**
Ou sou kontravansyon	**You're going to get a traffic ticket**
Si ou pa gen siyal	**If you don't get a signal**
Wa fè l ak dwèt	**You'll make it with your little finger**
[In French] Le pouce, l'index, le majeur,	**Thumb, index, middle,**
L'annulaire, l'auriculaire	**Ring finger, and pinky**
Ala la w bon dwèt se lemajè!	**The middle finger is such a great finger!**

D. P. Express sang about Michèle at the same Carnival. This song was so popular that Carnival 1981 is remembered by many as Kanaval Bibwon (Baby bottle Carnival). One critic called this song "a useless blasphemy" having "no place in a carnival."[95]

Madmwazèl, wa kenbe bibwon byen	Miss, hold on to the baby bottle well
Pou li pa chape	So he doesn't become independent
Menm si wa tonbe	Even if you fall
Kenbe bibwon pou li pa vole	Hold on to the bottle so he doesn't fly away

For the 1982 Carnival, Michèle lobbied for a luxurious stand to be built along the parade route with bar, toilet, and electricity. Bossa Combo criticized the stand as a symbol of waste and excess:

Gade kijan w kite mato a glize	Watch how you let the hammer slip
Li tonbe sou dwèt w Madmwazèl woo	It falls on your finger, Miss, whoa
Se pou w di mwen	You must tell me
Ak ki bwa w fè estann sa a	With which wood did you build the stand?
Kat pa kat se byen, wit pa wit se solid	Four by four is fine, eight by eight is solid
Sèz pa sèz, two gwo!	Sixteen by sixteen is too big!

In 1983, diatribes about Michèle were even more widespread, many dealing with her struggle with Roger Lafontant, one of the so-called superministers who, rumor had it, were running the country for Baby Doc.[96] Shoogar Combo sang:

Dyab pa fe dyab pè	The devil doesn't fear another devil
Gwo dyab manje ti dyab	The big devil is eating the little devil
Yo kloure Toto sou lakwa	They're nailing Toto [Duvalier] to the cross

Yo foure yon paydefè sou tèt-lie	They're putting steel wool around his head
Ala nèg inosan se Toto	What a naive guy that Toto is!

In many of these songs, Jean-Claude appears as a naive dupe of Michèle, his mother, or his ministers. The *mini-djaz* movement reflected a middle-class consensus, and the middle class was one of Baby Doc's traditional strongholds. The breakdown in the coalition that supported the dictatorship was gradual and was reflected in a slow refocusing of the critical rhetoric upon the dictatorship itself. To this purpose, Coupé Cloué used the following image to paint Jean-Claude as tragically credulous: *Yereswa, mwen rèv yon bourik kap souse yon piwouli* (Last night I dreamed a donkey was sucking on a popsicle). After Michèle decisively won a protracted power struggle with Jean-Claude's mother, Simone "Mama Doc" Duvalier, Dixie Band taunted "Mama Doc" by name with the song "Gwo Simone" (Big Simone): *He! Tu n'as pas de plume sur le ciboulet!* (Hey, you have no feathers on your noggin!).

Despite Michèle's efforts to recast herself in the public eye as a Haitian Evita with her own hospital charity project, her lavish spending and her shopping sprees in Paris fixed her image permanently in the public consciousness. Dixie Band (from Montreal) sang a *chan pwen* to Michèle at Carnival 1984:

Tout fanm se lougawou	All women are werewolves
Men pa devan Ti Maryann, o!	But not in comparison to Little Maryanne
Li gen dwèt long	She has long fingers
E li renmen kòb	And she loves money

As economic conditions worsened and inflation rose precipitously, food riots broke out first in Gonaïves, then in Cap-Haïtien. Things became so desperate for Baby Doc in 1985 that he offered all workers an extra two days off in order to begin Carnival on Friday. A common carnival expression is *ban nou pase* (let us pass), from the need for *bann madigra*-s (parade bands) to make their way through the crowds at Carnival. Without the direct reference to Toto, a nickname for Duvalier, the following lyrics might suggest an aggressive carnival "let me pass" song. Yet here they assume an angry *pwen* directed at Jean-Claude, demanding that he get out of the people's way. The rapid erosion of mechanisms of control had created a situation in which a *mini-djaz* (Dixie Band) could confront the dictatorship in a carnival song:

Tonnè boule m, bannou pase!	**Thunder burns me, let us pass!**
Si w pa rale kò w, m ap kraze w!	**If you don't get out of the way I'll break you!**
Kraponnaj sa a, mwen pa pran ladan l!	**I won't stand for this deception**
Ma manje w wi, ma devore w wi!	**I'll eat you, yes! I'll devour you, yes!**
Toto brikabrak! Cho biznis!	**Pawnshop Toto, Mr. Show Business!**
Ou son ou dasomann, retire kò w!	**You're just a gatecrasher—Get out of here!**

The atmosphere of dissent and rebelliousness at Carnival 1985 was one more indication of the steadily deteriorating base of support for Jean-Claude's presidency for life. Dixie Band's message was hardly ambivalent. The dictatorship was teetering: Jean-Claude had to go, or the people would force him to go. The middle classes from which the *mini-djaz* arose and the destitute urban working class which formed much of their audience at Carnival were, for the moment, united. The danger implicit in carnival now threatened presidential security—the danger of a crowd both *anraje* (worked up, enraged) and *angaje* (politically committed).

Duvalier declared 1985 "The Year of Youth," and it was indeed a year in which young musicians came to the forefront of the political and musical revolution. A young singer and guitarist, Beethova Obas (who performed occasionally with Manno Charlemagne), wrote a roots music song that became a "clandestine hit in his own neighborhood of Arcachon 34" called "Plezi mizè" (The pleasures of poverty). In a period when hunger riots were breaking out, Obas's lyrics painted *rara* festivities as a respite from the misery and hunger of peasant existence:[97]

De vaksin, de tanbou, Ayisyen anraje . . .	**With *vaksin*-s and drums, Haitians worked up . . .**
Nanpwen tan pou chodyè monte	**There's no time for the pot to heat up**
Vant timoun yo ap kòde	**The children's stomachs are knotted**

Denmen lè bann ap pase	Tomorrow when the rara band is passing
Na bliye vant kòde	We'll forget the knotted stomachs[98]

During the hot summer of discontent in 1985, Ansy and Yole Dérose organized and hosted a televised festival from the Sylvio Cator Stadium at which Eméline Michel, Guerda Hector, Pirogue, and other new generation artists were first presented to a large public.[99] Throughout the summer, groups such as Kajou, Pirogue, and Splash received major airplay on Port-au-Prince radio, and musical change, like political change, was everywhere evident.

In the years following the visit to Haiti by Pope John Paul II, a Catholic radio station named Radyo Solèy (Radio of the sun) became Haiti's main press organ for uncensored news. In response to the first large demonstrations in Gonaïves (November 27–28), the government shut down Radyo Solèy on December 5. During the next month, demonstrations spread to the universities and to provincial cities such as Cap-Haïtien, where 50,000 people turned out for an antigovernment march, singing:

Pa di mo, pa di mo	Dont curse, don't curse
Jan Klòd Divalye	Jean-Claude Duvalier
Ranje kò w	Get yourself ready
N ap dechouke w	We're going to uproot you
Nou pa pè gaz	We don't fear tear gas
Nou gen sitwon	We have limes [to counter- act it][100]

After the closing of Radyo Solèy, a young songwriter named Jean-Michel Daudier penned a protest song about the censorship of the station, "Lè m pa wè solèy la" (When I can't see the sun). The song drew on the currents of liberation theology, portraying the station as an instrument of divine will, an index of right and wrong, and an essential element in Haitian spiritual survival. Papa Djo, a popular deejay on Radyo Solèy, said of the song, "The sensibility in the heart of Jean-Michel allowed him to capture the sentiment of the Haitian people with "Lè m pa wè solèy la." They loved it, they sang it, they learned it by heart, and they found strength from it. He called the people together [rasanble] in a single work brigade [konbit] of truth and justice."[101]

Circulated on bootlegged cassettes, it made its way on to numerous radio broadcasts and became the anthem of Operasyon Dechoukaj (Operation "uprooting"), the movement to end the dictatorship:

Son bèl bagay ki Bondyè ka ban nou . . .
The Good Lord gave us a beautiful thing . . .

Ki pou n di sa ki byen, ki pou n di sa ki mal
To tell us what's right, to tell us what's wrong

Le n pa gen lafwa, le n ped lespwa
When we have no faith, when we lose hope

[Refrain]
[Refrain]

Lè m pa wè soley-la
When I can't see the sun

Mwen paka leve, paka kanpe
I can't get up, can't stand

Paka mache, paka kouri
Can't walk, can't run

Kè pa kontan, mwen pa sa vi
My heart isn't happy, I can't live like this[102]

Jean-Claude and his family left Haiti a week before Carnival 1986. It was widely assumed that the impending Carnival and the security risks that Carnival presented were critical in the timing of the departure. This contention was supported by Elizabeth Abbott in her popular history of the Duvaliers: "The race was against time. Carnival was scheduled for February 12,when millions of Haitians would take to the streets, unfettered, unafraid, a singing, dancing mass that could swiftly turn from revelry to violence. . . . In February, 1986, carnival would be the perfect catalyst to transform rebellious uprisings into full-scale revolution."[103] As the news of Duvalier's exile spread throughout the country, throngs took to the streets, stripping trees of their branches, and hoisting them high in the air as a symbol of renewal.[104] Crowds sang the French version of Burns's "Auld Lang Syne," a song of parting that takes on sarcastic overtones when bidding farewell to a humiliated or despised ruler.

Lumane Casimir with Jazz des Jeunes at the Théâtre de Verdure during the 1949 bicentennial of the founding of Port-au-Prince. The "folklore show," featuring Casimir, Jazz des Jeunes, and the Troupe Folklorique Nationale, was the cultural centerpiece of the event that helped to popularize Haiti's "indigenous" arts. (Photographer unknown; reprinted with permission from a playbill for the Théâtre National, May 29–June 7, 1987.)

Nemours Jean-Baptiste (center) in the studio with his two most celebrated band members, accordionist Richard Duroseau (left) and guitarist Raymond Gaspard (right), the originator of the term *konpa-dirèk*. (Cover art to the album *Les Trois Dangers*, Ibo Records ILP-127.)

Wébert Sicot and Super Ensemble Wébert Sicot, from the cover of the album *La Flèche d'or d'Haïti*. (Ibo Records ILP-132.)

The *mini-djaz* Les Fantaisistes de Carrefour perched on a luxury automobile, wearing paisley shirts in front of a government building—celebrating the middle-class life-style. (Album cover to *Haïti*, Ibo Records, ILP-143.)

Tabou Combo in a Brooklyn recording studio in 1973, from the cover to their album *Respect*. In recognition of their new cultural surroundings, the identifying tag-line "de Pétionville" is now very small in relation to their name, they have chosen an album name that works equally well in French or English, and members of the band sport dashikis and afros. (From the album *Respect*, Mini Records MRS 1039.)

Ti-Manno on stage with D. P. Express at the Ciné Triomphe, Port-au-Prince, at the time of the success with the album *David*. (From the cover art for *David*, Superstar Records SUP-111. Photo: Dominique F. Simon.)

The carnival float for the band D. P. Express, surrounded by an exuberant crowd. (Photo: Steve Winter, 1989.)

Political singers Les Frères Parent with a sign featuring the title of one of their songs. A *konbit* is a peasant labor association or work brigade that symbolizes a spirit of collective unity and discipline. From left to right, Alain Picard, Claire Lydie, and Jean-Jacques Clark Parent. (Photo: Steve Winter, 1989.)

The painting by Jude Thegenus graces the cover of Farah Juste's *La Voix des sans Voix*, in which she is pictured singing in the midst of a tableau dramatizing the plight of the Haitian boat people. (See page 154.)

Members of Groupe Sa in their practice space atop Morel's Bakery, Boulevard Jean-Jacques Dessalines, Port-au-Prince, in 1982. From left to right, Jean Raymond Giglio, "Aboudja" Derenoncourt, and Jean Robert. Note the combination here of the two *manman tanbou* (mother drums) and drum set. (Photo: Chantal Regnault, 1982.)

The *mizik rasin* (roots music) band Foula playing traditional *vaksin*-s (bamboo tubes) and drums. (Photo: Steve Winter, 1989.)

Manno Charlemagne performing at Miami's Tap Tap Restaurant. (Photo: Peter Eves, 1994.)

Posters for the election of Manno Charlemagne as mayor of Port-au-Prince. (Photo: Gage Averill, 1995.)

Fan club and rehearsal/performance space for the band D. P. Express and later for Ansyto Mercier and his group Digital Express. Because they had their own dance club, D. P. and later Digital Express could perform throughout periods of political crisis when other clubs and halls were closed. (Photo: Gage Averill, 1988.)

A *taptap* (bus) called "High Fidelity." Taptaps use their sound systems and audio tapes to attract patrons, and they constitute important sites for music consumption. They are typically covered with religious and secular messages and graphics, and many advertise favorite musical bands or songs. (Photo: Gage Averill, 1995.)

Boukman Eksperyans, under a *manman tanbou* (mother drum). (Photo: Steve Winter, 1989.)

5

"Watch Out for Them!"
Dechoukaj and Its Aftermath

Woy, dechouke yo	Wo, uproot them
N ap dechouke tout move zèb	We're uprooting all of the bad weeds
Pou nou kab mete tèt ansanm	In order to unite [put heads together]

The years following the exile of Duvalier challenged every sector of Haitian society, producing a revolutionary climate in which Haiti's various classes, political forces, and institutions (e.g., the army and the *makout*-s) struggled for political control and hegemony.[1] To *dechouke* a plant is to pull it up by its roots. It was a particularly apt metaphor for political changes after Duvalier, because it recognized that the dictatorship was more than an oppressive overlay kept in power by force alone, but that it had sunk its roots deeply into Haitian society and culture. The word was appropriated for actions such as killing *makout*-s and ransacking their homes, businesses, or offices. Violent *dechoukaj* left behind many burned-out, abandoned, and crumbling buildings. *Dechoukaj* could just as easily be applied to closing down or transforming institutions, firing Duvalierist managers, changing Duvalier-era laws, or even modifying beliefs. *Angaje* musicians counseled the popular movement and commented profusely on the politics of the period. *Men nan men* (hand in hand), *men kont* (hands clasped), *tèt ansanm* (heads together), *kole zepòl* (put shoulders together), and many other body metaphors joined agricultural images of planting, harvesting, and uprooting in the Haitian rhetoric of social change and progress.

The agreement brokered by the U.S. State Department to secure Jean-Claude's departure set up a National Council of Government (CNG) consisting of five military and civilian members (including human rights activist Gerard Gorgue) led by Lt. Gen. Henri Namphy. This was the first in a string of military-dominated governments that ruled Haiti up until the inauguration of Jean-Bertrand Aristide in 1991. The CNG officially abolished the *tonton makout*-s, but many *makout*-s simply changed uniforms and slipped quietly into the ranks of the army or police.

This period is also characterized by a continuing tumult in musical style. Occasionally, one heard the sentiment that *konpa*, too, should be uprooted because of its long association with the dictatorship (despite the proliferation of *angaje konpa* in the 1980s). Increasingly, musicians explored avenues other than *konpa*, including *nouvèl jenerasyon* (new generation music), *mizik rasin* (roots music), and imported forms like rap and reggae dancehall chanting (musics of African "diasporic intimacy").

The period following the departure of the Duvaliers also represented a watershed in the transnational integration of Haitians.[2] Former political refugees now were welcome in Haiti. Family members returned home with gifts and cash, boosting the hard-strapped economy. Haitian-American radio stations and programs retransmitted insular news programs, and Haitian newspapers from the diaspora expanded their circulation in Haiti. Haitians in the United States became increasingly radicalized in relation to Haitian politics and to diasporic struggles (AIDS stigmatization, INS policies, etc.). The transnational space was characterized by increased economic, social, political, and cultural integration. Despite sporadic resentment toward diaspora Haitians and their American mannerisms, many Haitians shared an optimism about the incorporation of Haitians abroad into the affairs of the country.

To summarize, after 1986 we find an increasing transnational integration in Haitian music, a more fully engaged role for musicians in political struggle, and new musical movements challenging the dominance of *konpa* in the market. Most important, peasants and the poor—through their popular organizations and through their effect on Haitian urban culture—moved still closer to the center of Haitian political and musical life.

"Uproot the Wrongdoing": Musicians Support
Operasyon Dechoukaj

Among the thousands of Haitian exiles flocking back to Haiti in the months after February 1986 were many *angaje* musicians who had fled Haiti during the crackdown in 1980 and some who had been in exile for much longer. Manno Charlemagne returned home on March 7 and promptly organized a group of percussionists and singers into the Koral Konbit Kalfou (literally, Chorale of the crossroads work brigade chorus) to advance the mix of political and roots music that the *kilti libète* (freedom culture) cultural organizations had pioneered in the 1970s.

Their first song was called "Gran rivyè" and contained the line *"N ap mennen pwen nou nan kalfou a"* (We're bringing our point to the crossroads). As I have explained, *pwen* is a multivalent term in Creole. It means "point" literally, but it is used to designate songs that censure or denigrate with signifying tropes. *Pwen* also means "fist," "point/perspective," and "magical spell" (similar to *a wanga*, which is often left for its intended victim at a crossroads). Thus *pwen* simultaneously draws on musical, spiritual, ideological, and physical power. Manno and the Koral's use of the crossroads as a place of reckoning in Vodou spirituality prefigures its celebrated use by Boukman Eksperyans at Carnival 1992.

N ap mennen pwen nou nan kalfou o	We're bringing out "point" to the crossroads
N ap pare tann yo ak dan sere o . . .	We're waiting for them with clenched teeth . . .
Nou pap janm zonbi k ap tann sèl o	We're not going to be zombies waiting for salt[3]

Why salt? There is a popular belief that zombies can be brought back to life (or put out of their soulless existence) with salt, and that as a result, their masters jealously keep salt away from them; this line proclaims a determination to resist zombie-like slavery. The references to Vodou are multiplied in Charlemagne's songs of this period, but in contrast to some roots music groups, Charlemagne was far more concerned with the religion's political or revolutionary potential: "Vodou can be a religion, a way of life for people, but it can also be a cultural arm. That's how I use it. I'm not going to discuss the religious part. I'm not going to say it doesn't exist. But I use, in a good way, the militant part of Vodou, and I use it for good. I call it, 'cultural resources.'"⁴

Charlemagne and the Koral debuted in April of 1986 at Haiti's Teyat Nasyonal (formerly Théâtre de Verdure, built originally for the 1949 exposition). This concert was the first of a string of explosive concerts at the theater over the next half-decade. One of the songs they performed was a revised version of a song from 1974, "Ayiti pa fore" (Haiti is not a forest), with new verses chastising Michèle Duvalier (called by her maiden name Bennet), the *tonton makout*-s, and the CNG:

Lè w fè sa ma pè w	When you do that, I'm so scared of you
Paske w se makout	Just because you're a *makout*
Ou konprann ou ka kraponen mwen	You think that you can fool me
Ou rale wouzi w, mwen rilax sou w!	You take out your Uzi machine gun, but I relax
Ou rale baton gayak la, mwen pi koul sou w!	You take out your wood club, I'm even calmer
Tone kraze m Michèl Bènèt, I am sorry for you	Goddamn it, Michèle Bennet! I am sorry for you
Se nan videyo wa gade pèp ayisyen	Only on video can you watch the Haitian people
Ou voye papa w a achte twa bonm	You send your father to buy three bombs
Pou vin bonbade lajenès an Ayiti	To come and bombard the youth in Haiti
Ki deklere ke dechoukaj la poko fini	Who declare that the uprooting isn't over yet
Konsèy Gouvenman chaje tonton makout	If the CNG is full of *tontons makout*-s
Konsèy Gouvanman gen Regala ladan l	If the CNG has General Regala in it⁵

The last refrain echoes an idée fixe in many of the political songs of *dechoukaj:* The struggle was far from over. Militant performers fought to maintain the intensity and focus of the popular struggle and to forestall any relaxation in the wake of Duvalier's exit. Their insistent chorus suggested that little had really changed in Haiti since February 7, 1986: Duvalierists still held state power, class relations were largely unchanged, and the transition in Haiti was being managed by the U.S. State Department precisely to forestall revolutionary change. To emphasize the complicity of imperialism in the crisis, Charlemagne entitled his live 1988 solo album, *Nou nan malè ak oganizasyon mondyal* (We're in poverty with the world system); the album became the hottest selling album in Haiti for a period in 1988. The initials of the production company that issued the album (Kolektif Ayisyen Konsekan Ozetazini) spell out the name of the peasant armed units that opposed the first American occupation (*kako*-s), and the catalogue number (1915) is the date of the original U.S. invasion. This was the last album Charlemagne released for over six years, during which he was, as he once described it, *"plonje nan kesyon politik"* (submerged in political struggle). Charlemagne took it upon himself to counsel patient building of popular organizations, certain that the army, the elite, and foreign powers had something other than the best interests of Haiti's poor at heart.

The *angaje* band Les Frères Parent, which had left Haiti during the crackdown in 1980, returned and quickly produced a cassette featuring a new movement song, "Operasyon Dechoukaj" (Operation uprooting). Their song "Konbit" (Work brigade) asked questions about the social order in Haiti (reminiscent of Manno Charlemagne's earlier "Pouki?" [Why?]). "Konbit" offered a method for rebuilding the country based on the cooperative peasant activity of work brigades, employing everyday images (ladders, cakes, chairs, Catholic communion) to make class oppression tangible. This song was featured in a Jonathan Demme film and provided the title for the compilation that Demme produced along with Fred Paul and myself.

Di pito se yon gato	**Rather, look at life as a cake**
Yon gato ki mal pataje	**A cake that's badly distributed**
Yon ti gwoup jwenn yon bann, yon bann	**A small group grabs the big chunk**
Men yon bann menm pa jwenn ditou . . .	**While the majority gets nothing . . .**
Poukisa nan lamès losti-yo toupiti?	**Why is the wafer so small at mass?**
Paske fidèl-yo pa gen twòp apeti	**Because the faithful don't have much appetite**

| Pouki fidèl-yo pa gen twòp apeti? | Why do the faithful have such a small appetite? |
| Paske tout lasemèn gaz fin apare yo | Because all week long they are bloated with gas[6] |

Reducing the disparities between classes was the key to progress in the view of the venerable Cap-Häitien ensemble Orchestre Septentrionale. Their song on the subject carried the same name as the 1980 Ti-Manno/D. P. Express song "Ansanm ansanm" (Together/united):

Si nou vle demokrasi se pou n konsanti	If we want democracy, we have to consent
Pou gwo nèg swiv	For the big people to follow
Menm disiplin ak piti	The same discipline as the poor
Pa gen demokrasi nan diskriminasyon	There is no democracy in discrimination
Nou pa janm avanse si nou divize . . .	We can't advance if we're divided . . .
Se pou n kraze fontyè	Break down the wall
Ant mas pèp ak boujwazi	Between the masses and bourgeoisie[7]

In addition to clarifying class relations in Haiti, *angaje* artists used their new-found freedom to criticize the greed, violence, and corruption of those who would perpetuate Duvalierism without Duvalier. Les Frères Parent characterized the struggle as one between light (information, innocence, generosity) and darkness (evil, corruption, violence). Like Charlemagne and author Franck Etienne, Les Frères Parent employed the metaphor of the *zonbi* (a potent metaphor of slavery to generations of Haitians) to characterize life under the dictatorship:

Gen de moun ki pa janm vle wè	There are folks who don't want to see
Yon pèp ki òganize	A people that is organized
Konsa yo toujou ap travay	That's why they're always working
Pou yo divize l	To divide them
Moun-sa-yo prefere yon pèp	These kind of people prefer a people
Tèt anba kou zonbi	With their heads bowed like zombies

| Ak sa yap toujou gen pouvwa | That way, they'll always have power |
| Fè nenpòt ki abi | To commit any kind of abuse[8] |

General Williams Régala, a military member of the CNG, mentioned in a song by Manno Charlemagne above, also made an appearance in a song by Beethova Obas:

Lè w tande yo gen pouvwa	When you hear they have grabbed power
Yo konprann se yo k sèl wa	They believe they're the sole law
Arete moun san manda	They arrest people without a mandate
Pour avoir críe "aba"	Just for having cried out, "Down with this!"
Divalye te fè l konsa	Duvalier did it like that
Jan Klod te fè l konsa	Jean-Claude did it like that
Regala te fè li konsa	Régala did it like that[9]

In 1986, Sakad, Nikol Levy's New York-based roots-rock band released the album *Rebati kay la* (Rebuild the home). In the title song, Sakad compared the process of *dechoukaj* to tearing down a rotten house to build a new one.[10]

In "Flanm difè" (Flames of fire) Sakad suggests that destruction and purification are a necessary part of the revolutionary process:

Gen youn flanm difè	There's a flame from a fire
Lè li pran gaye, gwo zotobre rele danje . . .	When it spreads, big shots cry "danger" . . .
Lè li eklate, malere se danse li danse	When it bursts, the poor are dancing[11]

Not all of the musical commentaries on *dechoukaj* were as supportive and uncritical concerning violence and destruction. Radio deejay and singer Master Dji (Georges Lys-Herard) recorded "Sispann" (Stop) with sampled sound bits and an African-American-style rap, to caution the popular forces. The song begins with a sample of the voice of Pope John Paul II demanding change in Haiti and then praises the spirit of change with a series of lines starting with "speak up." As the lyrics move on to the topic of "destruction and uprooting" and perceived excesses of revolutionary zeal, the song shifts tone, denouncing mob violence:

Yo pa sonje pe pou tande pou koute	They don't remember to listen, to hear
Pou yo manyen veye analize	To feel, to look around, to analyze
Non! Yo pito depale . . .	No, they'd rather rant and rave . . .
Sispann fè kachkach	Stop playing hide-and-seek
Sispann banm kout fwèt kach	Stop striking me with a hidden whip
Sispann fè apach	Stop being a hooligan
Montre m figi w si w pa lach	Show me your face if you're not a coward[12]

In the heated atmosphere of *dechoukaj,* musicians weighed in on every side of the conflict. Distrustful of the motivations of the bourgeoisie and military, Manno Charlemagne and Les Frères Parent counseled no letup on the pressure from the masses in the streets, but Master Dji, scornful of mob violence, cautioned against the politics of anger and vengeance. His middle-class audience, of course, had less tolerance for abuses committed in the name of righting historical wrongs.

Operasyon Dechoukaj brought the voice of a Salesian priest named Jean-Bertrand Aristide to international prominence. An advocate of *teyoloji liberasyon* (liberation theology) and a leader in the *ti-legliz,* Aristide came back from exile to preach to some of Haiti's most desperately poor at the St. Jean Bosco church in the slum called La Salines. Considered anti-American by the U.S. State Department, his sermons were taped and analyzed for years by the U.S. Embassy in Haiti. What is little known outside Haiti is that Aristide is also a guitarist and songwriter. Of the few songs by Aristide that have been recorded, one paid homage to the many who were tortured and killed in Duvalier's most notorious prison, Fort Dimanche (Fò Dimanch, in Creole). In this song, Pè Titid (Creolized diminutive of Father Aristide) suggested that the fort be converted into a school in memory of its victims:

Pou lonè tout Ayisyen yo maspinen,	For the honor of all Haitians they abused,
Masakre, Matilize	Mutilated, and tortured

Pou rèspè tout Ayisyen toufounen,	Out of respect for all Haitians beaten up,
Toupizi, nan kalfou lamò	Spun around on the crossroads of death
Younn fwa, de fwa, twa fwa	Once, twice, thrice
Anpil fwa anfen ansanm	Many times finally together
N ap priye ansanm	We'll pray together
N ap deklare ansanm	Declare together
N pral mande ansanm	We'll ask together[13]

Notice that Aristide used the *lonè-rèspè* formula (peasant greeting ritual, translated as "honor, respect") for the structure of the first two lines and that he used the idiomatic Creole means of emphasizing a point by counting to three. These kinds of devices, along with the use of proverbs and traditional storytelling techniques, are fundamental to Father Aristide's highly popular style of public address.

The choral songs of Gacin Garçon, remarkable distillations of liberation theology, appear on two albums. Aristide commented on the second, "Nou tout se legliz: solidarite, fòk sa chanje" ("All of us are the church: Solidarity, this has to change") with the following: "The marrow of this message is deep in my heart. The sugar of the music is deep in my blood. My heart dances, my blood marches. And I say: Bravo to *sanba* Gacin, *Ayibobo* to God."[14] By calling the evangelical composer a *sanba* and by praising God with the formula used in Vodou services (*ayibobo*), Aristide exemplified the subtle syncretism of Vodou and Christianity that he has championed and that allowed him to sport a Vodou ritual diagram (*vèvè*) on his vestments. In "Fòk sa chanje," Garçon used Pope John Paul II's famous phrase, set against a litany of obstructions to peace, with still another reference to the "honor-respect" formula:

Pa kab gen lape	We can't have peace
Lè moun ap eksplwate moun . . .	While people are exploiting others . . .
Lè moun ap viv nan lamizè . . .	While people are living in misery . . .
Lè yo gen la teren . . .	While they have the playing field . . .
Se onè respè ki kapab mete lape	It's honor and respect that can bring peace[15]

The explicitly *angaje* performers were joined by many commercial artists who welcomed political change, championed national unity, and drew on religious themes of liberation. Albums like *Tèt-ensem* (Unity) from Magnum Band, *Van libète* (Winds of liberty) from Skah Shah, *Fòk sa change nan lakou lakay* (Something's got to change in the courtyards at home) from Tropicana and *Haïti libere* by Toto Necessité all carried messages of political liberation. Using the uprooting metaphor, Dadou Pasquet and the Magnum Band chastised the rich and powerful in this 1986 excerpt from "Pran konsyans" (Take a conscientious stand):

Ou menm kap soufri se w menm
   map pale . . .
Mezanmi frè m yo fò n pote kole

Mechanste sa fò l dechouke . . .
Pèp la decide l ou met devore l

Lè ya rive pou l libère

Kontinye lite chase move je

Se pou bagay l sa chanje

You that are suffering, I'm talking to you . . .
Brothers and sisters, let's work together
To uproot the wrongdoing . . .
Even if they are devoured, the people have decided
The time has come to free themselves
Keep struggling to chase away the evil eye
To change this thing[16]

But "changing this thing" was proving to be a very protracted battle.

"Bitter Christmas": The Election Massacre

Facing sustained and sometimes violent protests demanding civilian government, the CNG finally proposed an election of a constitutional assembly for October 1986, leading to a new constitution and finally to new presidential elections. The new constitution, the subject of a sophisticated political debate among all sectors of Haitian society, was approved April 28, 1987. Among many other provisions, the constitution barred "notorious Duvalierists" from running for office and enshrined Creole as the official language along with French. The assembly set up an electoral commission called KEP (Provisional electoral committee) and scheduled elections for November 29, 1987. The November elections initially attracted over two hundred candidates for president, a fact that was grist for comedians and songwriters alike.

Les Frères Parent released an election song called "Veye-yo" (Watch out for them). The refrain was chanted often at progressive political rallies and was adopted as the name of an oppositional political organization. "Veye-yo" contained a Creole rap section with a line that captured the public's perception of the candidates: "Anyone who can express themselves in French thinks that they can be the next president." The following text is from the sung section of the song:

No, no, no ta pa posib	No, no. This shouldn't be possible
Pou l, yon ti peyi kou Ayiti	For a small country like Haiti
Gen tout kandida-sa-yo	To have all these candidates . . .
Pou nenpòt tèl malouk gen pou li pwezidan	For such a big shot to run for president
Veye yo, se pou nou veye yo . . .	Watch out, we should watch out for them . . .
Kandida de zouzou	Candidates of the big shots
Ansyen divalyis	Duvalierist candidates
Ansyen tonton makout	Former *tonton makout*-s
Restavèk Meriken	Lackeys of the Americans[17]

Les Frères Parent, invoking a parade of presidents, argued that social change would never come from the top:

Vensan lese Lèsko monte	Vincent let Lescot rise up
Lèsko pase pa Estime	Lescot was succeded by Estimé
Estime kite Pòl Maglwa	Estimé left Paul Magloire
Malere pa change	Our misery didn't abate
Maglwa bannou Divalye pè	Magloire gave us Duvalier the father
Divalye pè bay Divalye fis	Duvalier the father gave us Duvalier the son
Divalye fis bay CNG	Duvalier the son gave us the CNG
Sa pou n fè veye yo!	And that's why we have to watch them![18]

By the final filing date, the list of candidates had been pared to twenty-two. A few of the more credible candidates possessed anti-Duvalierist credentials, including Protestant minister Sylvio Claude and schoolteacher Gérard Gorgue; Marc Bazin (a former Duvalier minister of finance who had broken with Duvalier) was considered a technocrat with business sector (and U.S.) support. Father Aristide and many of the revolutionary organizations saw the elections as a

diversion from the work of building the popular movement and regarded the field of candidates as members of the same old *poli-ti-kay*
(little house of politics) that had long governed Haiti. Here is how
Manno Charlemagne and Rose-Ann Auguste described a prototypical
candidate who employs *koudyay* politics in a song about the ruling
class:

L ap toujou pale de linyon	He's always talking about unity
Kan w wè l ta anvi pwezidan	That is, when he wants to be pres-ident
Desann kanton lan bèl machin	Descending into a small town in a fancy car
Bay lajan pou de kout vaksin	Handing out money for a bit of *vaksin* playing
Vye frè pa pran lan mannigans	My brother, don't fall for this plan
Se sa yo rele la twonpans	This is what they call the de-ception
Kite visye lan pòtoprens	Leave the lying cheat in Port-au-Prince
Toujou vann tèt-yo pou anyen	Always selling them out for nothing[19]

In the song "Ase babye" (Enough nonsense), singer Beethova Obas was
no less harsh on leaders who employ populist rhetoric to mask their
personal political ambitions,

Poutan nou di se pou li n ap travay	You say it's for the people you're working
Ase babye, di w pwal chanje	Enough nonsense, you say it's going to change
W ap tann pouvwa pou li fé lalwa	But you're just waiting for power to make laws
Ou pa wè peyi-a demanbre	You don't see the country being ravaged[20]

The left and the *ti-legliz* opposed on principle elections supervised
by the army. The Haitian bishop closest to the *ti-legliz*, Bishop Willy
Romèlus, gave the antijunta sentiment a unifying theme when he
called on the junta in July 1987 to *"rache manyòk, bannou tè blanch"*
(pull up your manioc fields, give us a clean field), a reference to land

tenancy practices whereby a new landowner or tenant would take possession only after the former occupant uprooted his or her manioc plants. Romélus demanded, in other words, that the army give up the reins of power *before* elections to allow for a fair and free process. The call to *rache manyòk* was picked up by Father Aristide, by the entire popular movement, and even by some candidates. Fédia Laguerre, whose earlier recording, *Operasyon dechoukaj*, had earned her the nickname *La Première Dame du Dechoukaj*, released another timely movement song called "Rache manyòk ou yo." Talking of Haiti's current "big band of candidates," she said:

Yap lolo la vyè pwomès grebete	**They renege on old promises to starving children**
Gade yon kandida	**Look at a candidate**
Ou twòp opòtounis	**Such an opportunist**
Fò w aprann respekte nasyonalis	**He'll have to learn to respect nationalists**
Ayiti o, Bondyè pral delivre w	**Haiti, God is going to deliver you**
Lap vann moun onèt ki pou sispann mizè w	**He'll send an honest person to end your misery**
Jeneral o w twòp kriminèl	**Generals, you're such criminals**
"Rache manyòk ou yo	**"Pull up your manioc fields**
Bannou teren an blanch"	**Give us a clean field"**[21]

As if to prove Romélus correct about the likelihood of fair elections, army-sponsored violence against the popular forces skyrocketed in the months before the elections. Radio Lumière was set on fire, the main market in Port-au-Prince was attacked by gunmen, graffiti appeared everywhere saying "Aba KEP, Viv Lame" (Down with the electoral commission, long live the army), and *zenglendo*-s, former *tonton makout*-s who had turned to less-organized and less-predictable forms of violence and crime, terrorized poor neighborhoods.[22] In response, neighborhoods organized squads to protect them against *zenglendo* activity, and Haitians once again avoided going out at night except to play dominos on the roofs of buildings.

One of the worst outbreaks of violence was directed against the peasant organization Tèt Ansanm around the town of Jan Rabel. Along with the Hinche-based Mouvman Peyizan Papaye (Papaye peasant mouvement), Tèt Ansanm was one of the most active and important organizations in the popular forces, with cultural troupes in communal sections wherever they had significant strength. A recording of songs from some of the Tèt Ansanm groups was compiled and released in late 1987. The collection, *Nou se lavalas,* was named for a song on the album with the following chorus:

Yo pare pou nou	**They're preparing for us**
Nou pare pou yo	**But we're prepared for them**
Mezanmi nou se lavalas	**My friends, we're the deluge**
N ap pote y ale	**We'll wash them all away**[23]

This text exploited a particularly powerful metaphor for Haitian peasants and the poor. Rains fall heavily in the wet season in Haiti, and with so much of the land deforested, the rains wash down the steep hills in a true deluge, washing everything from topsoil to garbage (and sometimes houses) down into the ravines and out to sea. The *lavalas* is seen as an unstoppable cleansing force, another metaphor for destruction and purification.[24] It was this song that provided Aristide with the name for his movement in 1990. The songs on the Koral Mizik Tèt Ansanm album were accompanied by drums and *vaksin*-s in *rara* or *konbit* style. One song encouraged militants in the Tèt Ansanm organization: *"Tèt Ansanm leve pye w pi wo, Lè w gade wa wè peyi ap chanje"* (Tèt Ansanm raise your feet higher, If you look around you'll see the country is changing). The liner notes spoke to the importance of the project: "Today we have in our hands the record *Nou se lavalas,* which is a great step on the road of *angaje* music, for cultural and for political reasons. This time, it's the masses themselves who are singing what's in their hearts. It's been a long time since we've heard the people 'complaining' about their fate, especially in the points they're sending [*pwen li voye*] in their songs."[25]

In July of 1987, peasants armed with machetes attacked Tèt Ansanm movement activists near the town of Jan Rabel. Although the attack was described in press accounts as an internal land-reform conflict among peasants, there was no doubt that the *chefs de section* and the major landowners had helped to organize and finance the opponents of Tèt Ansanm to try to break the peasant movement, to label it a communist front, and to divide it from urban resistance movements. The violence and the gruesome photos of the corpses that circulated afterward sent the message that the army placed no limits on how far it would go to silence opposition.

The army worried all along about its lack of control of the electoral process, and Namphy had repeatedly tried to take control of (or do away with) the KEP. The army would presumably have been content with the election of Marc Bazin, a former finance minister for Jean-Claude who had worked briefly for the World Bank, or with Professor Leslie Manigat, an anti-Duvalierist who had in the meantime signaled his enthusiastic willingness to cooperate with the army. But given the popularity of Gérard Gorgue, the schoolteacher and human rights activist, and of Sylvio Claude, a Protestant preacher who had served jail time under Jean-Claude, the outcome was greatly in doubt. Consequently, *zenglendo*-s, with support from the police and army, attacked on election day, absconding with ballots while slaughtering defenseless voters inside polling places. General Namphy called off the elections, dissolved the KEP, and hinted at new, military-run elections. Some called the disastrous election the *elèksyon malatchong*, making a reference to a big collective loss in the unofficial lottery.[26] In the election massacre, the people had been given the *boul malatchong*, and the Army seemed to have won a major victory.

Occurring less than a month before Christmas, the massacre produced its most poignant commentary in a song by Beethova Obas, a former accompanist for Manno Charlemagne, called "Nwèl amè" (Bitter Christmas):

Ala yon koze, gade yon bagay	What an episode, look at this thing
Tande yon lòbèy . . .	Listen to the confrontation . . .
Kèk aganman se pa sa k manke	We have enough chameleons
Ensekirite mache boule	Insecurity goes around burning
Brigadye bwaze . . . moun ap kriye	The police flee . . . people are crying out
Brigan yo lage kaki gwoble	The unruly are released, khaki denims
Kot Tonton Nwèl souple?	Where is Santa Clause if you please?[27]

Farah Juste's "29 Novembre" struck a more militant tone, starting with a recording of shots and screams and ending with a call for justice.

Yo wè eleksyon tounnen yon eksek-isyon	They saw the elections turn into an execution
Yon imiliasyon pou tout lan nasyon	A humiliation for everyone in the nation
Pèp ayisyen nan gon asasen . . .	The Haitian people have an assassin . . .

| Kriminèl o listwa va jije w | Criminals, history will judge you |
| Kriminèl o pèp la pa bliye w | Criminals, people won't forget who you are[28] |

"You Deceive Me": The Army Digs in and the Movement Simmers

Sometime before or after the election, the army appeared to strike a deal with Leslie Manigat. While other major candidates (Bazin, Déjoie Jr., Claude, and Gorgue) boycotted the army's *seleksyon* ("selection" rather than "election"), Manigat emerged as the army choice and triumphed in an election with low voter turnout and a high degree of *magouy* (fraud). Manigat's pretense of ruling independently of the army lasted until June 18, 1988, when, in a move that backfired, he tried to remove General Henri Namphy, at which point Namphy declared himself president and exiled Manigat. In a series of provocative actions (in part because they began to look as though they had "permanent" written on them) Namphy and his wife moved into the palace and began a long tour through the provinces, where he was greeted by pro-army *koudyay*-s with signs reading *"Pa touche chouchou Namphy"* (Don't touch our sweetheart Namphy), *"Nou vle lame"* (We want the army), and *"Aristid se masisi kominis"* (Aristide is a communist "faggot"), and similar sentiments.

By now the populace was deeply and justifiably cynical about the army's ever handing over power willingly to a civilian government. When the New York *mini-djaz* System Band toured Haiti in the summer of 1988, their bitter love song, "Ou tronpe m cheri" (You deceive me, my dear) was interpreted by many progressives as a commentary on the army, especially because of the use of words like *mechan* (evil) and *trayi* (betray) in the song:

Gade kijan ou tronpe mwen	Look at how you deceive me
O w tronpe mwen	Oh, you deceive me
Konsa konsa	Like this, like this
Yes sir! Mechan!	Yes sir! Evil![29]

The venality and brutality of Namphy's military strongman rule was exposed when, on September 11, a group of military-backed *zenglendo*-s burst into a sermon by Father Jean-Bertrand Aristide, attempted to assassinate him, shot randomly into the crowd, and destroyed the Eglise St. Jean Bosco, only to brag about it immediately afterward on a live radio program. Aristide's uncanny ability to survive many such attacks only strengthened his reputation as a "savior" among *le loum-pen* (lumpen proletariate).

The polemics deepened around the relationship of artists to the struggle for popular control. Some leftist musicians dismissed the *nouvèl jenerasyon* (new generation) artists (e.g., Pirogue, Emeline Michel, Papash, Djakout Mizik, Skandal, Master Dji) as bourgeois and irrelevant. No single event demonstrated the fragile unity of progressive artists more than the antidrug benefit organized at the Théâtre National on September 2, 1989. The sponsoring organization, APAAC (Association for the prevention of alcoholism and other chemical dependency) invited Manno Charlemagne, Beethova Obas, Emeline Michel, and Master Dji. Members of Manno's party, ANOP (National association of workers and peasants), were outraged that their spokesman was appearing in the same show as "bourgeois" artists. The group started to shout profanities and abuse at the other artists, including *"masisi"* (homosexual) and *"bouzen"* (prostitute). Master Dji was accused of being a drug user. Members of ANOP jumped on stage with a "boom box" cassette player to play a recorded quote by Manno to the effect that "the only time I'll get up on a stage with Master Dji is to burn him." Manno himself grabbed the mic to insist that he had agreed with the selection of Obas and Michel on the program, but not with the choice of Master Dji. The audience began to leave the theater, and the concert was terminated in the middle.[30] It was now apparent that broad coalitions for programmatic issues were harder and harder to sustain in the highly factionalized and partisan climate. Haiti was three years into *dechoukaj* and still under a crushing military rule. It was one thing to sing about the unity of progressive forces and another thing to hold it together on stage.

"We're Not Afraid This Year": *Mizik Rasin* on the Offensive

Starting in about 1990, the new roots music (*mizik rasin*) movement took center stage on the Haitian music scene, playing a pivotal role in the political events of 1990–93. The heightened interest in roots, as I have already argued, emerged out of the crisis in national identity linked to the fall of Duvalier. Meanwhile, the temporal and political connections between Duvalierism and *konpa* led many to call for a musical *dechoukaj* of *konpa*. According to bandleader Richard Morse of Ram, "*Konpa* was always up when the country was down, during the worst periods. . . . I call it 'bad karma music.'"[31] This view encouraged the exponents of roots music, as related by "Lolo" Beaubrun: "There was a change in Haiti, even in the mentality of the people, because you can see now in Haiti how young people are dressing differently: they have *djakout* [traditional peasant bags], more traditional hats . . . all this is a part of the movement that Boukman helped to launch along with Foula and Sanba-yo. After '86, the youth began to get tired of the traditional *konpa*—they wanted a new music to represent what they were feeling. They wanted artists who could express this for them. They were listening to what we were saying."[32]

With its emphasis on peasant religion, its traditional forms of signifying, and its Simbi and Zaka saturated semiotics, the *mizik rasin* movement staked out a propeasant political identification. Although many of its performers were not from a significantly different class background than that of musicians of the *nouvèl jenerasyon*, they distinguished themselves from the other tendency by their class outlook. Bassist "Chiko" Boyer explained: "The new generation represents a bourgeois tendency. The bourgeois class in Haiti was working with the political class in Haiti, and they took a conscientious stand after the seventh of February '86 (the end of the dictatorship), when all the bourgeois wanted to become patriots too. Everybody was talking about democracy. It's an opportunistic music. Now, they're trying to play *rara* too."[33]

The first real roots hit was a jingle prepared by Sanba-yo for a UNICEF vaccination campaign. Aboudja spoke about the song:

> At that time we were involved with a guy called Jean-Jean Fabius. He told us that UNICEF is going to have a vaccination campaign, so maybe if we have a song ready, they may use the song. Azouke wrote the melody together with me; in the end, I did the lyrics, and Zawo took the song, and he did the arrangement. It was very catchy, it was easy to hear, and in less than three months, everybody in Haiti knew "Vaksine" because at that time they [the radio stations] were playing it. And also, we wanted to contribute something to the *rasin*, to the tradition. Because most of the time the bands take something from the traditional music and they play it. I was going all over Haiti, and I heard rara bands playing "Vaksine." This has always been my ambition, to contribute to the traditional movement instead of using tunes that were already there.[34]

"Vaksine" was a litany of the groups in Haiti that should participate in the program to vaccinate children, as in the following few lines:

Bon ginen kanpe, Bizango kanpe . . .	**Good Africans stand up, secret societies stand up . . .**
Katolik kanpe, Pwotestan kanpe . . .	**Catholics stand up, Protestants stand up . . .**
Vaksine timoun-yo pou yo pa mouri	**Vaccinate the children so that they don't die**[35]

The new generation of roots groups that had played for small audiences before *dechoukaj* found that, with the ouster of Duvalier, they were rapidly expanding the number of venues available to them. Boukman Eksperyans, Sanba-yo, and Foula began to play in nightclubs in the suburb of Pétion-Ville, in hotels, and in downtown theaters. Boukman Eksperyans won national renown for the first time in 1989, when the band won the 3ème Konkou Mizik (Music Contest) in Haiti with their first mature *rara*-rock piece. "Pran chenn, wet chenn" (Get angry, remove the chains). The contest victory constituted a new level of appreciation for *mizik rasin* by the musical "establishment": musicians, media representatives, and music industry people who were closely associated with the *nouvèl jenerasyon* tendency, some of whom had previously shown little interest in the roots phenomenon. The song explored the legacy of slavery, using the polyvalence of the phrase *"pran chenn"* (take the chains/get angry):

Pran chenn, wet chenn	**Get angry, remove the chains**
Wa kase chenn-nan ki fè n paka ini nou	**Break the chains that keep us from uniting**
Pou n ka sekle lakou n . . .	**So that we can weed out our homes . . .**
Depi Lafrik nap soufri	**Ever since Africa, we've been suffering**
Nan bò isit se pi rèd	**It's so much harder here**[36]

The contest opened up media coverage and radio play time to the band, and they had a string of hits with "Nou la" and "Se Kreyòl nou ye." Having won the Konkou Mizik and with a number of hits behind them, Boukman could lay claim to being the most popular band on the island, and they were certainly the most controversial. Other early roots bands also achieved a degree of success. Foula played festivals in Mexico and Louisiana. Sanba-yo's "Vaksine" and Sakad's "Rebati kay-la" were selected for the A&R records compilation *Konbit: Burning Rhythms of Haiti*. Both Foula and Sanba-yo appeared in Jonathan

Demme's documentary film, *Haiti: Dreams of Democracy*, and I covered the movement in *the Beat*, focusing on Boukman Eksperyans, Sanbayo, and Foula, in a 1990 article called "Watering the Roots."[37] In New York, percussionist Clifford Sylvain formed a roots band called Rara Machine and released an album, the title of which owed a debt to Boukman's "Pran chenn, wet chenn" called *Break the Chains.*

Even though the movement was in its germinal stages in Haiti, foreign audiences were taking note of *mizik rasin* in a way they never had for *konpa*, considering that some of the best *konpa* bands had been trying for decades to break through into venues now being offered to *mizik rasin* groups. *Mizik rasin*, apart from issues of quality and novelty, fulfilled foreign expectations for "authentic" Third World dance musics in ways that *konpa* and *nouvèl jenerasyon* hadn't. In the new aesthetics of "world beat," the more "African" the better. Americans, especially, wanted Vodou in their Haitian music. Over the next five years, the inordinate economic power and draw of foreign markets added to the local pressures to "go" roots.

The countercultural Simbi-Zaka look that the roots musicians popularized was catching on among larger audiences. The possibilities for new codes in personal appearance didn't negate the disdain in which many of the "counterculture" were held by more conservative Haitians, who saw them as drug addicts or communists. Indeed, after the army coup of September 1991, countercultural garb and Simbi/Rasta dreadlocks exposed young Haitians to renewed repression. The roots music phenomenon was also spurred on by the extreme interest of young Haitian residents of the diaspora. *Sanba*-like groups, both informal and commercially oriented, formed in Miami (Kazak), Boston (Batwèl Rada), New York (Rara Machine, Rara Djakout). McAlister has discussed the relationship of this movement to diasporic identity, characterizing it as a transnational, oppositional subculture that "performs" Afro-Haitian identity to achieve many simultaneous goals (e.g., separating from African-American society even while embracing a political pan-Africanism, achieving status and celebrity, competing with Rastafarian Jamaicans, etc.).[38]

In January of 1990, President (and General) Prospère Avril responded to the assassination of an army colonel with a state of siege and a round of arrests of opposition leaders. This instability came at a bad time for the military government, which was attempting to project confidence and a return to a normal state of affairs. Then came the major musicopolitical controversy over Boukman Eksperyans's carnival *rara* "Kè m pa sote" (My heart doesn't leap/I'm not afraid). This was to be only the second Carnival held since 1985, and banning Boukman Eksperyans could have had public relations consequences for the government. The Avril government was divided over the song's significance, although it was clear that it was causing quite a commotion wherever it was performed. The band had set a crafty trap for the government by using the traditional signifying practice of not identifying the target of the *pwen*. The song referred only to "those guys" and "assassins," "frauds," and so on, and nowhere was the military or the government identified in the song; by censuring the song, the government would have admitted publicly to being the intended recipients of the *pwen*. "Kè m pa sote" makes references to traditional singers, *sanba*-s, employing a style of delivery that imitates them:

Sanba sa fè mal o	**Samba, this hurts, oh**
Gade sa nèg yo fè mwen	**Look what those guys do to me**
Sanba san m ap koule	**My blood is running, samba**
Yo ban m chay la pote	**They give me a burden to carry**
M pa sa pote l	**I'm not going to carry it**[39]

The next thematic section of this complex carnival song proclaimed the band's fearlessness, their (triumphant) presence in Carnival, and their warnings against violence inside their carnival entourage (once again posited as a metaphor for society, especially for the popular forces):

Kè m pa sote wo, kè m pa sote wo	**My heart doesn't leap, I'm not afraid**
Kè-m pa sote ane sa	**I'm not afraid this year**
Boukman nan kanaval, kè m pa sote wo . . .	**Boukman in Carnival, I'm not afraid . . .**
Avanse pa frape nan bann lan	**Advance, don't fight in the band**[40]

Boukman incorporated a Vodou chant for the deity of war, Ogou Balendjo, based on traditional praise poetry for the deity to the effect that "poison can't harm those possessed by Ogou Balendjo." They followed this with a list of insults directed, or so at least the carnival audiences felt, at the group running the country, calling them *magouyè* (deceivers, frauds), *sendenden* (idiots), and *paranoye* (paranoiacs). The final line of the song was a rhythmic chant on a single pitch that translated roughly as "I didn't know you at all before, but now I know you too well!"

Avril, insiders said, was convinced that the elliptical message of the song could be ideologically co-opted by the state along the lines of "even though things are hard, everyone has to work together." The government relented, and Boukman appeared in the carnival parade and on stage at the Champs de Mars, picking up the award for best *mereng koudyay*. More important, the song passed into the repertoire of most street carnival and *rara* bands in the city and many in the countryside. A little over a week after Carnival, a young girl was shot by the military, and the popular forces launched a nationwide strike. "Kè m pa sote," now universally considered an anthem of courage in the face of a government characterized as a "band of paranoid frauds and idiots," helped propel the strike along. The protests grew into a popular uprising demanding Avril's ouster, and four days later, on April 10, Avril resigned. Major General Abraham then installed a civilian Supreme Court Justice, Ertha Pascal Trouillot, as provisional president. Her task as provisional president was to move toward elections in the fall of 1990.

The elections took on a more sinister tone with the return of various *makout*-s to the country during the summer and with the attempt by former President Leslie Manigat to run for his lost presidency. On October 18, Father Jean-Bertrand Aristide threw his hat into the ring in order to create a progressive alternative to the notorious *tonton makout* Roger Lafontant. Citing the song "Nou se lavalas," he called his movement Lavalas and elaborated the image into a memorable slogan: *"Yon sèl nou fèb, ansanm nou fò, ansanm ansanm nou se lavalas"* (Alone we're weak, together we're strong, united we're a deluge). Aristide was a candidate of a progressive coalition called the FNCD (National front for change and democracy). With the entrance of Aristide into the electoral process, a number of progressive artists, hitherto opposed to the foreign-supervised elections, joined forces to support Aristide. Manno Charlemagne and the Koral Konbit Kalfou played two rally concerts with pro-Aristide and prodemocracy songs.

Aristide coined the phrase Dizyèm Depatman (Tenth department) to symbolize the reincorporation of diaspora Haitians into national life. With nine major political-administrative units (*départements*) in insular Haiti, the reference to a tenth fictively extended the Haitian state to encompass its expatriates. Aristide believed the diaspora could form an important source of cash and expertise for his campaign and for the country, and he envisioned the involvement of Haitian-American technocrats to help rebuild Haiti. Progressive artists helped to popularize the notion of a Dizyèm Depatman, as in the song by that title sung by Farah Juste:

Lamoun Nouyòk leve kanpe	New York Haitians are standing up
Moun Bwouklin tranble . . .	In Brooklyn, they're like an earthquake . . .
M konnen gen granmoun	I know that there are wise people
Nan lakou dizyèm depatman-yo	In the "courtyards" of the 10th department
Ann fè yon rasanbleman, voye Ayiti monte . . .	We're assembling to make Haiti better . . .
Pa kite peyi a nan boutèy	Don't keep our country in a bottle[41]

The lyrics *"gen granmoun nan lakou"* (there are wise people in the courtyard/at home) paraphrase a well-known Vodou song. Juste provocatively employed the intimate and local form of social organization (the *lakou*) as the gloss for the immigrant communities, imagining the community and the nation more closely knit and familiar. In Juste's song, the transnational dispersion of Haitians has become a resource and a social force for rebuilding Haiti.[42] Again, we find a progressive musician employing the image of zombiism in the song's last line (the bottle is the repository of a zombie's soul removed from his body).

Case Study: "The Rooster Sings"—Lavalas Elections, Inauguration, and Carnival

The election and inauguration of Jean-Bertrand Aristide was a singular moment in Haitian history. As I was there in a special capacity as an election monitor for the Organization of American States (OAS) and witnessed both events up close, I take the liberty of using a first-person narrative for this case study.[43]

I arrived back in Haiti on a plane loaded with Haitians from the diaspora, many of them returning to participate in the electoral campaign. Aristide's campaign was extremely popular in the diaspora, where many Lavalas committees were organized. At the airport, I ran into the band Boukman Eksperyans who were arriving from France to get ready for the elections, Christmas, and Carnival. Port-au-Prince was buzzing. For one, it was full of foreigners in OAS and UN outfits riding in jeeps; it was a time of full employment for drivers in Haiti. There was also, I would quickly discover, an infectious, almost buoyant optimism that the elections would succeed. The possibility of *magouy* (fraud) was the chief reason for the foreign intrusion. For once, the presence of the foreigners seemed to ruffle few feathers, and the conventional hope was that the presence of the outsiders would forestall a *makout* or army move for the time being. Aristide had been praising the *ti-soldat* (little soldiers), the younger and more progressive troops in the army, and envisioned them as a base for progressive change within the armed forces. Perhaps the generals were less able to move against democracy, not fully confident that their troops would follow. On the road out of the city that first night I saw many *fanal*-s, the intricate cut-paper Christmas lanterns . . . looking like fragile beacons of hope and faith.

The election was already a regular refrain on the radio and television, with spots airing for the candidates and for the election itself. Because of the high rate of illiteracy in Haiti, radio is the most effective means for reaching people, and music—whether on radio, live, or on tapes—was the best delivery system for electoral information. For these reasons, the 1990 election was a very musical election. During the weeks of OAS training and waiting for assignment, I continued my music research, with special attention to the election material.

Many of the leading campaigns attempted to stake out a populist, mass appeal by crafting jingles based on the popular *rara* style that Boukman Eksperyans had pioneered. *Rara*, of course, carries strong traces of its lower-class origins, and with the textual and sonic signification of neo-*rara* campaign songs, candidates attempted to achieve political "downward social mobility," seeking a mass electoral base outside the Port-au-Prince middle class. Having already followed and chronicled the rise of the new *mizik rasin* movement, an anomaly in popular music even one year earlier, I was still shocked by what seemed to be its near-total triumph in late 1990, where it seemed to have become the new common musical tongue.

KEP (the Provisional electoral committee; CEP, using the French acronym) was engaged in organizing and promoting the elections within the context of a system that was actively working to undermine them. KEP needed to educate voters about the mechanics of the election, the constitution, and the notions of popular control and democracy. They advertised the election on radio with a *rara* called "Sèz Desanm" (December 16th).

Si n gen vwa sa, annou mande bon	If we have this voice, let's demand the best
Nan zafe eleksyon	For this election
Ane sa nanpwen blan	There are no foreigners dictating things
Ayiti pou devan	Haiti is taking the lead
Sèz desanm	December 16th
Pou montre yo, n ap vote	To show them, we're going to vote
Nan sèksyon, nan tout komin	In every section, in every commune
Tout depatman n ap vote . . .	In every department, we're going to vote . . .
Sayo nanpwen peyi	Those without a country
Sayo nanpwen pouvwa	Those without power
Se yo ki pou deside	It's they who must decide
Sèz desanm, pou deside al vote	December 16th, choose to vote
Pou peyi a aleliya	To give a hallelujah for Haiti
Pou bagay yo ka chanje	So that things can change
Konstitisyon se manman lwa	The constitution is the mother of the law
Si yo pa respekte l	If they don't respect it
Ya fè lwa nou monte l	Our law will raise it up [spirits will possess it]
Pou tout moun ka gen dwa	For all people to have rights
Nou pa vle kraze zò ankò	We don't want repression [breaking bones] again
Fòk chèf nou yo konn sa	Our leaders have to understand this
Se sa k fè nou pral vote	This is why we're going to vote
Pou nou ka avanse	In order for us to advance
Nou se leta	We are the state
Si n se sitwayen n al vote	If we're citizens, we have to vote
Leta se nou	The state is us.[44]

The text focused on the possibility for real change, on metaphors of popular control, and on reminders of the election date. This was a song of empowerment directed at disenfranchised and dispossessed groups by an official organization that was itself positioned in a quasi-adversarial role to the military and military-supported government. Note the play on the word *lwa*. One translation is "law," but the juxtaposition of the second usage with the word *monte* (to mount) also suggests the *lwa*-s or Vodou deities (this signifying trope is called a homonymic pun). Along with the reference to "Aleliya," the song alludes to both Christianity and Vodou.

The candidates endeavored to translate complex programs or platforms into short radio announcements; establish an identity for themselves (many of them were little known outside the capital); weave political icons (visual symbols, slogans, theme music, etc.) into memorable symbolic clusters; and provide practical voting information, such as ballot numbers, dates, party associations, and the placement of the candidate's name on a ballot. All of this was made more difficult by the lack of a history of such elections.

Marc Bazin, running on the ANDP ticket, was widely believed to be (once again) the favorite candidate of the U.S. State Department. ANDP was a newly formed alliance that included Bazin's own, better-known party. Some members of the Boukman Eksperyans anonymously recorded a *rara* for Bazin that was meant to impart a populist appeal to a man considered by the left to be a *restavèk bank mondyal* (lackey for the World Bank). The song was arranged by the group's assistant, and the band got $10,000 for the recording. (In turn, the band also produced a campaign song for Aristide.)[45]

Si n vle jwenn travay pou peyi-a chanje	If we want to find work for the country to change
N ap vote Bazin	We're voting Bazin
Nou a mete kwa-kwa pou gen nimewo twa	We'll put a cross on number three
N ap vote Bazin	We're voting Bazin!
Pèp-la bezwen w pou pwezidan. Bazin!	The people need you for president. Bazin!

The song then lists a number of ameliorations that a Bazin presidency would usher in: irrigation, an agricultural development bank, justice, health care, and good schools, and concludes by once again fusing the identity of the party, the candidate, and the number on the ballot.

ANDP se mèt kèsyon	ANDP is the answer!
Al vote al vote	Go vote, go vote
Vote nimewo twa	Vote number three
Vote ANDP . . .	Vote ANDP . . .
Voye Bazin monte . . .	Send Bazin up . . .

A lesser-known politician, Thomas Desulmé used a song with *rara* rhythmic influences (and the uprooting metaphor), but the orchestration was more pop oriented and contained *nouvèl jenerasyon*–style vocals and flutes:

Nou vle travay pou jwenn manje	We want work in order to get food
Nou vle travay pou jwenn sante	We want work to get healthy
Nou vle travay pou jwenn libete	We want work to achieve liberty
Desilme se travay	Desulmé is work
Ann dechouke lamizè avèk travay	We'll uproot poverty with work
Annou vote youn lidè ki konn travay	We'll vote in a leader who knows how to work
Annou vote Desilme	We'll vote in Desulmé

In similar fashion, Louis Déjoie and his PAIN (Parti Agricole et Industriel National), a mulatto agronomist and son of a presidential candidate that opposed Duvalier in 1957, used a two-measure *rara* chorus underneath his radio and television advertisements. The Aristide campaign used a somber peasant *konbit* song to bracket the following announcement, which communicated very detailed information on what Lavalas supporters were supposed to do in the voting booths: "Haitian people, stay strong. We have the right to vote with an electoral card in the voting booths. Don't let anything take away your resolve. We're going to bet [as in the lottery] on the FNCD fighting rooster number five because any other option is a bad number [*boul malatchong*, a lottery term]. And now, on every large paper ballot, under each column, exercise caution . . . look for the fighting rooster number five and make a cross in the little white ball above the head of the fighting rooster."[46]

Throughout the election season, there were recurring intertextual relationships to the Boukman Eksperyans song "Kè m pa sote." Whereas Boukman Eksperyans complained in the song that *"chay-la lou wo!"* (the burden is too heavy), the Lavalas campaign used a proverb to proclaim, *"Men anpil, chay pa lou"* (With lots of hands, the burden isn't heavy). Whereas Boukman sang, "Kè m pa sote woy!" (you don't scare us), in defiance of General Avril, banners for Aristide said, "Kè-m pa sote ak Titid" (We're not afraid with Aristide). Another spin-off of the *"chay-la lou"* theme involved candidate Louis Déjoie, or Ti-Loulou as he was nicknamed, and the American ambassador, Alvin Adams. Adams, who used a Creole proverb upon entering the country that earned him the nickname "Bourik Chaje" (Loaded donkey), quoted another proverb after the entry of Jean-Bertrand Aristide into the presidential race, *Apre fèt, tanbou lou* (After the dance, the drum is heavy).⁴⁷ This was taken as an expression of American misgivings about Aristide and fears over a Lavalas victory. In a joking reference to the ambassador's earlier nickname, some Haitians began calling him Ambasadè Tanbou Lou (Ambassador heavy drum). Playing with this, candidate Louis Déjoie on his radio announcement over campaign theme music punned, *"Tanbou-a pap lou nan men Ti-Loulou"* (The drum isn't heavy in Little Louis's hands).

Much of this play with proverbs (i.e., much of the streetwise shift in political rhetoric) was a result of the convergence of the Aristide candidacy with its rootsy political discourse and the effect of the music of Boukman Eksperyans and the *mizik rasin* phenomenon. What one discovers in the music and sloganeering of this period is a complex web of intertextual references connecting commercial popular music to campaign songs, mottos, slogans, and proverbs. This is a reflection of the shift in popular music that occurred near the end of the Duvalier dictatorship as commercial musicians adopted *angaje* political stances and roots-oriented sound structures and a reflection of the power of these songs to reach the population.

When the assignment came through, my OAS teammates and I were assigned to Gonaïves. Our driver thought it best to leave after dark on December 14 and travel inconspicuously. Gonaïves is the cradle of Haitian revolution and the first city to explode politically when times are rough. One observer, a Harvard-trained anthropologist, brought along a bullet-proof vest when he heard he was going to Gonaïves, remembering Haiti's last bloody (and failed) election. A few things had worried me, too, especially the rumor mill, which, even when the rumors (*zen* or *tripotaj*) are outrageous, has the ability to powerfully shape perceptions and thus events. I heard one rumor that the army's ammunition had disappeared and had been distributed to groups of *makout*-s around the country. I also heard rumors that the CIA had targeted Aristide for assassination and that the electoral computers (which came from the United States via the election in El Salvador) were programmed to report: "Bazin wins!" Even though neither rumor was credible, it struck me that if for some reason something happened to Aristide or to the electoral process, Haiti could quickly become very uncomfortable for Americans, on the strength of rumor alone.

All over the country, people were singing Aristide's campaign songs. Little kids danced around a fire by the side of the road in the slum

called La Salines: *"Lavalas!"* When they saw the OAS letters on the
jeep, they shouted *"kòk kalite!"* which roughly means "good fighting
rooster" and *"kòk-la chante!"* (the rooster will sing/crow). Ahead of us
on the dark, pothole-filled road, an overloaded truck was serving as an
impromptu dance floor, and we could hear shouts of "Titid," "Lavalas,"
and *"kòk kalite"* accompanying the dancers. Aristide had taken the
fighting rooster as his symbol. The rooster is a favorite theme in Haitian folksongs; it is associated with virility, and it is an extremely visual
and recognizable image, not likely to be forgotten when one is scan-
ning the ballots in the voting booth. One Lavalas partisan happily explained, "All over the country on Sunday morning (election day) you
will hear the roosters. It will be a new sun coming up on Haiti and the
cocks will be crowing."

Over and over that night in the jeep we heard a song on the radio
"Nwèl Lavalas" (Lavalas Christmas), by Pierre Louis Duval. It began and
ended with the sound of a rooster crowing, and its ominous line *"Menm
si gen danje"* (Even if there's danger) seemed to be a reply to Bazin's
charge that an Aristide victory would be fraught with danger for Haiti:

Tonton Nwèl o, Tonton Nwèl o	Santa Claus, Santa Claus,
Se denyè chans pou mwen	It's my last chance
Menm si gen danje fòk Lavalas desann	Even if there's danger, the Lavalas has to descend
Pou Ayiti gen pa-l	For Haiti to come into its own
Tonton Nwel, se chak ane ou pa koute	Santa Claus, every year you don't listen
Ou ban m manti	You give me lies
Ou pote kado se vwe men se pa pou Ayiti	You bring gifts it's true but not for Haiti[48]

As we approached Gonaïves in the dark, a *rara* band was moving
down the National Highway with women out in front sweeping the
street clean. A Haitian with us said, "Secret societies. Bizango is strong
up here, and most of them are for Titid." *Rara* bands had played for
all of the candidates, but the great majority had seemed to me to be
for Aristide. I had heard an account of a Bazin rally in the south where
they paid a *rara* band to play. Another band came by singing *"Magouyè
bay talon w, se kòk kalite kap pale"* (Deceivers, give up your spurs, the
fighting rooster will be the one speaking). The Bazin band reportedly
switched sides, and both took up the chorus *"Kiyès ki towo a se Aristid,
Aristid ak malere se marasa"* (Aristide is the bull, Aristide and the poor

are like twins). I fell asleep late, and already the roosters were beginning to crow.

On December 16, election day, we rose at 4:00 A.M. to open a polling station at a soccer field in Gonaïves. A house adjacent to the field was blasting music from Wagner's *Lohengrin*. I listened to the morning sounds. The surprising element in the hot and dusty morning was that, in spite of the heat and the ballots' being over an hour late in arriving, long lines of people were waiting patiently outside the soccer field. The army was lounging around, seemingly happy and relaxed. Where was the pushing and shoving, the nervous soldiers with weapons drawn? After the ballots arrived, we left for the mountains to monitor the voting in a town called St. Michel de L'Attalye. Along the way, peasant houses were displaying political posters, and we witnessed thousands of peasants trekking out of the hills to vote at the roadside polling places. The voting in St. Michel was a little confused because all the polling places had recently moved and the numbers and names had been jumbled. Yet everyone, from illiterate peasant voters to middle-class poll presidents to the representatives of the various parties, seemed intent on making the process work. Although ballots were late in getting to poor neighborhoods around the capital, the electoral commission announced that polls would stay open as late as necessary.

We picked one of the polling stations at which to watch the count. Our station was one of the lucky ones—it received a lightbulb at dusk, and we didn't have to count by flashlight. The counting process was completely aboveboard, theatrical, and very long-winded. I fell asleep many times on my feet. I called in the results (a coded version of our presidential tally) to Port-au-Prince over radio at 1:00 A.M., but the counting for senators, deputies, and other offices lasted until dawn. The coded results coming in from all over the country were staggering; anywhere from 50% to 90% for Aristide from the various polling places, in a race with fourteen candidates. Before dawn, the UN and OAS were posting a 67% margin for Aristide. By the time we reached Gonaïves the next day, crowds had gathered around OAS headquarters singing *"Mesi OEA"* (thank you, OAS). Hearing that a huge *manifesta-syon* (demonstration) called by Manno Charlemagne and others to forestall fraud had shut down the highway north of Port-au-Prince, we found a hotel and lay low.

Haiti progressed along the road to an Aristide inauguration despite the claims of Roger Lafontant and other *makout*-s that Lafontant's exclusion from the race invalidated the results. Lafontant and his supporters waited until January 6 to make their move. The coup was discovered by an acquaintance of mine, guitarist "Tit" Pascal, the brother of the provisional president Ertha Pascal Trouillot. "Tit" was visiting his sister when Roger Lafontant's tank parked on the street to take Ertha to the palace. "Tit" escaped and called General Abraham and the American embassy. Later that day, for one reason or another, the army (under General Abraham) decided not to back the coup, invaded the palace, and arrested Lafontant. In the end, the coup worked perfectly into Aristide's plans. It exposed the *tonton makout*-s, forced the army to take sides, and showed that the people (who had filled the streets during the confrontation to pressure the army) were willing to defend their gains.

In the highly charged atmosphere after the coup, rumors circulated of plots, coups, and conspiracies; one of these rumors resulted in the death of singer-guitarist Ti-Pierre (Pierre A. Pierre-Louis). Ti-Pierre, a blind guitarist and composer, had performed for many years with Claudette Pierre-Louis, but she had recently emigrated to Canada. The duo had been a popular one for some years at Duvalierist parties. On January 26, Ti-Pierre was playing at the home of a *makout* and *bokò* (sorcerer) when a rumor circulated of another *makout* coup. Pro-Aristide residents of the district Carrefour Marin broke into the house to confront the *makout* and to *dechouke* his house. Finding the party in progress, they attacked the guests with clubs and burnt the house down, killing Ti-Pierre and three others. The rumor the next day was that the intruders had mistaken Ti-Pierre with his dark glasses for a *makout*. *Dechoukaj* had claimed its first well-known musician.

In preparation for the inauguration, women residents everywhere swept the streets clean. Murals adorned almost every available wall space, and flags and garlands hung over houses and across streets. Even the pungent smell of urban Haiti (with noticeable contributions from citrus, urine, and blue car exhaust) was abated. Many planeloads of *dizyèm* (as diaspora residents were now called) were arriving each day, and a cast of *dizyèm* artists was scheduled to headline the preinaugural concert at the Stade Sylvio Cator on February 6, including Farah Juste, Martha Jean-Claude (in Haiti from Cuba for the first time since the 1950s), and Myriam Dorismé. The concert was called "Prélude au Changement" (Prelude to change) and was in some ways a musical consolidation of the progress made by *angaje* music of the last five years (to the day) since the overthrow of Duvalier. Exiles performed with resident artists. Jean-Michel Daudier reprised his historic "Lè m pa we soley la" (When I can't see the sun), with the crowd singing along and swaying. Boukman Eksperyans performed their new carnival song, "Gran bwa," dedicated to the upcoming festivities marking the 200th anniversary of the gathering of rebellious slaves at Bwa Kayiman (Cayman Woods). Farah Juste sang "Alelouya pou Ayiti" and "Ayiti demen" while a folkloric choir and orchestra backed up the political singers. After all these years in the opposition, some of the musicians must have felt odd indeed to be looking out on the full stadium as the cultural representatives of the new power structure.

By this time, the roots music scene had become much more crowded. At the end of 1990, three members of Boukman Eksperyans, including singer Eddy François, left the band to found Boukan Ginen (literally, fire pit of Africa; Boukan Ginen was also said by the band to be a praise name for a Rada *lwa*). Boukan Ginen produced a carnival *rara* song called "Pale pale w" (Talk) with dire warnings about the fate of the country. Their collective stage presence, led by the charismatic François and a strong Vodou percussion battery, had roots music enthusiasts excited. Haitian-American hotelier Richard Morse, who had hosted regular performances by Boukman Eksperyans and others at the Olaffson Hotel, launched his own roots group, Ram. Perhaps the most popular song on the street was a *pwen* from another new roots music group called Koudyay directed at outgoing provisional president Ertha Pascal Trouillot. Despite having presided over the first fully democratic process in Haiti's history, Pascal Trouillot was not well liked by lower-class Haitians, who held her responsible for the attempted coup and who saw her administration as a further plundering of the public coffers.

"Manman poul-La" (Mama Chicken) took up the bird symbolism so popular at the time:

Manman Poul-la Trouillot	**Chicken mama Trouillot**
Manman Poul-la	**Chicken mama**
Gade pintad-yo	**Look at the guinea hens**
Ki te antre nan kòlòj-mwen	**Who were let into my cage**[49]

The guinea hen (*pintad*) was the avian symbol of the Duvalier clan, which adorned the family flag. The lyrics accused Trouillot of allowing the Duvalieriest into the (national) cage, the presidential palace. As a *manman poul* (a widespread insult in the Caribbean for a fool), she was considered neither a *kòk kalite* (fighting rooster) nor a strict Duvalierist *pintad* but something in between. At another point in the song, the lyrics make a sexual pun on the president's name, which in Creole can be understood as *twou-yo* (holes). Of the many songs transformed by the masses in the street at carnival time, this proved to be the most highly adaptable, with legions of insults, including *manman kaka* (shit) and *manman bouzen* (whore), substituting for the *poul-la* of the original lyrics.

The carnival bands swirled around the palace in anticipation of Aristide's inauguration. Inside the green iron gates of the palace, the army brass band struck up a version of the beloved *mereng* "Haïti Cherie" for the new president's tour of the grounds and inspection of the troops. Just before Aristide's speech at the palace, a new Creole version of the Haitian anthem by singer Ansy Dérose was sung by Dérose, the National Folkloric Choir, Lionel Benjamin, Boulo Valcourt from Caribbean Sextet, and Myriam Dorismé. I participated in Carnival that year as a peripheral member of the lower Belair carnival band Ozananna, playing bell to accompany the trumpets, tubas, trombones, and drums of the musical ensemble of the band. At about dusk, we would take the group, then numbering many hundreds strong, on the route down into the city past city hall, and up the Champs de Mars past the palace. On inauguration night, a tiny Aristide could be glimpsed on one of the balconies, acknowledging the many *ochan*-s played in his honor. Ozananna's *ochan* was reciprocated; few, if any, of the bands in Port-au-Prince could match Ozananna for musical ability and sheer volume of sound.

On the morning after the inauguration, I joined a pilgrimage of thousands of people winding through a garbage dump to the remains of the despised Fort Dimanche, the army prison that was the home of many of the worst abuses of the Duvalier years. At a ceremony that morning, Aristide dedicated the fort as a museum to the memory of those who died there. Families of the victims carried portraits of those slain to contribute to the museum. Afterward, a concert in the courtyard of the fort itself. Accompanied by members of Sakad, Farah Juste sang Aristide's song "Fò Dimanch." Manno Charlemagne sang a few songs and launched into the virulent antiforeign "Kou langèt manman w blan," the title and chorus of which use the strongest insult available in Creole:

W ale lakay mwen	**You went to my country**
W bwè tafya mwen	**You drank my liquor**
Ou menm monte sou vant fanm mwen	**You even got it on with my wife**
Kou langèt manman w blan	**Fuck you [you mother's clitoris], foreigner!**

That afternoon the Carnival Chanjman (Carnival of change) began in earnest. From all over Port-au-Prince, *rara* bands, brass bands, stick-fighting *madigra* (Mardi Gras) "Indians," "Arabs," *zonbis* (zombies), devils, *chaloska* (menacing military parodies—from the Creole name of General Charles Oscar), and other bands and masques converged on the waterfront city hall before parading in front of the palace and past the carnival reviewing stands. Banners welcomed the *dizyèm*. *Vèvè*-s (ritual diagrams drawn on the floors of Vodou *peristil*-s with cornmeal) had been fashioned from chips and powder in the middle of city intersections for the foot and auto traffic to obliterate. Murals featured *kòk kalite*-s besting guinea hens and chickens.

The political transition and the spirit of change and social engagement made their way into many or most of the year's *mereng kanaval* (in addition to the entries by Boukman Eksperyans, Koudyay, and Boukan Ginen already mentioned), such as Papash's "Tanpèt" (Storm), Scorpio Universel's "Pa gen danje" (There is no danger), with the lyrics, "*Le coq chante, coq lavalas*" (the rooster crows, the *lavalas* rooster), and Almando Keslin's entry with the similar phrase, "*kok-la chante lavalasaman.*" *Lavalasaman* was a new adverb coined by Father Aristide to describe behaving with the patience and force of the *lavalas*. The carnival street band Ozananna incorporated this into a light-hearted satirical song: "*Nou mande nou mande, pou nou konyen kanpe, nou mande nou mande, lavalasaman*" (We're asking to fuck standing up, but we're asking *lavalas*-ly). After two more days of walking all day long in the hot sun and dancing all night at Carnival, I was exhausted, but I joined in one last time with Ozananna, playing bell, and swaying through the shoving, dancing, fighting, and celebrating throng, maintaining my energy with copious amounts of *kleren* (cane liquor). After another night of "*Manman poul-la Trouillot, manman kaka,*" I dropped exhausted into my cot, partly from a cold I was fighting, partly from a stomach disorder from eating *fresko* (shaved ice made with tainted water), and partly from having to head back to the United States the next day.

The year from Carnival 1990 to Carnival 1991 brought the most far-reaching political changes to Haiti in many generations. It was a remarkable moment in the history of Haiti, when, to a majority of Haiti's most desperate citizens, all seemed possible. Music empowered the struggle and *powered* the celebrations that followed the victory. The invigorating sound of *rara*—appropriated from Haiti's peasants and newly popularized in commercial music—evoked the struggle of the oppressed classes (who had inserted themselves into the national political equation), firing up emotions and imaginations in this period.

"Dangerous Crossroads": Coups, De-factos, Embargoes

Angaje musicians played a prominent role in the first Aristide-Préval government.[50] Clark Parent, of Les Frères Parent, won a senatorial race and served as one of the most pro-Aristide of FNCD senators. Aristide appointed Farah Juste to be the representative to the government from the *dizyèm*. Manno Charlemagne, in what some took as a tongue-in-cheek jab at the military, was appointed to be a salaried adviser to the Ministry of Interior and Defense. Musicians were heavily involved in the plans for the celebration of the bicentennial celebration of Bwa Kayiman. The celebration of Bwa Kayiman was viewed by the elite as an effort to place revolutionary violence against whites at the center of the independence narrative. Unaccustomed to their newly marginal role in affairs of state and always suspicious of Aristide, the economic elite grew more restive. Although Aristide publicly distinguished between the *patriyòt* (patriotic) elite and the *patripoch* (pocket-stuffing) elite, the numbers of the former (at least those willing to cooperate with the new government) dwindled daily. Many of the *rara* bands I marched with at Eastertime were singing songs consumed with plots and conspiracies.

In the face of elite resistance, foreign criticism, and rumors of plots against Aristide, activists grew desperate to save the movement and the fragile government. Pro-Aristide masses rekindled the spirit of *dechoukaj*. Crowds protested while carrying tires to suggest to the elite that they would suffer *pè lebrun* ("necklacing" by burning tire) if a coup were launched. Aristide at one point alluded to *pè lebrun* in his own elliptical way. Manno Charlemagne composed a song referring to *pè lebrun*, and one coup leader pointed to Manno's performance of this song at the palace as an immediate, precipitating factor for the coup. But coup plans had already been long under way. Seven families from the economic elite had raised a war chest and enticed the Port-au-Prince police unit (called the Cafeteria) under Colonel Michel François to spearhead the coup.

Afraid that the army or *makout*-s planned to spring Roger Lafontant from jail, Manno Charlemagne held nightly singing vigils outside the jail cell:

Starting on the day Aristide left the country [before the coup, to speak at the UN], I did four "vigilance concerts"—on the twenty-fourth, twenty-fifth, twenty-sixth—and on the twenty-seventh, we went to the airport to save his life, because they wanted to kill him in front of the airport when he returned. Now the first thing I'm going to say: Mr. [Jesse] Helms is lying. He's lying. Saying Aristide was a dictator, I am laughing. If he was a dictator, we could have avoided that coup d'état for sure. I'm a guy who can put 800,000 people on the street, and Aristide knows that. We also put people on the street when we felt they wanted to do some *magouy* [dirty tricks] to steal the election on the seventeenth of December, 1990 [the day after Aristide was elected]. We put people on the street.[51]

The *kou deta makawon* (ugly coup) came on Monday, September 30, 1991. General Raoul Cédras, General Philippe Biamby, and Colonel François emerged as the leadership of the coup. On October 1, following intense international pressure, Aristide's life was spared, and he was escorted by the French ambassador to a plane which flew him to exile first in Venezuela and later in the United States. The army, police, and *attachés* set about trying to reverse the directional arrow of *dechoukaj*, carrying out mass arrests, executions, beatings, and torture.[52] Vengeance killings of Aristide supporters multiplied, with the French ambassador to Haiti estimating at least 1,200 killed. In response to this effort to undo the popular changes of the last few years, progressives coined the expression *"Kreyon pèp la pa gen gonm"* (The people's pencil has no eraser), a revision of a Creole proverb about the "pencil of God." By this they meant that the progress made before the coup, including the taste of democracy experienced for the first time, was stored in the collective memory and could not be undone by the coup or by the terrorism of the *attachés*.

A number of incidents directly affected musicians and music industry personnel. On the day of the coup, soldiers burst into the home of Radio Caraïbe director Jacques "Jacky" Caraïbe, one of the most supportive members of the media toward roots music bands and the new generation. They beat and detained him, and he was later found dead. Daniel Beaubrun, bass player for Boukman Eksperyans, described the scene around the Beaubrun's home, "Around here was . . . Vietnam. Right on the streets here. On the corner up there, they had a big truck, one of those huge army things, and they kept dropping a couple of guys off on each block. Every block you have two or three in position like they were in a war or something. We basically spent the whole month of October at home. We never went out, even during the day. . . . The shooting never stopped for the first five days. Night and day. Oh boy, that was a nightmare."[53]

On October 9, with troops surrounding the Senate, Joseph Nerette, a supreme court justice, was sworn in as president; Jean-Jacques Honorat, a (former) human rights activist became prime minister a few days later. The military and elite now had a government in place and were free to mop up resistance; this government became known among those who didn't support it as the *gouvenman defakto* or simply *les defakto*. On the day after Nerette's assumption of the presidency, soldiers arrested Manno Charlemagne, accusing him of carrying weapons and of inciting violence. He was held by the Anti-Gang Service for forty-eight hours, threatened with execution, and then transferred to the National Penitentiary. Amnesty International and other human rights organizations lobbied for his release. After the Tribunal Civil ruled his arrest illegal, he was released on October 18 only to be rearrested an hour later in front of his family by plainclothes personnel who refused to produce an arrest warrant. When he was finally released on October 25, Manno was alerted that the army wanted him apprehended again, and so he and his family entered the Argentine embassy, where they requested and were granted asylum. The ambassador and embassy worried that *zenglendo*-s would break in to apprehend Manno. While at the embassy, Manno was the focus of a campaign in the United States called "Americans for Manno" (spearheaded by director Jonathan Demme) that attracted many celebrities (Harry Belafonte, Danny Glover, Michelle Pfeiffer, Sting, and others).

Clifford Sylvain, the leader of the New York roots group Rara Machine, composed a response to the coup in the two days after it took place, called *"Pan-n se pa-n"* (What's ours is ours), accusing the military of wanting to deprive Haitian peasants of their land. The song listed a litany of problems in the country and in the communities of Haitians overseas. It began with a gruesome audio reenactment of the coup and then asked the question,

Kisa pou n fè ave yo	**What can we do with them**
Mechan ipokrit ki nan lakou lakay o . . .	**Evil hypocrites at home . . .**
Pa-n se pa-n	**What's ours is ours**[54]

Boukan Ginen also wrote a carnival *rara*, "Boukan tou limen" (Boukan all fired up) in reaction to the coup, using a common Voudou

chant, *Yo ba mwen kou-a, kou-a fè mwen mal o* (They give me a blow
[coup], this blow makes me sick). Then, once again using the image of
the carnival band as a metaphor for the country, the group complains
in "Jou a rive" that "*Y ap elimine tout moun nan bann nan*" (They're
eliminating all the people in the band—a reference to the campaign to
root out and assassinate supporters for Aristide among the lower
classes).

Boukman Eksperyans were the recipients of continued threats and
intimidations, but not direct violence, presumably because of their international renown. The Mango Records release of their first album,
retitled *Voudou Adjae*, was nominated for a Grammy Award, the first
nomination ever for a Haitian band. During the early months after the
coup, the band produced a number of new songs, including two that
were called "violent" by the authorities: their 1992 carnival song, "Kalfou danjere" (Dangerous crossroads), and "Nwèl inosan" (Innocent
Christmas). In one incident, *attachés* with machine guns showed up at
a concert to keep them from performing "Kalfou danjere," "Nwèl inosan," or "Kè m pa sote." Here are some of the "incendiary" lyrics from
"Nwèl Inosan":

Timoun yo, gade gwo zam ap mete divisyon	Children, look at how weapons cause division
Gade kijan nou lage, nou pa pwoteje	Look how we give up, fail to protect ourselves
Gade ki wout yo vle n fè	Look at the route they want us to take
Pou n pedi libète-n	To lose our freedom[55]

Their song "Kalfou danjere" was perhaps the most-quoted Haitian
song of the decade, as it seemed to capture perfectly a moment of
political crisis, spiritual resistance, and cultural production.[56] It was
infused with Kongo religious imagery of the crossroads as a site of
spiritual judgment, implying that the Vodou deities and the Haitian
people would sit in judgment of the actions of those who carried out
the coup.

Ou manti, ou chaje ak pwoblèm	Liars, you'll be in deep trouble
Nan kalfou, kalfou nèg Kongo	At the crossroads of the Congo people
O wou o, Kalfou nèg Kongo	O wou o, the crossroads of the Congo people

Touye, nou pap touye	We're not doing any killing
Jwe, nou pap jwe la . . .	We're not going to play that game . . .
Ginen pa Bizango	Ginen is not Bizango[57]

Bizango is one of the secret societies (sometimes called *sectes rouges*, or red sects) that emerged from the colonial era, and which are known for their sometimes violent reprisals.[58] In "Kalfou danjere," Boukman Eksperyans contrasted their violent reputation with the kind of spiritual resistance they believe to be in accord with the concept of Ginen. The band also reprised a familiar trope for carnival songs, the identification of the carnival band as a symbol of the people:

Se fran Ginen kap pase la	The true Ginen are passing
Se bann Boukman kap pase la . . .	The Boukman entourage is passing . . .
Woy men moun-yo	Woy, here are the people[59]

"Kalfou danjere," released over four months before carnival, was banned from the so-called Carnival de l'Unité (Carnival of Unity), and the video was refused airplay on TNH (Télévision National d'Haïti), where it was called "dangerous." The song nevertheless became the unofficial favorite that year, and, contrary to many reports in the American press, it did receive a lot of airplay from some of the more progressive stations in Haiti such as RFI Haïti, and PVS Antenne 16.

Like Boukman Eksperyans, the roots band Ram (under the leadership of Haitian-American hotelier Richard Morse) was resident in Haiti. Their song, "Fèy," based on a traditional Vodou song that Richard's mother (Emerante de Pradines) had sung decades earlier, is an excellent example of indirect signification on the political situation. The song is based on the proverb *Jou yon fèy tonbe nan dlo, se pa jou a li pouri/koule* (The day a leaf falls in the water is not the day it rots/sinks), which is a warning not to count someone out because he or she is down. The last two lines got the band into trouble with the authorities, who interpreted the lyrics about the boy leaving the country as a reference to the exile of Aristide:

| Fèy yo gade mwen nan branch mwen | Leaves look at me on the branch |
| Yon move tan pase li voye m jete | A storm passes and tears me off |

Jou w wè m tonbe, se pa jou a m koule . . .	The day you see me fall is not the day I sink . . .
Yon sèl piti gason-m-nan	The sole young boy of mine
Yo fè l kite peyi al ale	They make him leave the country[60]

The army, the *makout*-s, and the elite were so nervous about pro-Aristide sentiment and organizing in the lower-class neighborhoods that they arrested a carnival band in the neighborhood of Bel Air for singing "*Nou pa gen pè*," which would typically translate as "We have no fear," but because *pè* also meaning "father," the song was understood as a *pwen*, an encoded version of "We have lost Father [Aristide]."

A message from Aristide to the Haitian people denouncing the coup, entitled "Tanbou rezistans" (Drum of resistance), drew heavily from musical proverbs and imagery: "After the election ball [dance] of December 16th, the drum of democracy was not heavy, because with many hands, the load isn't heavy. After the coup d'état of September 30, the drum of complicity was heavy in the hands of those responsible. They may beat the drum, but the people don't dance."[61] In the proverb Aristide quoted, "*Jan ou bat tanbou, se konsa nou danse*" (How you beat the drum is how we dance), the drummer stands for the figure of power, obeyed as a matter of course. Praising and encouraging resistance, Aristide argued that the people were engaging in *mawonaj*. I quote this piece of Aristide's to demonstrate how consistently his political discourse incorporated musical metaphors.

The OAS and United States responded to the coup with an embargo against the *defakto* regime that went into place in November of 1991. By all accounts, the embargo seemed to cause minimal problems for the elite, at whom it was ostensibly directed, while deepening the desperation of Haiti's poor. In the spring of 1992, over 10,000 refugees sought asylum each month, the largest flow in history. The United States responded by depositing those it intercepted at a makeshift refugee camp at the naval base at Guantanamo, Cuba. The facility reached maximum holding capacity, with approximately 15,000 Haitians housed in tents on abandoned airstrips, before the United States resumed the process of indiscriminant repatriation.

The embargo created a very difficult situation for the progressive forces. As the army and *defakto* government held on to power and the embargo took its toll on the poor, many came to see it as a weapon to divide the progressive movement from the people. If the left opposed the embargo, they joined tactical forces with the *defakto* government and the *attachés*, whereas if they supported the embargo, they aligned themselves with the imperialist United States and turned their backs on the suffering of the peasants and urban poor. Many artists in Miami, including Farah Juste, Manno Charlemagne, and Kiki Wainwright, signed an open letter opposing the embargo.

Ram used the embargo as the topic of their carnival *rara* for 1992, "Anbago." Along with a politically ambiguous phrase about Haiti's being stuck in an embargo, the group incorporated a line from the old *rara* song "Kote moun yo?" (Where are the people?), which had been popularized nationally by Jazz des Jeunes in the 1950s. The song has always had a political association and a link to the adversarial texts in *rara*. In its original context, it meant, "Where are the people [our political enemies] who are speaking badly of us?" but in the context of the coup and embargo, it drew on new signifying possibilities:

Anbago, ye . . . Ayiti pran sou anbago	Embargo, hey . . . Haiti is stuck in an embargo
Ayiti pran sou anbago	Haiti is stuck in an embargo
Kote moun you m pa wè moun yo	Where are the people? I don't see the people[62]

Morse described to me the circumstances surrounding the group's performance of the song at the military-sponsored carnival of 1992. The army asked Morse to come downtown, and then put him in a room with "a bunch of red-eyed guys . . . it was probably *zenglendo* payday!"[63] Some musicians from Bossa Combo were there as well. Coupé Cloué, Sweet Mickey, and Mizik Mizik had already played at the Carnival, but to very small crowds, and the military told Morse that they wanted Ram to play and that they'd arrest him if there wasn't a good crowd. Morse responded that he'd play, but that the audience was their problem. For the Ram concert, the staging area at the Champs de Mars filled up, but there were a score of soldiers on the stage and truckloads of police. Ram played their set without saying anything, but then asked the crowd to sing along with "Angago." "Everyone sang 'Where are the people?' like four months after the coup! Where are all those people who can get us out, like Aristide, who's left the country, and where are family members who've been lost, and where are those who are afraid to stand up and talk? The military got bugged, man, and they switched off the power. Music is powerful.

Someone once said to me '*Mizik-la se sewòm*' . . . music is a serum, like an injection of blood."[64]

At that point in the performance, Morse realized that the army was arresting people who were *de men nan lè* (two hands in the air) and worried that the band was being used to ferret out Lavalas supporters. When the power went off, the crowd, fearing violence, dispersed even while the band began an acoustic *petwo* percussion jam while singing *pwen*-s. After the concert, Morse was interrogated by some of the military there about his views on the political crisis. Two *zenglendo*-s followed him home to the hotel he manages to complain that he stopped playing too soon and to demand money and band T-shirts. Later, a member of the bourgeoisie told him that many in the elite lined up alongside the palace in their Pajeros (a popular Jeep-like recreational vehicle among the elite) and that they could, "hear [him] real good! especially on 'Kote moun yo?' and what did that song mean anyway?"[65]

In early 1993, OAS negotiator Dante Caputo outlined a possible international civil mission to restore legitimate government, and this gave the army ammunition to stir up a nationalist outrage over possible foreign "occupation." When Caputo arrived in the country on February 1, he was met by a *koudyay* demonstration featuring music by the *defakto's* principal musical supporters, *konpa* singer Michel Marthelly, known as Sweet Mickey, and the *mini-djaz* Digital Express. Placards read, "Down with Aristide, out with Caputo," and T-shirts were handed out that read, "Yes to sovereignty, no to occupation." To counter the international support for Aristide, the Haitian military and its supporters successfully marshaled nationalist and xenophobic sentiment in the name of Haitian sovereignty. The Haitian Army, which was created by the American Marines during the first occupation, now cast itself as the "saviors of national sovereignty" and painted the president as a puppet of foreign powers bent on enslaving Haiti.

Haitian-American rap and reggae artist Papa Jube, based in New York, wrote his own song about the embargo:

Chak jou ki jou Ayiti pedi yon pyebwa	Every day, Haiti loses trees
Se lamizè, grangou, ak lamalsite ki fè sa	Poverty, hunger and sickness do it
Pouki gwo msyè vle touye yon piti . . .	Why do powerful men want to kill the weak

| Depi 1804 yap kenbe Ayiti anba dlo | Since 1804 they've kept Haiti under water |
| 1992 yo kenba nou sou Anbago | In 1992, they keep us under an embargo[66] |

Although Papa Jube's text seemed unambiguously to oppose the embargo, identifying it as a mechanism of foreign repression, his own published English summary translation worked against his text: "While we know of its political necessity / The people and the youths still suffer."[67] "Knowing of its political necessity" was not a sentiment expressed in the Creole lyrics, suggesting that Papa Jube was playing to two different audiences: a Haitian audience cynical about U.S. intentions, and an American audience sympathetic to the internationalist "New World Order" rhetoric of the embargo.

Interest in the Carnival de la Fraternité at the end of February 1993 was dampened by the ugly mood of the country and by a nautical disaster, the sinking of the ferry *Neptune*, in which over 400 lives were lost. Carnival Saturday was declared a day of mourning by the Bazin government, but Carnival resumed on Sunday. Tabou Combo was in the country at the time and had to cancel their Carnival appearance owing to the period of mourning. With one member of the band closely related to *defakto* Prime Minister Marc Bazin, the group was targeted by Lavalas partisans as being too cozy with the *defakto*-s, and a boycott of Tabou concerts was threatened in the diaspora. In the partisan atmosphere of the *defakto* years, Lavalas militants branded Tabou, Zin, and even Phantoms (pro-Aristide) as *makout*-s for traveling to Haiti under the *defakto*-s. The roots music groups didn't perform at Carnival 1993, with the exception of Vodou Azor, which featured the drummer Wawa. Because of the band's willingness to play at the *defakto* carnival, Wawa was promoted by those supporting the *defakto* government as a counterweight to more political roots bands such as Boukman Eksperyans and Boukan Ginen. One government supporter told me of his amazement as audience members along the route went into trance under the effect of Wawa and Azor's music, much as some audience members were doing for Boukman Eksperyans and other groups. Clearly the gods were divided in their political loyalties.

The winner of the 1993 carnival prize was the band Mizik Mizik, another group accused by Lavalas supporters of pro-*defakto* sympathies, with their "Carnival de ger" (Warlike carnival), which captured not only the intensely competitive carnival spirit but also the spirit of a divided country run by a military dictatorship, a country on a perpetual warlike footing. The song featured harsh rhythmic "punches," an occasional military snare drum, and such militaristic language like "attack," all of which reinforced the aggressive and warlike tone.

De men ale fanatik pran pozisyen pou n ale	Hands in the air, fans get ready to go forward
Mizik-Mizik la rive, Lari Potoprens bloke	Mizik Mizik arrives, the city's streets are blocked
Leve drapo-nou byen wo pou n voye	Raise the flag high to show
Tout moun dezyèm	Everybody in the second-place group
Nan Mizik-Mizik gason pa kanpe	In Mizik-Mizik, guys can't stand
Tout moun anraje, se ponyè ki pale	Everybody's enraged, our fists do the talking
Si w santi w dezyèm met kò w sou kote	If you feel you're with the others, get lost!
Pran yo, pran yo, pran yo	Take them, take them, take them!
Atake atake atake	Attack! Attack! Attack![68]

Boukan Ginen had a precarnival run-in with the authorities from the Bon Repos police station, who demanded that they cut off their dreadlocks and who told them that if they continued to play their style of *angaje* music, the police "would arrange to have [them] 'disappeared' from the scene."[69] Boukman Eksperyans's entry for the 1993 carnival was "Jou malè" (Day of shock), in which the band sounded its own warlike theme. Much of the song is a kind of dialogue between two warrior avatars of Ogou, Ogou Badagry and Ogou Feray. As a carnival song, it harkens back to the 1991 "Kè m pa sote," with its invocation of another Ogou avatar, Ogou Balendjo. The avatars are different, but the idea is the same—The people, with the protection of Ogou and the other *lwa*, are invincible:

Se nan gran chimen map kanpe la	I'm standing on the great path
Mape mande kilès ka va kanpe	I'm asking who else will stand up
Tout moun yo pran kouri	Everyone runs for cover
Se nèg lagè m ye, se baton fè anye	I'm a man of war, an iron club
Kisa yo ka fè mwen? Kanno pa fè mwen pè	What can they do to me? Cannons don't scare me

Ogou Badagri, sa w ap fè la?	Ogou Badagri, what are you doing there?
Se veye, yo mete m veye	Watching, they put me on the watch
M p ap domi, Feray, M p ap domi	I'm not sleeping Ogou Feray, I'm not sleeping[70]

Their song was once again banned from Carnival. A couple of months after Carnival, a tribute concert to comic actor Theodore Beaubrun Sr. ("Lolo" and Daniel's father, aka Languichatte), at which Boukman was performing, was disrupted by men screaming, breaking glasses, and climbing on stage, and by soldiers shooting outside the nightclub. On April 24, 1993, a Boukman Eksperyans concert at a *lycée* (high school) in Port-au-Prince was teargassed. The military had come out in force for the concert, and during the performance of "Nwèl inosan," the soldiers seemed to be readying their weapons. Concert promoters pleaded with the band to stop, but after explaining the situation to the audience, the band continued, launching into "Kalfou danjere." Soldiers began pumping tear gas into the audience. Some fled (reporting beatings at the hand of soldiers outside), but others remained, tying bandannas over their mouths and crowding the stage. This was the same year that *Kalfou danjere* held the number one position on the *Billboard* world-music charts for eighteen weeks. Just as with "Kè m pa sote," "Kalfou danjere" became a popular song among neighborhood and rural *rara* bands. In this period, Boukman Eksperyans's plight and their travails were increasingly used in press reports abroad as a window into the Haitian situation. Their politics and spiritual beliefs were often projected onto the nation by journalists for whom the band became the symbol of Haitian resistance.

The United States and OAS were pressuring both sides for a compromise solution to the standoff. On July 3, 1993, they succeeded in getting the military and Aristide to sign an agreement in New York City called the Governor's Island Agreement, specifying the return of Aristide after a new prime minister took over the reins of government. Robert Malval was the choice as prime minister. In this period, the neo-Duvalierist party called FRAPH, acting with military support, began to terrorize the city. On the day after President Clinton made a strategic retreat in Somalia, FRAPH militants and *attachés* blocked the waterfront in Port-au-Prince to keep American troops from landing. Their immediate objective was to create the appearance of "another Somalia" for the United States and undercut popular support in the

United States for action in Haiti. The Governor's Island Agreement had served its purposes well for the military; it had divided Aristide from supporters opposed to any agreement with the coup leaders, and his restoration had been avoided after all.

In the midst of the military's campaign for support against American, UN, and OAS threats, supporters of the *defakto*-s and their opponents were busy trading places on issues of nationalism and anti-imperialism. Some around Aristide, conscious that their future was now linked to American support, toned down their anti-imperialist rhetoric just as those who supported or tolerated the coup were sharpening theirs.

Manno Charlemagne maintained throughout the *defakto* period and afterward that the central goal was to build the political movement, not to "hitch the people's wagon" solely to one individual, or to depend on foreign powers to solve Haiti's crisis. He produced an album with the title song "La fimen" (The smoker) to counsel patience on the part of popular forces: "*La fimen* means 'the smoker,' and the smoker is the guy who oppresses people in Haiti. But if I smoke, when you open up your window, you don't have a smoke problem. The smoke leaves and you stay. You see? So in the song I am saying, these oppressors are smoke. The people, you are the masters of the land. *They* have to go. Don't be desperate. I say, *La pèsonn kanzo plisyè fwa*, meaning the people do *kanzo* many times. *Kanzo* is a word referring to a Vodou initiation ceremony [which uses fire]. So I'm saying, this is not the first time that they have survived a coup d'état. We've done it many times, and we will do it again."[71]

With the United States threatening an invasion, sanctions against Haiti were intensified, including a ban on travel visas that wreaked havoc on the touring schedules of Haitian groups. Boukman Eksperyans, forbidden from entering the United States from Great Britain, instead headed to Jamaica, where they recorded their third album at Tuff Gong studios. Their bass player died in Haiti after not receiving medication for bacterial meningitis because of the embargo. Boukan Ginen stayed put in Montreal, and other bands languished in Haiti or Mexico.

Reacting to invasion rumors and threats, the new *defakto* president, Emile Jonaissaint, declared a state of emergency, and he and General Cédras attempted to prepare the country to resist an invasion. On September 18, the imminent invasion was averted by a last-minute agreement between American negotiators (former President Jimmy Carter, General Colin Powell, and Senator Sam Nunn) and Raoul Cédras (and then signed by Jonaissant) that permitted the American forces to land unopposed. On October 15, President Aristide returned to the country, and in his return speech at the National Palace, broadcast by CNN to the entire world, he once again drew on musical imagery: "Nap relaks sou konpa. Met lòd sou dezòd . . . , balanse sou konpa demokrasi a, dousman, kalmaman, koul. Kadanse, balanse, koul." (We're relaxing into the *konpa* [beat]. Put order on to disorder . . . , sway to the *konpa* of democracy, sweetly, calmly, cool. Dance, sway, be cool!)[72]

Epilogue
"Carnival of Hope"

As I completed this book in the summer of 1995, Manno Charlemagne, a central figure in the musical and political upheavals of the 1980s and 1990s, was elected mayor of Port-au-Prince (arguably the second most important elected office in the country) on the "Bò tab-la" ticket. "Bò tab-la" means "at the side of the table," and the phrase had served as the title of Manno's composition for the 1995 Carnival, the Kanaval Lespwa (Carnival of hope). The phrase resonated sympathetically with the political rhetoric of Aristide, who claimed that the days were over when the rich ate *at* the table in Haiti and the poor collected scraps from underneath. The new Haiti was to be one in which all Haitians sat together at the table. After staying nominally above the fray for most of the campaign, Aristide made a last-minute endorsement of "Bò tab-la" and of its standard bearer, his long-time ally Manno Charlemagne.

I was in Haiti in the summer of 1995 to attend a roots music festival (called "Bouyon rasin," meaning "roots soup") and the signing by President Aristide of the Berne Convention, an international agreement on intellectual property rights. The international military occupation was in evidence everywhere, with armed convoys in the streets and helicopters flying low above the tin roofs of the city. As I walked up to the Sylvio Cator stadium grounds to check out preparations for the festival, a convoy of UN soldiers arrived on a routine patrol. The bewildered leader radioed in to headquarters, "Do we know that there's a big music festival about to happen here at the stadium? Are we supposed to be providing security for this thing?" Waiting for an answer, the tanks and armored personnel carriers deployed around the festival grounds, and the soldiers took up defensive positions around the crews who were hastily erecting sound systems and painting sponsors' logos on billboards ringing the stadium. One of those sponsors was the Ministry of Education and Culture, an innocuous enough sponsorship in most countries, but in Haiti, it provided concrete proof to the opponents of Aristide that this was a Lavalas propaganda event, bought and paid for by the state. I cite this viewpoint as one last example of the difficulty of severing the realm of expressive culture from that of power and politics in this period in Haiti.

The festival was testament to the growth of roots music as a musical and social phenomenon of both local and international significance. A New York radio station oriented toward African-American and immigrant populations broadcast the festival live, and many of the groups appearing (and one that didn't) had secured recording contracts overseas (Boukman Eksperyans, Boukan Ginen, Ram, Kanpèch, Simbi, and Rara Machine).[1] Groups based in Haiti and in the diaspora mixed with a foreign group or two (e.g., the Swedish Vodou-rock ensemble Simbi). First-time visitor to Haiti Célia Cruz performed with the Haitian folkloric diva Martha Jean-Claude, who had been living in Cuba for forty years, and Jean-Claude's former singing partner, Emerante de Pradines Morse (who had introduced Martha to Haitian audiences at the Rex Theater in 1944), joined her on stage for a short set.[2] Their performance in two-part harmony of "Choucoune" and "Erzulie" (the latter by Emerante's father, "Kandjo" de Pradines) provided a sonic link to earlier roots music movements, to the era of Jazz des Jeunes, the Bicentennial Exposition of 1949, and the "Generation of '46." Ram, led by Emerante's son Richard Morse, followed and was in the midst of playing a carnival *méringue* when torrential rains started to fall. Audience members opened their arms wide to receive the blessing and benediction of the rains and of the music.

In the last chapter, we saw how a carnival song helped bring down a government, how a populist priest and future president borrowed the title of a peasant song as the name for his political movement, how progressive musicians served the president and held assembly seats, and how military coup leaders implicated a musician as a precipitating factor in the coup. I could go back in time to the role played by troubadour "Kandjo" in bringing down the occupation government of Louis Borno in 1930, or to the role that Jazz des Jeunes played in paving the way for the triumph of *noirisme;* put simply, musicians have long been deeply dug in the political trenches in Haiti, honing political rhetoric and generating political meaning through musical texts and through the evocative and associative power of musical sound.

Certainly, a portion of this book has been given over to a historical survey of the deployment of the arts of musical resistance or *mawonaj* in neotraditional musical movements. Musicians have employed instruments (e.g., the *lanbi*, or conch shell, and the *vaksin*, bamboo trumpet) and genres (*rara, kongo*, carnival *maskaron, twoubadou*, etc.) that carry political symbolism, and they have harnessed the aesthetic of indirect signification and even playful obscenity found in the songs of Carnival, *koudyay*, and *rara* (many of which might best be termed *chan pwen*-s) to castigate or censure the powerful. The *indigène* movement, *noirisme*, Vodou-jazz, *kilti libète, mizik angaje*, and *mizik rasin* have all drawn on this reservoir of traditional elements to build an arsenal of musicopolitical signification capable of serving the needs of resistance, oppositional, and countercultural movements. These practices have colonized spaces typically viewed as the domain of commercial relations constructed on a Euro-American model of show business: hit parades, recording contracts, fan clubs, and airplay. I would suggest that the closer one looks at the popular musics of countries and social groups on the so-called margins of the world's music industries, the more one will see hybridizations of globally circulating practices, values, and beliefs with those that are more properly "local."[3]

But of course the argument in this book is not restricted to neotraditional musics nor to the use of music as an instrument of resistance; it ranges rather more broadly to characterize music as a medium of the negotiation and communication of power. Traditional events called *ochan*-s and *koudyay*-s have been incorporated in interesting ways into the praxis of commercial musicians (note the *ochan*-s played by *konpa* bands on flatbed trucks in front of the palace during carnival and the participation by some *konpa* bands in anti-UN *koudyay*-s during the years of the *defakto* government). In these two musical demonstrations, musicians ally themselves with the politically or economically powerful and, in return for increased access to patronage and the spoils of power, help to deliver key constituencies (neighborhood audiences, mass audiences).

Throughout much of the story of popular music in Haiti in the twentieth century, the peasants and lower classes have occupied a marginal position. Though they begin to consume popular music at Carnival and on radio and later on cassettes, they do not participate in it actively as major consumers of musical commodities (while they may be secondary beneficiaries, their purchasing power is not helping to shape the product at the point of purchase). In addition, the large majority of musicians in commercial groups have been—and still are—

drawn from the ranks of the middle class. At the same time, middle-class musicians have been incorporating elements of lower-class musical life ever since the inception of urban, popular music in Haiti (witness "Kandjo" de Pradines's evocation of Vodou song in "Erzulie" at the turn of the century). In this way, peasant culture has traditionally been the *object* of elite and middle-class fascination and authenticating gestures. However, rather than viewing this relationship simply within a framework of elite appropriation of cultural authenticity, I tend to view the variable presence of lower-class symbols in popular music as an index of the importance of the "class question" in Haiti. The movement of peasant and lower-class musics and expressive culture to center stage has paralleled a stubborn bid for political centrality on the part of the oppressed. It can be said in the 1990s that they are no longer simply the passive objects of middle-class romantic fascination; rather, the peasants and poor have organized and projected their voices onto national debates, making demands on power while inserting themselves into the center of the struggle for a democratic future in Haiti. Like Boukman Eksperyans, they are saying it is no longer a "day for the hunter" but a "day for the prey."

One last Haitian proverb: *Manti mèt kouri jan l kouri, laverite ap toujou kenbe l* (Lies run around the way they will, but truth always catches them). I have come to believe that music will play a central role in this "catching"—in other words, that music (commercial as well as noncommercial music) will further the productive critique and struggle that are refashioning social, cultural, and political life in Haiti. Haitian popular, commercial music has the opportunity to make a great *ochan* to Haiti even while it crosses over into global music markets.

Notes

Preface

1. I subsequently discovered that many peasants view the reforestation projects as part of what they call the "American Plan." A notion of an American Plan has emerged over the years as peasants and popular organizations witness a certain synergy among foreign government aid programs and international donor organizations such as the IMF and World Bank. These programs, they say, result in the migration of peasants from their lands and into the cities to work as low-paid factory employees. Reforestation, they claim, is intended to replace peasants with trees just as the food aid is intended to undercut peasants' market prices for agricultural goods.

2. Orchestre Septentrionale, "Plezi Chanpèt," *Bwa Kayman*, Maxnelle Productions MH001.

3. "Bwa Kayman," *Bwa Kayman*.

4. Averill 1994a, pp. 224–225.

5. This was the recording *Rara in Haiti, Gaga in the Dominican Republic* on Folkways Records (Folkways 4531), which was later reissued by Smithsonian Folkways under the name *Caribbean Revels: Haitian Rara and Dominican Gaga*, annotated by me and Verna Gillis (Smithsonian/Folkways SF 40402, 1991).

6. Marcus and Fischer, p. 176.

7. Averill 1993, 1995a.

8. Averill 1989, 1994a, 1994b.

9. Pacini Hernandez, p. xv; Austerlitz.

10. Guilbault and Hill.

11. Waters, p. 305.

12. Moore 1994, pp. 32–54, and 1995, pp. 165–98.

13. "Hey, Miami, Listen Up!: The Music and Musicians of Little Haiti," *New Times* (Miami), 2(39): 11–15, 1988.

14. This would be the realm of power more familiar to readers of Foucault, from whom I have borrowed the term "capillary." See Foucault.

Chapter One

1. Dirks, Eley, and Ortner, p. 5.
2. Ibid.
3. Giddens, p. 30.
4. Bourdieu, 1977, p. 9.
5. Nattiez, pp. 3–37. Where I part with Nattiez is in regard to the analysis of the "trace." Calling this level of analysis the "neutral level," he implies that there are neutral analytical processes that can be brought to bear on the material trace; I would view such an effort as a simple substitution of the analyst for the receiver, and I would argue that the analysis is simply another subjective (nonneutral) form of reception.
6. See Weber, and the revised notion of class proposed by Ralf Dahrendorf.
7. I would refer readers interested in Haitian racial categorizations to the excellent work of Micheline Labelle, who elicited racial terminologies (and their meanings) from different social sectors (i.e., informants from different classes, racial groupings, and locales) in the south of Haiti. Following her section on the ideology of racial categorization, Labelle treats the "discourse of difference," the ways in which members of different social sectors attach values, stereotypes, and personality traits to the various racial categories.
8. See Bellegarde-Smith; Dupuy; Nicholls 1979 and 1985; and Trouillot for much more detailed social histories of Haiti, all of which deal extensively with issues of class formation, racial ideology, and the nature of the Haitian state.
9. Fass, p. 2, employs the term "kleptocracy"; Lundahl, p. 297, uses the term "predatory state," and in the same spirit, Trouillot has titled his book *Haiti: state against Nation.* Dupuy (p. 211) emphasizes the role of the "triple alliance" of dictatorships, bourgeoisie, and U.S. interests in perpetuating problems of underdevelopment and poverty.
10. Yih. *Lizay* can mean manners, politeness, or diplomacy, but it can also imply a "two-facedness" bordering on deceit. Yih translated the word as "manners," and I have taken liberties in interpreting it less charitably.
11. Manno and Marco, *Lapli.* Lyrics appear in Chalmay, pp. 28–29.
12. My doubts concerning elite hegemony have been reinforced by the theoretical critique of "paper thin hegemony" offered by James C. Scott (pp. 77–90). Scott argues that the apparent consent of the oppressed to their own oppression so often chalked up to hegemony and false consciousness more often results from a failure to privilege the private discourses of the subordi-

nated, which he terms "hidden transcripts." Readings based only on "public transcripts" offered by the oppressed and their oppressors will produce pictures of consent and compliance (and of hegemony).

13. Courlander, pp. 170–78. *Malis* comes from the French *malicieux* (malicious), while *Bouki* comes from the word *bouk,* meaning small town (from the French *bourg*).

14. Buchanan, pp. 289–90.

15. Brown.

16. Yih, pp. 467–78.

17. Briyant Solèy, Léogane, recorded by the author in April 1991.

18. Rara Modèle d'Haïti, Carrefour du Fort, recorded by the author in April 1991.

19. André Pasquet, words by Yvon Mondesir. *Piké Devan.* Reissued by Mini Records, MRS 1120, 1989.

20. The pessimistic view of Haitian history is best represented in Diederich and Burt; Heinl; and Rotberg.

21. Dash, 1981, p. 5.

22. This is part of an argument that David Yih and I are formulating in an article called "Militarism in Haitian Music."

23. Interview, Jean-Baptiste "Baba" Pierre. Pierre was director at the time of the *mini-djaz* Scorpio d'Haïti.

24. Interview, José Tavernier. Tavernier is a former member of the New York *mini-djaz* Ibo Combo.

25. Interview, Guesley "Ti-Gous" Morriseau. Morisseau is a former member of the Cap Haïtian *mini-djaz* Les Diables Bleus.

26. Coupé Cloué, "Souvenirs D'Enfance," *Maximum Compas from Haiti,* Virgin/Earthworks CDEWV 27, 1992. Translation from Creole by Ralph Boncy.

27. Laguerre, 1980, p. 144.

28. Brown, p. 94.

29. See the discussion of this practice in Velez.

30. Comhaire-Sylvain, p. 78.

31. Ibid.

32. Abrahams, in Gates, p. 74.

33. Scott, p. 19. Michel de Certeau (pp. 24–26) developed a theory of cultural trickery, poaching, ruses, and guerrilla warfare by the subjugated. As an example, he offers a practice called *"la perruque"* (the wig) whereby workers poach time at work for their own purposes. This framework was elaborated by John Fiske.

34. In this way, the *chan pwen* differs from the functions assigned to the Puerto Rican *plena* (sometimes dubbed *el periódico cantado,* i.e., the sung

newspaper), the historical British broadside, or the Mexican *corrido,* all of which are said to have a primary function of disseminating information. The West African hereditary *jali* is similarly charged with preserving and disseminating complex historical and genealogical accounts. In contrast, the Haitian *pwen* is usually short, and its response sections should be capable of being learned and sung easily by an ad-hoc chorus of participants.

35. For a more detailed description of this phenomenon, see the discussion of *betiz* in the dissertation by Elizabeth McAlister. She connects the sexual politics of *betiz* lyrics to the subject position of what she terms the *rara* "small men," marginalized by their relations of power to other more powerful men and to women, who have a more central role in both domestic and market affairs.

36. Ibid.

37. The *manbo* Lola, central figure of Karen McCarthy Brown's *Mama Lola,* is possessed by a member of the Gede family called Ti-Malis, the same name as the figure of Haitian morality tales.

38. Ibid., p. 363.

39. See Fiske, p. 15.

40. My concern with affect, the body, and ethnoaesthetics is echoed in a number of works on African and African-diasporic music. See, e.g., Chernoff; Keil and Feld; Waterman.

41. Blacking, p. 6.

42. Brown, pp. 374–75.

43. Ibid. Emphasis my own.

44. Interview, Wagner Lalanne.

45. This section revisits some territory I covered in "Haitian Music in the Global System."

46. Sklair, p. 42.

47. For a discussion of early recording projects in the Third World, see Gronow; Wallis and Malm; or Shelemay.

48. Interview, Marc Duverger.

49. Interview, Anderson Cameau. Cameau is the former trumpeter for Skah Shah and a number of other bands.

50. Interview, Fred Paul. Paul owns Mini Records.

51. Interview, Jeff Wainwright. Wainwright is a partner in the Miami-based record company Melodie Makers.

52. Interview, Robert Martino. Martino played guitar for Les Difficiles de Pétion-Ville, Les Gypsies, Scorpio, and Miami Top Vice.

53. Interview, "Baba" Pierre.

54. Nemours Jean-Baptiste et son Super Ensemble, *Les Trois Dangers.*

55. Ensemble Nemours Jean-Baptiste, "Compas Mondial," *Nemours-New-Sound*, Ibotone/Anson Music Center, AMC 1201. 1966.

56. Interview, Mushi Widmaïer.

57. Loederer, p. 195.

58. Herskovits, p. vii.

59. Rara Machine, liner notes to *Break the Chain: Kase Chenn*, Shanachie Records, 64038.

60. Dash 1988; Lawless.

61. Davis 1985.

Chapter Two

1. For the early history of the *méringue*, I rely on Fouchard, who in turn relies on commonly cited travelers' journals, such as those of Moreau de St. Mery. The literature on the *méringue* should still be considered problematic; it has been immersed in nationalist polemics, with scholarship in the Dominican Republic, and predisposed toward parlor and art music examples of the genre.

2. *Kata* derives apparently from the Ki-Kongo word meaning "to cut." It is applied throughout the African diaspora for rhythms beaten out with sticks to accompany drums, and it is used in Haiti for the highest pitched drum in some Vodou batteries. In the English-speaking Antilles, the similarity of the Ki-Kongo word (both in sound and in meaning) to the English word *cutter* allows for the substitution of the latter. In later chapters, we will encounter the word *kata* used to designate the rhythm played on the high hat cymbals in *konpa* (the rhythm is the same as the *méringue* five-stroke pattern). See McDaniel for a review of the term in the Caribbean musical literature.

3. Carpentier, p. 130.

4. The Dominican Republic won its independence in 1844 not from a European colonial power but from Haiti, and, ever since, the bilateral relations between these two neighbors sharing a single island have been complicated by issues of racism, nationalism, and a deep mutual distrust. See Austerlitz for an overview of Dominican scholarship on the origins of *merengue*.

5. Alberti, p. 71.

6. Fidélia, p. 3.

7. Haitian art music, or *mizik savant*, is the subject of two major works: Dumervé, which comprises extensive biographies of Haitian musicians and composers; and Largey, which is both an ethnography of elite musical practice and a social history of art music in Haiti. Largey's work sheds light on both the European-oriented musical tastes of the elite and on the nativist ideologies that inspired composers to work with Haitian peasant musics.

8. Jailler and Lossen (p. 32) distinguish between the *orchestres de famille* and the *bastrinque* in turn-of-the-century Martinique. The *orchestres de famille*, also known as *sérénades*, comprised string instruments (violins, mandolins, and guitars) and were perambulatory, serenading at the houses of friends and for newlyweds. The *orchestres de bastringue* featured piano, clarinet, trombone, drum battery, cello, and string bass. These typically performed at soirees and *bals.*

9. *Time*, "Haiti: End of Intervention," August 13, 1934, p. 20; emphasis added.

10. Seabrook, 1929, p. 81.

11. Fouchard, p. 119.

12. A Harlequin recording, *Jazz and Hot Dance in Martinique* (Harlequin HQ 2018), contains a single, intriguing recording of Salnave's group from 1933, a fox-trot called "Brown Love." The other saxophonist on the recording is Emile Chancy, also a Haitian, but the drummer was the Martinican bandleader Flauvius Notte. This orchestra was considered an Antillean group, rather than a Haitian band per se, and it may have had a Cuban trumpet player.

13. Craige, p. 168.

14. Lists of personnel and instruments in the various groups in this chapter can be found in an unpublished manuscript by Félix Herissé, *Les ensembles musicaux*, in the archives of L'Ecole Ste. Trinité in Port-au-Prince. I was kindly directed to this manuscript by Michael Largey.

15. See Corvington 1987, esp. pp. 281–82; and Fouchard, pp. 118–19. I rely on Corvington's excellent history of the occupation throughout this section and wish to acknowledge its influence.

16. Gilroy.

17. Haiti has long exported laborers for grueling work, especially for sugar harvests in Cuba and the Dominican Republic. These migrant laborers were typically thought of as landless peasants or newly urbanized poor, but Nicholls (1985, p. 181) argues that for many peasants with ties to the land, migrant labor has fed a cash economy supplementing rural barter and trade practices. Cane cutters, in this view, can be seen as moving between rural, urban, and foreign settings, bringing to Haiti a particular form of Caribbean cosmopolitanism.

18. In Dash 1981, pp. 83–84.

19. *L'Essor*, March 5, 1924, in Corvington 1987, p. 308.

20. Corvington 1987, pp. 163–64.

21. Craige, pp. 139–40, 148.

22. See Dash (1981) for an excellent analysis of the contribution of literary figures to *indigènisme* as well as for a more detailed history of the move-

ment than is possible in these pages. Robin Moore's (1994) analysis of the effect of *afrocubanismo* and *négritud* on the ideology and work of Cuban ethnologist Fernando Ortíz calls into question the lack of an embracing, cross-cultural history of Afrocentric movements in the Caribbean (also Brazil and the U.S.) and of their legacy to scholarship. Although Dash has linked literary production in Haiti to that of the Harlem Renaissance and vice versa, it would appear that this project could be vastly expanded.

23. Price-Mars.

24. In the wake of Edward Said's deconstruction of Western discourses on the Orient, a few scholars have attempted to explain how Africa (and by extension, the African diaspora), like the Orient, has been imagined and constructed in Western discourses. See, e.g., Mudimbe; Miller; and Torgovnik.

25. In Dash 1981, p. 71.

26. From *La Revue indigène*, no. 2, 1927, p. 53. Quoted in Dash 1981, p. 80.

27. Largey, p. 106. My translation departs slightly from Largey's.

28. Corvington 1987, pp. 198–99.

29. Comhaire-Sylvain, p. 79.

30. Fouchard, p. 116.

31. Paul, p. 180.

32. Corvington 1987, p. 63.

33. Occide Jeanty's "1804" and Geffard and Lhérisson's "La Dessalinienne" (named for General Jean-Jacques Dessalines, first president of Haiti) were both composed for the centennial of Haitian independence in 1904. "La Dessalinienne" was the winner of a contest to choose a national anthem for the occasion.

34. Interview, Emerante de Pradines Morse. Much of this chapter's material on her father, Kandjo, is informed generally by this interview with Mme. de Pradines Morse.

35. Ibid. song title not given

36. Ibid.

37. Ibid.

38. Corvington (1987, pp. 305–6) also lists a number of Kandjo's hits, including "Sa ki fè sa dous konsa" (What makes this so sweet), "Se la raj" (It's all the rage), "Qu'est-ce qui frappe à ma porte" (Who's knocking at my door?), and "Mete fren" (Put on the brakes).

39. Both the Vincent song and its rejoinder are included in Courlander, p. 160.

40. Fragat, 1989 and 1986. Fragat reports that the G. B. in the name Otofonik G. B. may stand for Grande Bretagne, the source of most 78 rpm re-

cordings at the time, *gwo bouzen* (big prostitute), or an obscure Masonic reference (Masonry is popular among the Haitian elite, and its symbols and mysteries have been incorporated into Vodou).

41. *Mereng koudyay*, essentially indistinguishable from *mereng kanaval*, evolved out of fast, celebratory songs of the early Haitian military sung on the occasion of a military victory, which were later adopted at carnival-like festivities. *Mereng kanaval* has continued as the inclusive term for all carnival compositions even though some later compositions were essentially fast *konpa*, *mini-djaz konpa*, or neo-*rara* roots music.

42. *Le Nouvelliste*, 1934.

43. Heinl, p. 511.

44. Boisvert.

45. Interview, H. Widmaïer.

46. Corvington 1991, pp. 280–87. This chapter helps to fill out the information in that section on Port-au-Prince nightlife.

47. Canez, p. 1.

48. Corvington 1991, p. 306.

49. Ibid., p. 308.

50. *La Relève*, nos. 2–4, 1938; quoted in Dash 1981, p. 105.

51. This is most apparent in the tract written by Lorimer Denis and Duvalier called *Le Problème des classes à travers l'histoire d'Haïti* (1965 [1938]), a lengthy historical argument for the conflation of class and race in Haiti.

52. Price-Mars, pp. 182–83. His reference to plainchant, an early musical practice of the church in Europe, implied that Vodou music should serve as a source and foundation for the evolution of a Haitian art music much as European sacred plainchant served as the starting point for the development of European common practice harmony.

53. See Largey for a list of works by—and biographies of—the most famous *folklorique* composers: Elie, Lamothe, Jaegerhuber, Jeanty, and Lassague.

54. Some of the information in this paragraph related to the band's personnel is taken from Ed Rainer's article. The remainder is based on interviews with St. Aude.

55. This song was written in the 1950s. I am using it here because it fills in important elements of the band's ideological stance. Although it paints a dismal portrait of the "disdainers," i.e., members of the elite and political class who were not in agreement with the black political movement, it was also aimed at Jazz des Jeunes's main competitors in the late 1950s, the Ensemble Nemours Jean-Baptiste. The lyrics were included in a thesis at l'Université de l'Etat by Saint-Cyr.

56. Super Jazz des Jeunes, *Saturday Night in Port-au-Prince,* Marc Records, MARC-MDVG 203. While this song is an articulate defense of nativist music, its lyrics are in French, not Creole, and the song is based on a Cuban melody. By a number of important indices, Jazz des Jeunes stands out as the most popular orchestra of the years between the end of World War II and the opening of the Duvalierist epoch. They seem to have surpassed the popularity of Les Gais Troubadours in the mid-1940s and had only the Orchestre Casino International as principal competitors until the ascendancy of the *konpa-dirèk.* Their compositions were widely listened to over the radio and in their Théâtre National performances. However, because there was no true recording industry, the indices by which their popularity can be judged are all mediated by the media and by government tourism and cultural offices. They were certainly the most written-about band of the period, they were often chosen to represent Haiti abroad, and the era is often dubbed the "Epòk Dejèn" (Epoch of des Jeunes), but these are middle-class media and bureaucratic impositions. I mention this only to caution the reader concerning some problems of historical methodology, namely that the most controversial and the most written-about performers are not necessarily those that were the most popular.

57. Ibid.

58. This is taken from an unpublished recording featuring Issah el Saïeh and some members of his orchestra that was recorded in Havana at Radio Progresso with the orchestra of Issah's good friend Bebo Valdez. It was kindly given to me by Herby Widmaïer.

59. Again, see Yih for a fuller description of this phenomenon in songs of Vodou.

60. Jazz des Jeunes, "Kote Mon Yo?" *Super Jazz des Jeunes.*

61. *Haïti-Observateur,* September 9–16, 1988, p. 14; translated from French.

62. Heinl, p. 551.

63. Beaubrun.

64. Radio Port-au-Prince (formerly HH2S), Radio Caraïbes, HHRO, HHCA, HH3W, Radio-Haïti, and MBC. See Corvington 1991, pp. 158–68.

65. Jean Magloire, the Chief of the Propaganda Service to the General Commissariat of the Exposition, discussed the functions of the exposition in his book (written to defend the Estimé presidency), p. 59.

66. Ibid., p. 62.

67. Mathurin, pp. 165–91. Also performing were the Cuban Trio Aguila, Cuban pianist Rosario Franco, Martinique's Moune de Rival, French pianist Gilles Gilbert, Puerto Rican vocalist Daniel Santos, and a Guatemalan ma-

rimba orchestra (which played the ubiquitous "Panama m tonbe"). The theater was host to the Quebequois choir Choeur La Vallée Smith, which performed Haitian and Canadian folk songs in addition to opera. A Puerto Rican choir, A Ca Pela, performed at the Club Militaire with the Orchestre de l'Armée, at the presidential palace, and at the Haitian-American Institute.

68. Friedlander. Visitors included many of America's black intelligentsia and celebrities: fighter Joe Lewis, Ella Philipps Stewart (president of the National Association of Colored Women), and Doctor Virginia Nyabongo from the Tennessee Agricultural and Industrial State College.

69. See Fleurant and Wilcken for a more complete account of the folkloric dance movement in Haiti and its legacy.

70. Jazz des Jeunes, "Anciens Jeunes," *Saturday Night in Port-au-Prince.*

71. Pedro Saavedra Aleman; quoted in Mathurin, p. 158.

72. Courlander, p. 161. The second line of the song quoted ("Hold on to the country, don't let go") appears in a song for Duvalier in Chapter 3 and is a common refrain in the music of presidential praise singing.

73. Heinl, p. 564. Unlike the term *banbòch*, which designates a "wild" party, a *kèmès* is an early evening concert party, and its use here suggests a casual, continuous round of drinking and socializing.

74. Martin.

75. "Twa fèy," sung by Gérard Dupervil. *Vous en souvenez-vous?*

76. Interview, H. Widmaïer.

77. By the onset of the war, Widmaïer had built a modern climatized studio with a small theater and a fifty-meter antenna that carried the signal (broadcast on three different wavelengths) to all parts of Haiti. During the war, he affiliated the station, renamed 4VRW-Radio d'Haïti, with the Columbia Broadcasting System and the Paix des Nations Unis in order to carry news from the teletype machines.

78. Interview, Tacite Lamothe. 1986.

79. *New York Times*, 1954. The event is commemorated with a full-color volume, *Tricinquantenaire de l'independence d'Haïti.*

80. Interview, Charlemagne.

Chapter Three

1. In 1962, Duvalier institutionalized the militia, calling it the Volontaires de la Sécurité Nationale (VSN), but the nickname *tonton makout*-s persisted.

2. It is impossible to cover adequately the political history of the Duvalier reign in a chapter of this size. The reader is directed to academic treatments of Haitian history and political economy that contextualize the dictatorship and explore its ideology and practice, esp. Nicholls 1979 and 1985; Trouillot 1990; Bellegarde-Smith 1990; Dupuy 1989; Fass 1990; and Lundahl 1983.

There are many popular histories of Haiti that make fascinating reading, but all rely greatly on rumor and gossip, and some draw an overly sensationalized portrait. See Diederich and Burt 1986; Abbott 1988; Wilentz 1989; Rotberg 1971; and Heinl 1978.

3. "Duvalier Nan Bataille," by Luc Beaubrun, played by the Ensemble Nérette, Institut Musical d'Haïti, p. 48. Because these songs were written down in a form of Creole orthography, I have not updated the Creole, but have left it as it appeared in the original document. I draw extensively from this volume, because it elegantly expresses many of the cultural strategies and rhetorical gestures of early Duvalierism. I do not mean to suggest that these songs were widely popular; although many of them were written by well-known and popular performers, there is no evidence to suggest that any of these songs were ever "hits" for the groups performing them.

4. Ibid., p. 2.

5. "Dr. François Duvalier," ibid., p. 42. As for the final line about staying in office to complete the term, I remind the reader of a similar song about President Estimé.

6. "Duvalier Ou Pi Du," ibid., p. 24.

7. "Rete Tranquil" (Pétro rhythm), ibid., p. 36.

8. "Réactionnaire," by Les Frères Unis de la 5ième Avenue de Bolosse, ibid., p. 28.

9. As McAlister (1995) notes, this same formula was employed by the masses for Jean-Bertrand Aristide, often as "Aristid, peyi-a se pou w, kale bounda-w jan ou vle" (Aristide, the country is yours, bare your butt however you want).

10. "Bonjou Duvalier, Papa Moin," by Inovia Simon, Institut Musical d'Haïti, p. 38.

11. "Quimbé Pays ya Duvalier," by Jazz des Jeunes, ibid., p. 37.

12. "Min Président Peuple Là," by Aurèle Rosseau, ibid., p. 46.

13. "Haïti Reci Sauvé" (Haiti receives its savior), by Aurèle Rosseau, ibid., p. 47.

14. Jazz des Jeunes didn't record until 1956, and their early sessions were produced by their agent, Jean-Claude Abraham, owner of the club Djoumbala, who put together a small label (Palace Records) to market the records. Later, Jazz des Jeunes recorded for Marc Records.

15. For an analysis of the class roots of Dominican popular music (and its relation to national politics), see Pacini Hernandez 1995, and Austerlitz 1996.

16. Viloria was also instrumental in popularizing *merengue* in New York in the early 1950s. See Roberts 1979, p. 145. Information on Lira del Yaqui is from Alberti 1975, p. 58.

17. Interview, H. Widmaïer.

18. Interview, Charles Dessalines.

19. Fouchard 1988, p. 120.

20. This song made its way onto the compilation *Konbit: Burning Rhythms of Haiti*, A&M Records, CD 5281, 1989.

21. Désinor 1985, p. 7.

22. Interview, Wagner Lalanne. Lalanne was the keyboard player who joined Nemours in 1963–64, when he revamped the lineup of the band.

23. Ibid.

24. Lyrics from Saint Cyr, pp. 73–74.

25. "Anciens Jeunes," Super Jazz des Jeunes, *Saturday Night in Port-au-Prince*.

26. "Cafou," ibid.

27. I follow the conventions of popular discourse in Haiti by referring to Nemours Jean-Baptiste by his given name and to Wébert Sicot by his family name. Sicot and Nemours soundly dominated commercial music in Haiti for a decade and managed to inspire interest among a widely divergent class base. Part of the triumph of commercialism in this period is due precisely to the erasure of class-based consumption and its replacement with mass consumption. However, because of the peasants' economically marginal status, it cannot be said that they participated in any meaningful way in the cash economy and in commercial consumption. They were, however, exposed to popular artists on the radio where radio receivers were available (more common after the arrival of transistor radios). The urban poor, even if unable to attend concerts throughout the year, were able to (and did) hear popular music at Carnival.

28. Interview, Fred Paul.

29. Interview, Wagner Lalanne.

30. Ensemble Nemours Jean-Baptiste, *Musical Tour of Haiti*. I was first alerted to this song (and to the two that follow it) by Smith and Lamothe (1987, 1988) in their series on the history of *konpa* in the *Reggae and African Beat* (later, *the Beat*).

31. Ensemble Wébert Sicot, *Cadence Rampa*.

32. Ensemble Nemours Jean-Baptiste, *Haïti Cherie*.

33. Désinor, p. 7.

34. Ensemble Wébert Sicot, *Zeponis*.

35. Ensemble Nemours Jean-Baptiste, *L'As du Rhythme*.

36. Ibid.

37. Some time after lead singer André Dorismond left Nemours's ensemble to join the Sicot organization, Nemours was wounded by the break with his accordionist Richard Duroseau, one of the *"twa danje"* (three dangers,

i.e., Jean-Baptiste, Gaspard, and Duroseau), probably the instrumentalist most critical to the sound of the early *konpa-dirèk*. Although Sicot and Nemours proclaimed a reconciliation in the late 1960s, they were unable to escape the "eternal rivalry" that had been set in motion and internalized by their audiences. As late as 1982, over twenty-five years after the rivalry began, a Haitian newspaper in New York headlined a concert preview: "Showdown 1982: Confrontation Nemours Jean-Baptiste—Wébert Sicot!," *Haïti-Observateur* 1982b.

38. *Le Nouvelliste* 1967.

39. *Le Nouvelliste* 1959.

40. *Le Nouvelliste* 1958.

41. See "Spatial Stories" in de Certeau, pp. 115–30.

42. *Le Nouvelliste* 1959a. The common slogan "Don't touch Duvalier" was used in a *méringue* in praise of Duvalier from the 1958 competition mentioned earlier in the chapter.

43. *Le Nouvelliste* 1962.

44. Figaro. Yaws is a syphilitic disease that resulted in gaping sores on the bodies of the afflicted. Duvalier had participated in a U.S.-sponsored campaign to eradicate yaws in Haiti.

45. Ensemble Nemours Jean-Baptiste, "Ti Carole." Antha, 1991.

46. Interview, Wagner Lalanne.

47. Interview, Anonymous.

48. Interview, Guesley "Ti-Gous" Morisseau.

49. Diederich and Burt, pp. 169–70.

50. Ibid., pp. 211–13.

51. *Le Nouvelliste* 1965a.

52. *Le Nouvelliste* 1965c.

53. Burks, p. 7.

54. *Le Nouvelliste* 1968b.

55. Ibid.

56. *Le Nouvelliste* 1968a, p. 2.

57. Diederich and Burt.

58. From the notes to the album by Atis Endepandan, *Ki Sa Pou-N Fe? What Is To Be Done?* (Paredon P-1031). This account may be biased toward the political perspective of Vaksin, as it draws on testimony of former members of Vaksin who later formed the group Atis Endepandan (Independent Artists).

59. Ibid.

60. Abbott, p. 148.

61. Interview, Jean-Claude Desgranges and Farah Juste, 1989. Also, see Fleurant, 1995.

62. *Le Nouvelliste* 1962a.

63. Fidélia, pp. 2–3.

64. Some variant of the term *"yeye"* was used throughout much of Europe and Latin America to designate the new forms of rock and roll popularized in international markets by the Beatles. See Perrone for a discussion of the influence of *iê-iê-iê* on Brazilian popular music.

65. Interview, Alix "Tit" Pascal and Pierre "Bobo" Ciné.

66. Interview, H. Widmaïer, 1988.

67. Interview, José Tavernier.

68. Original Shleu-Shleu, *Poté Colé.*

69. The retreat from the Caribbean horn line represented possibly the most dramatic break with the musical past. The horn lines from the orchestras represented an archaic sound to the younger generation, who were confronted by imported American and European groups that either dispensed with horns or used a single saxophone.

70. [Chleu-Chleu, sic], *Haiti, mon pays.*

71. Interview, Georges Loubert Chancy. Chancy went on to become the lead saxophonist of Skah Shah.

72. Interview, Alfred Michel, 1988.

73. Interview, Nicole Lévy, 1988.

74. Jallier and Lossen, p. 95.

75. [Chleu-Chleu, sic], *Haïti, mon pays.*

76. Les Fantaisistes de Carrefour, *Haïti.*

77. Shleu-Shleu, *Tèt chove à New York.*

78. "Machan Yo," Ibid.

79. Interview, Alix "Tit" Pascal and Pierre "Bobo" Ciné.

80. Heinl, p. 663.

81. *Haïti-Observateur* 1975. Durosier's actions during the first years of Jean-Claude's regime, along with owning a Mercedes and carrying a pistol, were responsible for his reputation as a *tonton makout.* When he later went back into exile and attempted to reestablish a concert career in the diaspora, he was met at one event with a violent demonstration.

82. Trouillot, p. 189.

Chapter Four

1. Abbott, p. 165. Elizabeth Abbott, former sister-in-law of the Haitian general and president Henri Namphy, provides many glimpses in her account of the Duvaliers into the personal life of occupants of the palace. Because her sources are seldom specified, some skepticism about the details of her accounts is justified.

2. Interview, Ricardo, "Ti-Plume" Franck. "Ti-Plume" suggested that Dato, the name of the album's label, was a nickname for Duvalier.

3. Interview, Alfred Michel; translated from Creole.

4. Interview, Robert Denis; translated from French.

5. I find myself using the medical analogy here that was so popular among the opponents of Duvalier. One anti-Duvalier guerrilla movement of Haitian exiles named itself the Camoquins (Creole: *kamoken*) after an anti-malarial medicine. The term *kamoken* was used later to designate any fervent opponent of the regime.

6. Conservative equilibrium theories hold that population movements result from disequilibria in income and resources between regions or countries and restore equilibrium in the process, but the theories typically say little about the genesis or maintenance of these patterns of political inequality (Stepick 1984, p. 338). Lundahl (pp. 39, 42–43) has argued that no equilibrium is reached in the Haitian situation, because migration itself contributes to a downward socioeconomic-environmental spiral that he calls "cumulative causation." Equilibrium models also tend to marginalize the role of economic, cultural, political, and institutional barriers to migration in the country of origin as well as resistance to immigration on the part of the magnet country, as though migration were somehow frictionless in both source and host societies. Dependency theorists maintain that this flow of human resources from the periphery to the core is a critical product of core-periphery dynamics in the global political economy, working to the benefit of the core through a process financed by the migrants themselves. See, e.g., Locher, and Fass. Benefits in Haiti include reduced pressure on scarce land and jobs, reduced political pressure for amelioration, and the substantial remittances from family members abroad. According to Fass (p. 48), remissions have accounted for up to 33% of Haiti's total exports.

7. Factors affecting rural decline included the disappearance of Haiti's forests, burned for charcoal, and, as a result, the loss of much of the island's topsoil and agricultural productivity. The political situation (e.g., the appropriation of lands by Duvalier's *chefs de section* and his militia, the *tonton makout*-s) also conspired to make life intolerable for many.

8. Migration statistics have been culled from Bellegarde-Smith, p. 125; Nicholls 1985, p. 193; Laguerre 1984, pp. 169–70; Stepick, p. 1; and Schiller et al., p. 184.

9. See Buchanan, p. 173, for an analysis of class conflicts that beset a Haitian church congregation in New York and for her discussion of the notion of *koloni*.

10. Interview, José Tavernier. Ibo Combo was formed by Haitians already residing in the United States, most of whom were here as students.

11. Laguerre 1984, p. 93.

12. Interview, Fred Paul. Nearly all of the major Haitian producers from the late 1950s in have been based in the diaspora, including Joe Anson (Ibo Records), Marc Duverger (Marc Records), Fred Paul (Mini Records), Jerome Donfred (JD Records), René St. Aude (St. Aude Records), Giroboam Raphael (Geronimo Records), and Melodie Makers.

13. The *méringue* known as "Haïti Cherie" (originally "Souvenir d'Haïti") was composed by Robert Durand using a text by Othello Bayard. Bayard wrote his nostalgic poem dealing with exile while he was a student in Berlin during the 1920s.

14. Skah Shah 1, "Haïti," *Les Dix Commandements.*

15. Fleurant, p. 72. The *kilti libète* (freedom culture) groups were not commercial by nature and never sold large numbers of albums. Their influence was more properly in developing a synthesis of roots music and politics and in training artists who would later have careers as *angaje* artists.

16. Atis Endepandan, enclosed booklet to *Ki-sa Pou-n Fe?* pp. 4–5.

17. Ibid.

18. Ibid.

19. Fleurant, p. 72.

20. Manno Charlemagne, *Konviksyon,* STLP 314227, 1984; and Farah Juste, *Lespwa,* LPFJ-5231, 1983. The text was included in Chalmay [Charlemagne], pp. 46–47. To "break our bones" means to face repression.

21. Fleurant, p. 72.

22. See Part 2 of Guilbault, pp. 47–113, for commentaries by myself, Edouard Benoit, Gregory Rabess, and Jocelyne Guilbault about the relationship of Martinican and Guadeloupean *kadans, kadans-lipso* from Dominica, and Haitian *konpa* and *kadans ranpa.*

23. Boncy et al., p. 167.

24. Bossa Combo, *Accolade.*

25. D. P. Express, "Ansanm Ansanm," *David.* This was from one of the best-selling Haitian albums of all time.

26. Tabou Combo, "Hommage à Nemours Jean-Baptiste," *Baissez-Bas.*

27. Interview, Ricardo "Ti-Plume" Franck.

28. Wébert Sicot, *Gina;* José Tavernier and Mini All Stars, *My twenty-five years in Music;* Mini All Stars, *Pure Gold: Fifteen titres d'or de Nemours Jean-Baptiste;* Jean Yves Volcy, *Chansons d'hier et d'aujourdhui;* Gerard Dupervil, *Vous en souvenez-vous?* Even after Nemours's death in 1985, the anniversaries of the founding of *konpa* were celebrated with events in New York. The guest of honor in 1988 was Richard Duroseau, Nemours's original accordionist, with his group Top Compas.

29. Liner notes, Caribbean Sextet, *Caribbean News;* translated from French.

30. Ibid.

31. Boncy et al., p. 169.

32. Haïti 2000, *Tet san kò.*

33. Cited in Dash, p. 204.

34. Zèklè. *Stop.*

35. Interview, Mushi Widmaïer.

36. Ibid.

37. *Haïti-Observateur* 1984.

38. Zèklè, *Stop.*

39. Ibid.

40. Interview, Manno Charlemagne, 1993. This interview is excerpted from my column in the *Beat: "Konpa Demokrasi-a:* The Rhythm of Democracy," 13(6): 54–55, 86 (1994). The interview was conducted by Mark Dow. Manno frequently creolizes his name, and it is thus often spelled "Mano Chalmay."

41. Boncy et al., p. 112.

42. Manno and Marco, "Lapli." Lyrics appear in Chalmay, pp. 20–21. The word *jebebe* can also serve as a noun, meaning a fool. Although I have translated *vakabon* as scoundrel, its meaning varies widely from something close to a criminal, rogue, or lowlife, to something like a playboy, wastrel, or loafer.

43. Ibid., pp. 26–27.

44. Ibid., pp. 28–29.

45. Toro (a member of Atis Endepandan).

46. D. P. Express, "David," *David,* Superstar Records SUP 111.

47. D. P. Express, "Corije," *David,* Superstar Records SUP 111.

48. Gemini All-Stars de Ti-Manno, *Exploitation.*

49. Mini All Stars, "Raraman," *Raraman,* Mini Records, MRS 1191.

50. Interview, Alix "Tit" Pascal.

51. Interview, Nikol Levy.

52. The term *sanba* is used widely in the countryside for a variety of composers and song leaders, for example those in work brigades and *rara* bands.

53. Cressole.

54. Interview, Theodore "Lolo" Beaubrun Jr. In general, the information in this section on the origins of the latest roots music movement in Haiti is derived from interviews with "Aboudja" Derenoncourt, "Lolo" Beaubrun, "Chiko" Boyer, Jean-Raymond Giglio, "Tido" Laveaud, and from many informal discussions with participants like Eddy François and others.

55. Interview, Ronald "Aboudja" Derenoncourt.

56. Ibid.

57. Boukman Eksperyans, "Nou Pap Sa Bliye," *Vodou Adjaye*, Mango Records, 16253 9899-2.

58. Apart from Aboudja, others in the band took "roots" names: e.g., Kebyesou, Kafrik, and Amoila.

59. Interview, Ronald "Aboudja" Derenoncourt.

60. Boukman Eksperyans, "Nou pap sa bliye," *Vodou adjaye*.

61. Interview, Theodore "Lolo" Beaubrun Jr.

62. Interview, Nikol Levy.

63. Gonzalez.

64. Boukman Eksperyans, "Se Kreyòl nou ye," *Vodou adjaye*.

65. Interview, Theodore "Lolo" Beaubrun Jr.

66. Boukman Eksperyans, "Jou nou revolte" (The day we revolt), *Kalfou Danjere* (Dangerous Crossroads). This, and some of the other texts in this section, were written after the fall of Duvalier, but they describe the spiritual outlook of many of the exponents of this movement, and so I have taken the liberty of citing them in this section of the book.

67. Interview, Theodore "Lolo" Beaubrun Jr.

68. This concept is perhaps best exemplified by a compilation recording, *Rhythms of Rapture: Sacred Musics of Haitian Vodou*, produced by Elizabeth McAlister, that contained recordings of the commercial roots bands interspersed with "field" recordings from *rara* bands and Vodou societies. The project was conceived of as a collective effort, bringing together notes and field recordings from members of the roots movement such as Mimerose Beaubrun and Azouke Sanon as well as from scholars such as myself, Lois Wilcken, David Yih, Gerdès Fleurant, and McAlister.

69. Manno Charlemagne, "Leta, laboujwazi, lepèp," *Konviksyon*.

70. Manno Charlemagne, "Oganizasyon mondyal" (World System), *Nou nan malè ak organizasyon mondyal*.

71. See Anglade, pp. 68–71, and Dewind and Kinley, for analyses of the foreign aid situation in Haiti. Duvalier appears to have followed a strategy of curtailing state expenditures for social services and infrastructural development by neglecting the problems or by convincing donor nations, churches, and (NGOs) to intervene. With many sectors of the Haitian economy and administrative apparatus under foreign NGO or governmental control, some nationalists objected to Jean-Claude's strategy as a negation of sovereignty.

72. Farah Juste, "Diaspò," *Alelouya pou Ayiti*.

73. See Schiller et al.; Schiller and Fouron; Basch, Schiller, and Blanc, for a historical review of the political self-consciousness and organizing strategies in the diaspora.

74. Gerard Merceron, liner notes to Gemini All Stars de Ti Manno, *Sort Tiers Monde.*

75. Gemini All Stars de Ti Manno, "Nèg kont nèg," *Sort Tiers Monde.* Almost all of Ti-Manno's albums were major hits in the diaspora, where his lyrics formed popular topics of conversation in Haitian barbershops and restaurants. His albums continued to be circulated on cassette (often clandestinely) in Haiti.

76. "Sort Tiers Monde," ibid. The last line quoted contains a pun on the word *fakilte,* which means both a "school" or "faculty" and an "ability." A literal reading might produce, "They confuse a faculty with a university." Ti-Manno here disparages the middle-class and elite fetishization of academic degrees as a measure of self-worth.

77. Schiller and Fouron; also see Averill 1989 and 1995a.

78. Tabou Combo, "Partagé," *Ce konsa ce konsa,* Tabou. Skah Shah, and later System Band were the three *konpa* bands that could credibly claim to being the most popular bands in the diaspora.

79. *Haïti-Observateur* 1982a.

80. This case study was first presented at a special symposium of the International Council for Traditional Music called "Music and Dance in the Lore of the Sea," July 16, 1992, Grand Cayman Island, organized by Ricardo Trimillos.

81. The African homeland of the spirits in Haitian religion is called by a synechdoche, Ginen (from Guinée). *Anba dlo* (under the waters) more typically refers to under land-based water sources such as pools and waterfalls.

82. Lasirenn (the siren) is a Haitian manifestation of Wata Mama, a nearly ubiquitous deity in the Caribbean during the slave trade, who is also found in parts of West Africa. Lasirenn is generally represented iconographically as a mermaid (from the bowsprits of European ships), although she may also be represented as a whale, in which case she is called Labalenn. These two may be considered avatars of each other or as related, but distinct, deities.

83. In 1992, with hundreds of boats being built to carry emigrants, prices dropped in some places to as low as $20 per passenger.

84. The situation and strategies changed dramatically after the 1991 coup, when the United States refused temporarily to repatriate Haitians and instead held them in camps on the U.S. Navy base at Guantanamo Bay, Cuba. The account I give of the passage describes it at those other times when repatriation was nearly assured.

85. See DeWind and Kinley for more details concerning numbers of nautical migrants and their destinations.

86. Atis Endepandan, "Papa m monte yon bato," *Ki sa pou-n fè?*

87. Rodrigue Milien et son Coumbite Creole, "Rackêt," *Rackêt*.

88. Kiki Wainwright, *23 nèg vanyan*.

89. Ibid.

90. Gemini All-Stars de Ti-Manno, "Nan danje," *Sort tiers monde*.

91. Magnum Band, "Libète," *Adoration*.

92. Buell, p. 130.

93. Averill 1994a. This section is largely adopted from that article.

94. *Haïti-Observateur* 1989, pp. 17–18, 25.

95. *Superstar Magazine*, p. 9.

96. This is the same Roger Lafontant who ran for president in 1990 and then launched a coup to forestall Jean-Bertrand Aristide's inauguration. His political career began in the 1960–61 student strike against François Duvalier (see Chapter 3), with Lafontant leading a faction of students that deserted the strike, only to emerge soon after as well-paid *makout* leaders.

97. Boncy, p. 74.

98. From a recording by Emeline Michel, *Douvanjou Ka Leve*.

99. Boncy, pp. 74–75.

100. As recounted in *Joseph*. Note the early use here of the "uprooting" metaphor.

101. From the liner notes to Jean-Michel Daudier's *Solèy la*.

102. Jean-Michel Daudier, "Lè m pa wè solèy la." Although this song was originally circulated on cassettes, it was the centerpiece of a later recording featuring Daudier entitled *Solèy la*.

103. Abbott, pp. 322–24. Abbott claims that Duvalier announced his decision to leave while talking to his minister Georges Saloman: "The fact is, Minister Saloman, we are finished here. We must leave before carnival, before more people are killed." Again, Abbott's details about life in the palace should be considered hearsay.

104. The use of branches in political demonstrations is an outgrowth of the carrying of palm fronds for Palm Sunday; its political significance is one of renewal and cleansing.

Chapter Five

1. Epigraph is from Jacques Fattier and Haïti '86, "Dechouke," *Dechouke*. *Dechouke* is the verb; the IPN spelling of the noun would be *dechoukay*, but because the more French-like *dechoukaj* is used so consistently in the literature and in song titles, I have adopted this variant spelling here.

2. See Basch, Schiller, and Blanc; and Averill 1995a.

3. Manno Charlemagne, "Gran rivyè" (Great river), *Nou nan malè ak oganizasyon mondyal*. Text appears also in Chalmay, pp. 126–27.

4. Interview, Manno Charlemagne, by Mark Dow.

5. Manno Charlemagne, "Ayiti pa fore," *Nou nan malè ak oganizasyon mondyal.* Compiled on *Konbit: Burning Rhythms of Haiti,* A&M Records CD5281, 1989. Text appears also in Chalmay, pp. 84–85.

6. Les Frères Parent, "Konbit," *Konbit: Burning Rhythms of Haiti.*

7. Orchestre Septentrionale, "Ansanm Ansanm," *Bwa kayman.*

8. Les Frères Parent, "Chimen limye" (The path of light).

9. Beethova Obas, "Fò n sot lan sa" (We have to leave this behind us), *Si.* . . . Text appears in Chalmay, pp. 118–19.

10. Sakad, "Rebati kay la," *Rebati kay la.* Compiled on *Konbit: Burning Rhythms of Haiti.*

11. Sakad, "Flanm difè," *Rebati kay la.*

12. Master Dji, "Sispann," *Assali, Zeklè, Pirogue, Masterdji.* Later included on *Politik pa m.*

13. "Fò Dimanch," by Father Jean-Bertrand Aristide, on Farah Juste's *Alelouya Pou Ayiti.*

14. Liner notes to Koral Gacin Garçon, *Nou tout se legliz: Solidarite, fòk sa chanje.*

15. "Fòk sa chanje," ibid.

16. Magnum Band, "Pran Konsyans," *Tèt-Ensem,* Tida 35719; later re-released as Melodie Makers Inc., MMI 1026.

17. Les Frères Parent, "Veye-yo," *Veye-yo.* The word *restavèk* comes from *rester avec* (stay with) and refers to a child who has been sold by a poor family to a wealthier family to work as an unpaid household laborer. In political discourse, it is synonymous with "lackey."

18. Ibid.

19. Manno Charlemagne, "Lan malè m ye" (I'm mired in poverty), *Nou nan malè ak oganizasyon mondyal.* Text appears also in Chalmay, pp. 84–85.

20. Beethova Obas, "Ase babye," *Si.* . . .

21. Fédia Laguerre, "Rache manyòk ou yo," *Le Soleil luit pour tous.* The last two lines constitute the full version of the Creole message from Bishop Romélus.

22. *Zenglendo* comes from *zenglen* and means "broken glass," which suggests something dangerous.

23. Mizik Koral Tèt Ansanm de Jan Rabèl, *Nou Se Lavalas,* Alternative Culturelle, STLP 314229, 1987.

24. *Lavalas* is not an easy term to translate. I have seen it given as "downpour," "flood," "avalanche," "flash flood," "heavy afternoon rains," "inundation," "torrent," as well as "deluge," my preferred translation.

25. Liner notes to Mizik Koral Tèt Ansanm de Jan Rabèl, *Nou Se Lavalas.*

26. The unofficial, or "popular," lottery in Haiti caught on during the reign of François Duvalier. It is run out of small shops and carts called *bòlèt*-s

that often use the English term "bank" in their names, e.g., Freddy Bank
or Carmen Bank. Many poor Haitians consider playing the *bòlèt* an investment, and they try to improve their chances by dreaming of numbers or by
consulting an *ougan* or *bokò*. Although nominally regulated, there are a number of corrupt and risky practices associated with the *bòlèt* business. If the
bòlètman has secretly sold many identical numbers (usually because a rumor
has spread that someone with a lot of luck dreamed it was a winning number) and if that number comes up as the winning one on Dominican radio,
the *bòlètman* goes broke and everybody loses. The number where everybody
(even the winners) lose is known as a *boul malatchong* (probably from the
Spanish *malhechón*, meaning very badly made or bad mistake). For an excellent analysis of the *bòlèt* and of other folk financial practices, see Laguerre
1983.

27. Beethova Obas, "Nwèl Amer," *Si.* . . . The khaki and denim refer to
the uniforms worn by the army and the *makout*-s, respectively.

28. Farah Juste, "29 Novembre," *La Voix des sans voix.*

29. System Band, "Ou tronpe m cheri," *Ou tronpe m.* The author of the
song told me that the song was definitely not intended as a political commentary.

30. I was not at the concert, but pieced this description of it together
from a number of accounts of people who were there. Raphaël Féquière
wrote of the concert in an article, "Que faut-il en penser?"

31. Personal communication, Richard Morse, July 31, 1995.

32. Interview, Theodore "Lolo" Beaubrun Jr.

33. Interview, Yves "Chiko" Boyer.

34. Interview, Ronald "Aboudja" Derenoncourt.

35. Written by Sanba-Yo. On *Konbit: Burning Rhythms of Haiti.*

36. Boukman Eksperyans, "Pran chenn, wet chenn," *3ème Konkou Mizik,*
later included on *Vodou Adjae* 1991.

37. Averill 1990, p. 60.

38. McAlister.

39. Boukman Eksperyans, "Kè m pa sote," *Vodou adjae.*

40. Ibid.

41. Farah Juste, "10è département," *10è Département.*

42. I remind the readers of an earlier song of Farah Juste ("Diaspò") in
which the dispersion of Haitians in a diaspora was portrayed as a crime
against the Haitian people by international organizations.

43. Parts of this case study appeared in my column in the *Beat.* See Averill 1991.

44. This song, and the election jingles that follow, existed only on promotional cassette tapes for distribution to media outlets. I am indebted to Radio

Metropole in Port-au-Prince, where I was given access to the recordings and where I was allowed to copy the relevant public service announcements.

45. Personal communication, Oli Nicolas, July 29, 1995.

46. Translated from Creole.

47. Ambassador Adams's experience with Haitian proverbs was a lesson in the slippery terrain of allusive, metaphoric, and indirect signification. On arrival in Haiti, he quoted a Haitian proverb, *Bourik chaje pa kab kanpe* (The loaded donkey can't stand up), supposedly to signal his government's concern with the plight of Haiti's overburdened poor. His use of the proverb, however, was nearly universally understood as meaning that Haiti was too burdened with riches and that the United States was prepared to lighten the load by taking much of Haiti's wealth. Adams's nickname became Anbasadè Bourik Chaje (Ambassador loaded donkey).

48. Pierre Louis Duval, "Nwèl Lavalas," no catalogue number, 1990.

49. Koudyay, "Manman poul la," carnival recording, not released commercially.

50. René Préval, an agronomist and small businessman, was Aristide's first prime minister.

51. Interview, Manno Charlemagne, by Mark Dow, 1994.

52. The word *attaché* came back into common use in the coup period. It had originally been applied to all of the *makout*-s who "attached" themselves to the armed forces so as to escape *dechoukaj*. During the reign of the coup leaders under General Raoul Cédras, it more commonly referred to any plainclothes operatives acting in support of the government and with the aid of (or under the orders of) the military.

53. Rochlin, pp. 85–86.

54. Rara Machine, "Pan n se pan," *Voudou nou.*

55. Boukman Eksperyans, "Nwèl inosan," *Kalfou danjere.*

56. In addition to being the title of this section, the song title was used as the title of a volume of the journal of NACLA (North American Council on Latin America) and a book on global popular musics and politics by George Lipsitz. Numerous journalistic articles on music or politics in Haiti borrowed the phrase as well.

57. Boukman Eksperyans, "Kalfou danjere," *Kalfou danjere.*

58. In practice, the purview and quotidian activities of Bizango societies are typically much more mundane. For example, the groups hold ceremonies (often dedicated to *lwa*-s of the Gede family), sponsor *rara* bands, and provide support and aid for society members. Their "enforcement" image is enhanced by the issuance of *paspò*-s (passports), entitling the bearer to safe passage in society-controlled territory.

59. Boukman Eksperyans, "Kalfou danjere," *Kalfou danjere.*

60. Ram, "Fèy," *Aïbobo*, Cine.

61. Aristide, "Tanbou rezistans."

62. Ram, "Anbago," *Aïbobo*.

63. This entire account is based on personal communication, Richard Morse, April 31, 1995.

64. Ibid.

65. Ibid.

66. Papa Jube, "Anbago," *Liberasyon*.

67. Press release accompanying *Liberasyon*.

68. Mizik Mizik, "Kanaval de ger," *De ger*.

69. Interview with Boukan Ginen band members on Radio Metropole, February 17, 1993; reprinted in *Haïti Progrès* 1993.

70. Boukman Eksperyans, "Jou malè," *Libète* (*Pran pou pran l!*) (Freedom [Let's take it!]).

71. Interview, Manno Charlemagne, by Mark Dow, 1994.

72. Address to the nation, Jean-Bertrand Aristide, October 15, 1994.

Chapter Six

1. See Averill 1994b and 1995b for discussions of the effects of globalization on Haitian music, and especially on the viability of *mizik rasin*.

2. Celia Cruz has always been very popular in Haiti despite never having toured in the country. Haitians especially appreciate her recording in the 1950s of a Haitian Vodou song, "Gede zareyen." Celia's consistent involvement in—and popularization of—Cuban Santeria struck a responsive chord in a Haitian audience that came to see music inspired by Santeria's closest relative in the Caribbean, Haitian Vodou.

3. I am not suggesting here that we essentialize our notions of the "local" and "global," as I see these two categories as mutually constitutive. Haitian "local" practices are, of course, the product of a long creolizing process applied to cultural legacies from Africa and Europe; thus these are hardly candidates for an essential "locality."

Glossary

Anba tonnèl: Under the arbor, i.e., under the makeshift thatched shelters that are constructed in the countryside for dances and gatherings. By association, it refers to the spectrum of music that one would find played at these gatherings.

Angaje: Engaged, committed. Politically motived music.

Anraje: Enraged, turned on (sexually), enthusiastic. Used to describe the affective state of carnival and *koudyay* crowds.

Ansamm: Musical group or ensemble. See also *djaz, òkès*.

Ayibobo: Praise exclamation from Vodou songs.

Bal: Ball (elite dance).

Balanse: (1) To rock back and forth, (2) to decide between options, (3) to rehearse and "heat up" an ensemble, (4) a specific command and step in *kontradans* (contredance) and *kadri* (quadrille).

Bal bouzen: Prostitute dance; a dance held in a brothel.

Banbòch: Big party or fete. *Banbòche* (v.). To party. See *fèt*.

Banbou: Struck bamboo idiophone used in some dance bands, or the bamboo trumpets (associated with *rara* bands) also known as *vaksin* and rarely as *bwa bourik*.

Bann apye: Band on foot. A generic term for carnival parade groups not mounted on floats.

Bann avan: Band in front. The front section of a dance band that includes the singers, melodic instruments, and chordal instruments.

Bann dèyè: Back band. The section of a commercial dance band that includes instruments such as drum set, congas, bass guitar, bell and floor tom, and occasionally bongos.

Bann madigra: Carnival parade band.

Banza: Banjo. Any of a variety of stringed instruments with skin-covered resonators, usually with four strings. These are only rarely found in contemporary Haiti, sometimes as a children's instrument. Commercially constructed banjos from the United States are used in some *twoubadou* groups.

Bastreng: Turn-of-the-century public dance hall.

Bèl Epok: Beautiful era. An evaluative designation of a period of cultural efflourescence, variously designated as the 1930s or 1940s through the 1950s.

Betiz: Obscenity. This usually refers to a playful and satirically oriented obscenity popular in *rara*, carnival and *twoubadou* music.

Bokò: A specialist in ritual magic; usually reserved for less-reputable practitioners than a type of Vodou priest known as an *ougan*.

Bolewo: Bolero, a slow Cuban dance popular in Haiti, where it is played by dance bands (often arranged into medleys or potpourri boleros) and where it has also entered the repertory of some Vodou and folkloric drummers.

Cadence Rampas: See *kadans ranpa*.

Chaloska: A carnival masque patterned after Charles Oscar, an infamous early twentieth-century general.

Cha madigra: Carnaval float.

Chante pwen: To sing a "point" or powerful message at an opponent or competitor; related to *voye pwen*, meaning to send a "point" or magical spell. To sing songs, often coded, that sanction members of the community. Such songs may be called *chan pwen* or simply *pwen*.

Chica: A colonial-era dance of Kongo origin.

Chofe: To heat up or provoke.

Djaz: Dance band. See: *òkès, ansanm, mini-djaz*.

Douz edmi: Turn-of-the-century public dance, named for the price (12½ centimes) of admission.

Egzèsis: Exercises. Practice session of a carnival or *rara* band before the events, taken from military exercises.

Endyen Madigra: "Mardi Gras Indians," a carnival masquerade with elaborately costumed "Indians," who engage in stick fights.

Fanfa: Fanfare, a military-style brass band. Also *Kò mizik*.

Fèt: Party, holiday.

Fèt champèt: A festival in the countryside.

Fèt patwonal: Celebrations that take place in villages, towns, and cities on the occasion of patron saints' days.

Fi fwontyè: Literally, frontier girls. Dominican or Hispanic dancers in dance clubs who often served as prostitutes. Also *Fi enpòte* (imported girls).

Filin: An import from English, this term describes the sentiment that one invests in the production and interpretation of music and has an element of foreign sophistication to it. It also has a sexual connotation as in *bay filing* (to give feelings, i.e., to turn on).

Gagann: A carnival pushing contest.

Gede: A family of feared Vodou deities that have special importance in issues of life and death, crossroads, and cemeteries. Their prediliction for obscenity, word play, and for censure make them a particularly powerful model for carnivaleque behavior and music.

Ginen: A name for Africa, or more abstractly for the ancestral home and home of the spirits.

Grenn siwèl: Loquat fruit. *Mizik grèn siwèl* refers to "rustic" ensembles and music also known as *twoubadou*, playing instruments that have been transculturated from Cuban trios and quartets: guitars, maraccas, malinba, congas, claves, etc. Banjos and accordions substitute for guitars as lead instruments. The style, with quick call-and-response choruses and occasional parallel vocal harmonies, is reminiscent of Cuban country *son* and *son changüi*. The reference to loquat fruit implies a rustic country style with music both bitter and sweet.

Gwiye: To roll the pelvis in some dances, especially *banda*. The nominal form is *gouyad*.

Kadans: Generically, rhythm or cadence. A shortening of the label *kadans ranpa* in Guadeloupe and Martinique, where it became a synonym for *konpa* and was the commercial label for most French Antillean dance music of the 1970s and early 1980s.

Kadans ranpa: The dance music popularized by Wébert Sicot (c. 1958 and later) and patterns on the *konpa-dirèk* of Nemours Jean-Baptiste. Spelled *cadence-rampas* in French.

Kanaval: Carnival or Mardi Gras. The three days of carnival, which preceed Ash Wednesday, are called Dimanch Gra, Lindi Gra, and Madi Gra (Madigra).

Karabinye: A dance dating to the time of the Haitian revolution (c. 1804) that was a couples dance derived from a section of the *kontradans*. Considered a forerunner of the Haitian *méringue*.

Kare: Square. Describes the popular two-step dance style that accompanied early *konpa-dirèk* in the 1950s.

Kase: "Break." In music, this refers to rhythmic breaks on the drum that change tempo or rhythm using an intervening rhythmic formula. A primary function in many ceremonies is to induce spirit possession. See also: *koupe*.

Kata: Deriving from the Ki-Kongo verb meaning "to cut," *kata* is applied variously in different ensembles. It may refer to the invariant pattern played on the smallest drum in a Petwo ensemble or to the drum itself. In Kongo performance and in *rara* bands, the *kata* is the pattern played on the *fè* (iron) or is beaten by the *vaksin* trumpet player on the side of the bamboo instrument. In *konpa-dirèk* (commercial dance music), the *kata* refers to the pattern played on the ride cymbal in a drum set. A kata player is called a *katayè* or *katalyè*.

Kèmès: Originally a bazaar or fair, the term was used to describe early-morning church fundraisers (10 A.M.–2 P.M.). These were moved to a later time (4 P.M.–8 P.M.) to attract an older crowd to dances with live music. Subsequently, the term was applied to all dances held in this afternoon period, chiefly on Sundays, or even to early evening dances.

Kilti Libète: Freedom culture. The preferred term for the cultural work of the music, dance, poetry, and theater ensembles in the Haitian diaspora that opposed Duvalier rule in Haiti. The best known groups were Tanbou Libète, Atis Endepandan, Solèy Leve, and Troupe Kwidor.

Kleren: Cheap cane liquor, the drink of choice at most musical events. Also: *tafya*.

Klòch: Bell, played along with a tamtam (floor tom) in konpa bands. A *klòch* is also the small bell held by the *ougan* and played with the *ason* (sacred rattle) during ceremonies.

Kole kole: Literally "pasted together," a reference to close dancing.

Kole mabouya: Glued together and swaying the hips (in a dance).

Kò mizik: Military regimental band, from the French *corps de musique*. Typically, these bands combine wind and percussion instruments and maintain a repertory of arranged military, patriotic, and dance music, and they can be distinguished from the other kind of military band, the *batterie sonore*, which features fife or bugle in a marching percussion ensemble. Also *fanfa*.

Konbit: A collective labor society, and a gathering of such a society. These groups, when large enough, typically employ musicians to accompany the work. The nature of these groups and the terminology employed varies by region. Other variants on the work group include: *eskwad* (squadron), *sosyete* (society), *kovè* (corvée).

Konè: Coronet, the tin horns that accompany the *vaksin* in *rara* bands.

Konpa: See *konpa-dirèk*.

Konpa-dirèk: From *konpa*, meaning beat or rhythm, and *dirèk* (direct), this was a dance and music popularized by Nemours Jean-Baptiste and originated by his band, the Ensemble aux Calebasses, later called the (Super) Ensemble Nemours Jean-Baptiste. It was patterned largely on the style of *merengue* played in the Cibao region of the Dominican Republic called *merengue cibaeño* or *perico ripiao*. French spelling, *compas-direct*.

Kontradans: The descendent of the French *contredanse*, the *kontradans* included an assortment of figure dances directed by a caller and was popular among freed slaves of the colonial era. Rural variants survive to the present.

Koral: Choir, chorus.

Koudyay: From the celebratory or victory compositions played by military bands (*batteries sonores*)—compositions that were called (in French) *coups de jaille,* meaning a spontaneous bursting forth. These became the models for popular, festive songs that animate torchlight parades before national and church holidays, carnival, and political demonstrations. These events, their music, and the ambience of energetic celebration are all called *koudyay.*

Lage kò w: Let go of yourself, used to describe the exuberance of Carnival.

Lakou: Multifamily residential courtyard that was a principal form of settlement pattern in the Haitian countryside.

Lanbi: Conch, or a conch shell with a hole drilled in one end, that is blown like a trumpet. It was used extensively as a signal instrument from the period of the slave rebellions to the present. One finds it used in *konbit*-s, some Vodou and *kongo* ceremonies, and in rites for Agwe, deity of the sea.

Langaj: A ritual, spiritual language that appears in certain Vodou song texts (roughly equivalent to "speaking in tongues"). Also known as *pale Ginen.*

Lese frape: Let hit. The reaction, generally during carnival, of excited individuals who career through the crowd flailing their arms and bumping into others. In Guadeloupe, this is known as *blese bobo* and in Trinidad as breakaway.

Lwa: Vodou spirit. A *lwa rasin* (root spirit) is inherited from one's family. Also *mistè, zany.*

Madigra: Mardi Gras, carnival. Also *kanaval.*

Majò jon: Baton twirler in a *rara* band, from *majeur jongleur.*

Malinba: Large box-like lamellophone with three to seven flattened metal tongues, used as a bass-like instrument in *twoubadou* ensembles.

Manbo: A Vodou priestess.

Maskawon: A carnival dance, rhythm, and the drum battery that accompanies it.

Mereng: A dance/song tradition (derived from the French *contredanse* figure via the *karabinye*) whose best known variant is the refined parlor music called *mereng-lant* (slow *méringue*), also known as the *mereng salon* (salon *méringue*).

Mereng kanaval: A fast-tempo carnival *méringue,* now equivalent to the *mereng koudyay.*

Mereng koudyay: See *mereng kanaval.*

Mèt: Director or sponsor of a *bann rara* or *mini-djaz.*

Mini-djaz: Moderately small commercial music ensembles that evolved in the mid-1960s and featured electric guitars, bass, trap-set, congas, bell/tom, and sometimes a saxophone.

Mizik angaje: Political or socially concerned music.

Mizik dansant: General term for popular, commercial dance music.

Mizik savant: Art or classical music.

Mizik rasin: Roots music. The most common name for various neotraditional commercial musics as played by groups from the 1980s on.

Mizik tipik: Typical or old-fahsioned peasant music, generally referring to secular dance and diversion music of the countryside. See *anba tonnèl.*

Natif natal: Native (born or originated in Haiti), used to distinguish autochtonous cultural phenomena.

Nouvel jenerasyon: New generation. An urban, commercial musical movement that originated in the 1980s, associated with a generation of Haitian youth who were not old enough to participate in the *mini-djaz* movement in the late 1960s and 1970s. The extensive use of synthesizers, influences from Antillean *zouk,* participation of women singers and instrumentalists, and a lighter texture than *konpa* all helped to characterize the movement.

Ochan: From *aux champs,* a military drum signal pattern of the French army that signified "forward march." In Haiti, this has evolved into a variety of songs, drum patterns, and instrumental pieces that are used to salute dignitaries or important deities. The songs, whether played by a Vodou battery, a *kontradans* band, or a commercial *mini-djaz,* are often identifiably French and military in origin, featuring a variety of drum rudiments. Carnival bands often play *ochan*-s in front of the presidential palace and city hall.

Okès: Large musical ensemble, orchestra.

Okès bastreng: Turn-of-the-century public dance-hall band composed of string instruments and a few wind instruments such as the clarinet.

Otòfonik: Originally from the Victrola orthophonic 78 rpm records, this creolized version came to mean phonograph and later the old-style carnival groups that used megaphones (similar to old phonograph horns) to project their lead singers.

Ougan: Vodou priest.

Petwo: A category of Vodou deities and the dance music associated with them. Most Haitian *lwa*-s can be divided into Rada and Petwo families. Petwo is believed to have originated in the New World in the decades leading up to the Haitian slave rebellion and is commonly thought to have been named after a slave leader named Don Pedro. Many of its features have been traced to the Lemba healing cult of the Kongo region. Its deities are regarded as "hot" and militaristic.

Ploge: Plugged, or dancing in a very tight embrace with the man's arms holding the woman's buttocks.

Polemik: Ongoing controversy or argument (polemic).

Poto mitan: Central pole in a Vodou peristyle, considered to be a point of sacred contact through which the *lwa*-s enter the ceremony.

Pwen: Point of energy and contact between the mundane and sacred world in Vodou. Also spell, fist.

Ràboday: To the brim. A carnival and *rara* dance rhythm.

Rada: Category of Vodou deities and the dance rhythms associated with them.

Radyo teyat: Radio broadcasts, usually of a variety nature, recorded in the Ciné Paramount in Port-au-Prince on Sunday afternoons for Radio d'Haïti.

Rara: A seasonal festival related to Vodou belief that takes place all over Haiti during Lent, when *rara* groups take to the streets for days of exhausting processions. *Rara* groups can form at other times of the year for political events, spontaneous celebrations, etc.

Sanba: Rural singer associated with the *konbit*, or work parties, and with *rara* bands.

Sine teyat: Music concerts in movie theaters on Sunday afternoon.

Spèktak: An urban music/dance concert featuring many performers.

Swaè: A late-evening dance, generally lasting from 1 P.M. until 3 A.M. or later.

Tanbou: A generic term for drum.

Tèt kole: Glued heads. Cheek-to-cheek dancing.

Teneb: A political protest through noise. During a *teneb*, Haitians bang on or blow whatever noise-making object is at hand (car horns, tin pans, fences and light posts, conch shells, etc.) to create a powerful cacophonic protest.

Twoubadou: A style of music brought to Haiti from Cuba in the early twentieth century. Guitar-based trios and quartets with maraccas and *tanbou* are typical.

Vakans: Summer vacation (July–August), when families head for the mountains or beaches. A time of many important *fèt*-s.

Vaksin: Traditional bamboo trumpet that is also struck on its side with a stick. It is commonly used in hocketed three to five piece ensembles in *rara* bands.

Vèvè: A ritual pattern traced on the ground (usually with corn meal or chalk), generally representing a deity (but which may also represent a ritual object or metaphysical concept) and that is considered to be a *pwen* (point of contact with the *lwa*-s).

Vodou: Afro-Haitian religion.

Yanvalou: Rhythm and dance used extensively in Rada ceremonies.

Yeye: Rock-and-roll derived ensembles popular in the early 1960s in Haiti.

Bibliography

Abbott, Elizabeth. 1988. *Haiti: The Duvaliers and Their Legacy.* New York: McGraw Hill.

Alberti, Luis. 1975. *De musica y orquestas bailabes dominicanas, 1910–1959.* Santo Domingo: Editora Taller.

Anglade, Georges. 1982. *Atlas critique d'Haïti.* Groupe d'Etudes et de Recherches Critiques d'Espace, Département de Géographie, Université du Québec à Montréal, et Centre de Recherches Caraïbes de l'Université de Montréal.

Antha, Pierre. 1991. "Nemours Jean-Baptiste et Wébert Sicot: Le legs de la compétition à l'anthologie." *Haïti-Observateur,* April 24–May 1, p. 26.

Aristide, Jean-Bertrand. 1992. "Tanbou rezistans." *Haïti Progrès,* June 10–16, p. 1.

———. 1994. "Address to the Nation." October 15. Television broadcast.

Atis Indepandan. 1975. Liner notes to *Ki sa pou-n fè?* Paredon Records P-1031.

Austerlitz, Paul. 1996. *Dominican* Merengue *in Regional, National, and International Perspectives.* Philadelphia: Temple University Press.

Averill, Gage. 1988. "Hey, Miami: Listen up! The Music and Musicians of Little Haiti." *Miami New Times,* March 16–22, pp. 10–15.

———. 1989. "Haitian Dance Bands, 1915–1970: Class, Race, and Authenticity." *Latin American Music Review* 10(2): 203–35.

———. 1990. "Watering the Roots." The *Beat* 9(3): 60–61.

———. 1991. "The Season of Living Dangerously: Elections, Coups, and Carnival." The *Beat* 10(2): 20–23, 69.

———. 1993. *"Toujou Sou Konpa:* Issues of Change and Interchange in Haitian Popular Dance Music." In Jocelyne Guilbault et al., *Zouk: World Music in the West Indies.* Chicago: University of Chicago Press.

————. 1994a. "*Anraje* to *Angaje:* Carnival Politics and Music in Haiti." *Ethnomusicology* 38(2): 217–47.

————. 1994b. "'*Se Kreyòl Nou Ye'/*We're Creole": Musical Discourse on Haitian Identities." In Gerard H. Béhague, ed., *Music and Black Ethnicity: The Caribbean and South America.* New Brunswick, NJ: Transaction.

————. 1994c. "*Konpa Demokrasi-a:* The Rhythm of Democracy." The *Beat* 13(6): 54–55, 86.

————. 1995a. "'*Mezanmi, Kouman Nou Ye?* My Friends, How Are You?' Musical Constructions of the Haitian Transnation." *Diaspora* 3(3): 253–72.

————. 1995b. "Haitian Music in the Global System." In Alvina Ruprecht and Cecilia Taiana, eds., *The Reordering of Culture: Latin America, the Caribbean and Canada in the Hood.* Ottawa: Carleton University Press.

Averill, Gage, and David Yih. Forthcoming. "Music and Militarism." In Ingrid Monson, ed. *The African Diaspora: a Musical Perspective.* Garland Publishing.

Basch, Linda, Nina Glick Schiller, and Christina Szanton Blanc. 1994. *Nations Undone: Transnational Projects, Postcolonial Predicaments and Deterritorialized Nation-States.* Langhorne, PA: Gordon and Breach.

Beaubrun, René. 1957. *Combite,* December 31.

Bellegarde-Smith, Patrick. 1990. *Haiti: The Breached Citadel.* Boulder: Westview Press.

Birdwhistell, Raymond. 1974. *Introduction to Kinesics.* Louisville: University of Louisville Press.

Blacking, John. "Some Problems of Theory and Method in the Study of Musical Change." 1977. *Yearbook of the International Folk Music Council* 9:1–26.

Boisvert, Luc. 1978. "Ricardo Widmaier: Pionnier de la radiodiffusion en Haïti." *Haïti-Observateur,* September 29–October 6, pp. 11–12.

Boncy, Ralph. 1992. *La Chanson d'Haïti,* Vol. 1: *1965–1985.* Québec: CIDIHCA.

Boncy, Ralph et al. 1987. "Nouvelle Musique Haïtienne: De Nemours . . . à Beethova." *Conjonction.* Suppl. 176:160–76.

Bourdieu, Pierre. 1977. *Outline of a Theory of Practice.* Trans. Richard Nice. Cambridge: Cambridge University Press.

————. 1984. *Distinction: A Social Critique of the Judgement of Taste.* Cambridge, MA: Harvard University Press.

Brown, Karen McCarthy. 1991. *Mama Lola: A Vodou Priestess in Brooklyn.* Berkeley: University of California Press.

Buchanan, Susan Huelsebus. 1980. *Scattered Seeds: The Meaning of the Migration for Haitians in New York City.* Ph.D. dissertation, New York University.

Buell, Frederick. 1994. *National Culture and the New Global System*. Baltimore: Johns Hopkins University Press.

Burks, Edward C. 1965. "Ex-Aide's Murder Stirs Haiti Town." *New York Times*, March 11.

Canez, Velorio. 1942. "Notre folklore musical." *Haïti Journal*, November 26, pp. 1, 4.

Carpentier, Alejo. 1972 [1946]. *La musica en Cuba*. Mexico City: Fondo de Cultura Economica.

Chalmay, Manno. 1989. *Le poukwa le kouman*. Port-au-Prince: "Organization Culturelle" Konbit Kalfou.

Chapple, Elliot D., and Martha Davis. 1988. "Expressive Movement and Performance: Toward a Unifying Theory." *TDR: The Drama Review* 32(4): 53–80.

Chernoff, John Miller. 1979. *African Rhythm and African Sensibility: Aesthetics and Social Action in African Musical Idioms*. Chicago: University of Chicago Press.

Comhaire-Sylvain, Suzanne. 1951. "La chanson haïtienne." *Présense Africaine* 12:61–87.

Copelan, David. 1985. *In Township Tonight! South Africa's Black City Music and Theatre*. New York: Longman.

Corvington, Georges. 1987. *Port-au-Prince au cours des ans: La capital d'Haïti sous l'occupation, 1922–1934*. Port-au-Prince: Imprimerie Henri Deschamps.

———. 1991. *Port-au-Prince au cours des ans: La ville contemporaine, 1934–1950*. Port-au-Prince: Imprimerie Henri Deschamps.

Courlander, Harold. 1973 [1960]. *The Drum and the Hoe: Life and Lore of the Haitian People*. Berkeley: University of California Press.

Craige, John Houston. 1933. *Black Bagdad*. New York: Minton, Balch.

Cressole, Michel. 1983. "Voyage en Haïti cherie et maudite 4: L'espoir samba." *Liberation*, January 6, p. 21.

Dahendorf, Ralf. 1959. *Class and Class Conflict in Industrial Society*. Stanford: Stanford University Press.

Dash, J. Michael. 1981. *Literature and Ideology in Haiti, 1915–1961*. Totowa, NJ: Barnes and Noble.

———. 1988. *Haiti and the United States: National Stereotypes and the Literary Imagination*. New York: St. Martin's Press.

Davis, Wade. 1985. *The Serpent and the Rainbow*. New York: Simon and Schuster.

de Certeau, Michel. 1984. *The Practice of Everyday Life*. Trans. Steven Randall. Berkeley: University of California Press.

Denis, Lorimer, and François Duvalier. 1965 (1938). *Le problème des classes à travers l'histoire d'Haïti.* Port-au-Prince: Imprimerie de l'Etat.

Désinor, Carlo A. 1985. "Petite histoire et légende du compas direct et de Nemours Jean-Baptiste." *Le Nouvelliste,* May 28, p. 7.

Dewind, Josh, and David H. Kinley III. 1988. *Aiding Migration: The Impact of International Development Assistance on Haiti.* Boulder: Westview Press.

Diederich, Bernard, and Al Burt. 1986 [1968]. *Papa Doc and the Tonton Macoutes.* Port-au-Prince: Editions Henri Deschamps.

Dirks, Nicholas B., Geoff Eley, and Sherry B. Ortner. 1994. Introduction to Dirks, Eley, and Ortner, eds., *Culture/Power/History: A Reader in Contemporary Social Theory.*

Dumervé, Constantin. 1968. *Histoire de la musique en Haïti.* Port-au-Prince: Imprimerie des Antilles: Princeton, N.J.: Princeton University Press.

Dupuy, Alex. 1989. *Haiti in the World Economy: Class, Race, and Underdevelopment since 1700.* Boulder: Westview Press.

Fass, Simon M. 1990. *Political Economy in Haiti: The Drama of Survival.* New Brunswick: Transaction.

Féquière, Raphaël. 1989. "Que faut-il en penser?" *Tap-tap,* September 14, p. 3.

Fidélia, Georges. 1960. "Autour du carrousel." *Le Nouvelliste,* April 28, pp. 1–2.

Figaro, Georges J. 1965. "Le Carnaval 1965." *Le Nouvelliste,* February 28, pp. 1, 4.

Fiske, John. 1989. *Understanding Popular Culture.* Boston: Unwin Hyman.

Fleurant, Gerdès. 1995. "The Song of Freedom: Vodun, Conscientization and Popular Culture of Haiti." *Compost* 5:69–73.

Foucault, Michel. 1980 [1972]. *Power/Knowledge: Selected Interviews and Other Writings.* New York: Pantheon. Ed. and trans. Colin Gordon.

Fouchard, Jean. 1988 [1973]. *La meringue: Danse nationale d'Haïti.* Port-au-Prince: Editions Henri Deschamps.

Fragat, Jean. 1986. "Hier Encore: Otofonik G. B.—Marié po dis—Po Bisuit." *Haïti-Observateur,* October 31–November 7, pp. 17, 22.

———. 1989. "La trève carnavalesque." *Haïti-Observateur,* February 3–10, pp. 17–18, 25.

Friedlander, Paul J. C. 1949. "Haiti's Exposition: Bicentennial World's Fair Is Attracting More Tourists to the Caribbean Area." *New York Times,* December 25, section 2, p. 1.

Gates, Henry Louis Jr. 1988. *The Signifying Monkey: A Theory of African-American Literary Criticism.* New York: Oxford University Press.

Giddens, Anthony. 1984. *The Constitution of Society: Outline of the Theory of Structuration.* Cambridge: Polity Press.

Gilroy, Paul. 1993. *The Black Atlantic: Modernity and Double Consciousness.* Cambridge, MA: Harvard University Press.

Gonzalez, Fernando. 1992. "The Rhythm of the Roots." *Boston Globe,* March 20, p. 39.

Guilbault, Jocelyne et al. 1993. *Zouk: World Music in the West Indies.* Chicago: University of Chicago Press.

Haïti-Observateur, 1975. "Guy Durosier rejeté à New York." July 18–25.

————. 1982a. "L'orchestre de J -C Duvalier collecte des dollars dans la diaspora." April 30–May 7.

————. 1982b. "Showdown 1982: Confrontation Nemours Jean-Baptiste–Weber Sicot." June 18–25.

————. 1984. "Zekle annonce-t-il l'Orage?" October 20.

————. 1988. "Invitation du Jazz des Jeunes." August 20–27.

Haïti Progrès. 1993. "Le Carnival par et pour Bazin." February 24–March 2, p. 3.

Haiti Tourist Information Bureau. 1953. *Tricinquantenaire de l'independence d'Haïti.* New York: Haiti Tourist Information Bureau.

Hall, Edward T. 1984. *The Dance of Life: The Other Dimension of Time.* Garden City, NY: Anchor Doubleday.

Heinl, Robert Debs. 1978. *Written in Blood: The Story of the Haitian People, 1492–1971.* New York: Houghton Mifflin.

Herissé, Félix. [n.d.] *Les ensembles musicaux.* Unpublished manuscript, collection of L'Ecole Ste. Trinité, Port-au-Prince, Haiti.

Herskovits, Melville J. 1973. *Life in a Haitian Valley.* New York: Knopf.

Hill, Donald R. 1993. *Calypso Calaloo: Early Carnival Music in Trinidad.* Gainesville: University Press of Florida.

Institut Musical d'Haïti. 1958. *Chansons populaires composées en l'honneur du chef spirituel de la nation.* Port-au-Prince: Imprimerie Serge Bissainthe.

Jallier, Maurice, and Yollen Lossen. 1985. *Musique aux Antilles: Mizik bô kay.* Paris: Editions Caribéennes.

Jeanty, Edgar A., and Carl O. Brown. 1976. *Parol granmoun: 999 Haitian Proverbs in Creole and English.* Port-au-Prince: Editions Learning Center.

Joseph, Jocelyn. 1986. *Operasyon Dechoukaj, Bande Dessiné.* N.p. N.d.

Keil, Charles and Steven Feld. 1984. *Music Grooves.* Chicago: University of Chicago Press.

Labelle, Micheline. 1978. *Idéologie de couleur et classes sociales en Haïti.* Montreal: University of Montreal Press.

Laguerre, Michel S. 1980. *Voodoo Heritage.* Beverly Hills: Sage Publications.

————. 1983. *Urban Life in the Caribbean: A Study of a Haitian Urban Community.* Cambridge, MA: Schenckman.

––––––. 1984. *American Odyssey: Haitians in New York City*. Ithaca: Cornell University Press.

Largey, Michael D. 1991. *Musical Ethnography in Haiti: A Study of Elite Hegemony and Musical Composition*. Ph.D. dissertation, Indiana University.

Lawless, Robert. 1992. *Haiti's Bad Press*. Rochester, VT: Schenckman.

Lipsitz, George. 1994. *Dangerous Crossroads: Popular Music, Postmodernism and the Poetics of Place*. London: Verso.

Locher, Uli. 1984. "'Migration in Haiti.'" In Charles R. Foster and Albert Valdman, eds. *Haiti, Today and Tomorrow: An Interdisciplinary Study*. Lanham, MD: University Press of America.

Loederer, Richard A. 1935. *Voodoo Fire in Haiti*. Garden City, NJ: Country Life Press.

Lundahl, Mats. 1983. *The Haitian Economy: Man, Land, and Markets*. New York: St. Martin's Press.

McAlister, Elizabeth A. 1995. "Men Moun Yo" [Here Are the People]: Rara Festivals and Transnational Popular Culture in Haiti and New York City." Ph.D. dissertation, Yale University.

McDaniel, Lorna. 1986. *Memory Songs: Community, Flight, and Conflict in the Big Drum of Carriacou*. Ph.D. dissertation, University of Maryland.

Magloire, Jean. 1950. *Dumarsais Estimé: Equisse de sa vie politique*. Port-au-Prince: Imprimerie de l'Etat.

Manuel, Peter, with Kenneth Bilby and Michael Largey. 1995. *Caribbean Currents: Caribbean Music from Rumba to Reggae*. Philadelphia: Temple University Press.

Marcus, George E., and Michael M. J. Fischer. 1986. *Anthropology as Cultural Critique: An Experimental Moment in the Human Sciences*. Chicago: University of Chicago Press.

Martin, John. 1951. "Program of Native Songs, Dances and Music Launches Celebration Here of Haiti Week." *New York Times*, May 9, p. 29.

Mathurin, Augustin. 1975. *Bi-Centenaire de la fondation de Port-au-Prince, 1749–1949. Exposition Internationale, 8 Decembre 1949–8 Juin 1950, à la memoire du grand Président Léon Dumarsais Estimé*. Port-au-Prince: Imprimerie des Antilles.

Miller, Christopher L. 1985. *Blank Darkness: Africanist Discourse in French*. Chicago: University of Chicago Press.

Moore, Robin. 1994. "Representations of Afrocuban Expressive Culture in the Writings of Fernando Ortiz." *Latin American Music Review* 15(1): 32–54.

––––––. 1995. "The Commercial Rumba: Afrocuban Arts as International Popular Culture." *Latin American Music Review* 16(2): 165–98.

Mudimbe, V. Y. 1988. *The Invention of Africa. Gnosis, Philosophy, and the Order of Knowledge.* Bloomington: Indiana University Press.

Nattiez, Jean-Jacques. 1990. *Music and Discourse: Toward a Semiology of Music.* Princeton: Princeton University Press.

New York Times. 1954. "700 at Haitian Fete Mark Independence." January 4.

Nicholls, David. 1979. *From Dessalines to Duvalier: Race, Color, and National Independence in Haiti.* Cambridge: Cambridge University.

———. 1985. *Haiti in Caribbean Context: Ethnicity, Economy, and Revolt.* New York: St. Martin's Press.

Le Nouvelliste. 1934. "A propos du concours pour une méringue carnavalesque." January 22.

———. 1958. "Pour un carnaval artistique et populaire." February 13.

———. 1959a. "Les festivités carnavalesque." February 12, pp. 1–3.

———. 1959b. "Pour un carnaval original." January 15.

———. 1962a. "En chantant le Barbancourt-twist." April 12.

———. 1962b. "Groupes et bandes carnavalesques." January 12.

———. 1965a. "Communiqué de la Mairie." February 17.

———. 1965b. "Le Carnaval 1965." March 1–3.

———. 1965c. "La méringue carnavalesque." February 17.

———. 1968. "Le Carnaval 1968: Un très grande succès." February 1.

Ortíz, Fernando. 1994.

Pacini Hernandez, Deborah. 1995. *Bachata: A Social History of a Dominican Popular Music.* Philadelphia: Temple University Press.

Paul, Emmanuel C. 1962. *Panorama du folklore Haïtien: Présence Africaine en Haïti.* Port-au-Prince: Imprimerie de l'Etat.

Peña, Manuel. 1985. *The Texas-Mexican Conjunto: History of a Working-Class Music.* Austin: University of Texas Press.

Perrone, Charles A. 1989. *Masters of Contemporary Brazilian Song: MPB 1965–85.* Austin: University of Texas Press.

Price-Mars, Jean. 1919. *La vocation de l'élite.* Port-au-Prince: Imprimerie Edmond Chenet.

———. 1983 [1928]. *So Spoke the Uncle.* Trans. Magdaline Shannon. Washington, DC: Three Continents Press.

Rainer, Ed. 1995. "Pleins feux sur Charles René St.-Aude: La longue route d'un géant." *Haïti-Progrès,* December 28 [1994]–January 3, p. 19.

Roberts, John Storm. 1979. *The Latin Tinge: The Impact of Latin American Music on the United States.* New York: Oxford University Press.

Rochlin, Brian. 1992. "Boukman Eksperyans: Fighting the Hate That Haiti Produced." *Option* 46 (September–October): 82–86.

Rotberg, Robert I. 1971. *Haiti: The Politics of Squalor.* Boston: Houghton Mifflin.

Said, Edward. 1978. *Orientalism.* New York: Pantheon.

Saint-Cyr, Jean Franck. 1978. *La musique populaire Haïtienne, son évolution au cours des années 1947–1960.* Thesis. Faculté d'Ethnologie, l'Université de l'Etat d'Haïti.

Schiller, Nina Glick et al. 1987. "All in the Same Boat? Unity and Diversity in Haitian Organizing in New York." In Constance Sutton and Elsa M. Chaney, eds., *Caribbean Life in New York City: Sociocultural Dimensions.* New York: Center for Migration Studies of New York.

Schiller, Nina Glick, and Georges Fouron. 1990. "'Everywhere We Go, We Are in Danger': Ti Manno and the Emergence of a Haitian Transnational Identity." *American Ethnologist* 17(2): 329–47.

Scott, James C. 1990. *Domination and the Arts of Resistance: Hidden Transcripts.* New Haven: Yale University Press.

Seabrook, W. B. 1929. *The Magic Island.* New York: Harcourt, Brace and Company.

Shelemay, Kay Kauffman. 1991. "Recording Technology, the Record Industry, and Ethnomusicological Scholarship." In Bruno Nettl and Philip V. Bohlman, eds., *Comparative Musicology and Anthropology of Music.* Chicago: University of Chicago Press.

Sklair, Leslie. 1991. *Sociology of the Global System.* Baltimore: Johns Hopkins University Press.

Smith, C. C., and Gerard Tacite Lamothe. 1987. "Legends of Haitian Music. Part 1: Locking Horns." *Reggae and African Beat* 6(2): 14–18.

———. 1988. "Legends of Haitian Music. Part 2: Compas! Compas! Compas!" *Reggae and African Beat* 7(2): 30–37.

Superstar. 1983. "Carnaval 83." February 14, pp. 8–9.

Stepick, Alex et al. 1984. "The Roots of Haitian Migration." In Charles R. Foster and Albert Valdman, eds., *Haiti, Today and Tomorrow: An Interdisciplinary Study.* Lanham, MD: University Press of America.

Time. 1934. "Haiti: End of Intervention." August 13, p. 20.

Torgovnik, Mariana. 1990. *Gone Primitive: Savage Intellects, Modern Lives.* Chicago: University of Chicago Press.

Toro. 1979. "Mini-diaz." *Sel* 43:26.

Trouillot, Michel-Rolph. 1990. *Haiti: State against Nation—The Origins and Legacy of Duvalierism.* New York: Monthly Review Press.

Valdman, Albert et al. 1981. *Haitian Creole—English—French Dictionary.* Bloomington: Indiana University Creole Institute.

Velez, Maria Teresa. 1996. *The Trade of an Afro-Cuban Religious Drummer: Felipe Garcia Villamil.* Ph.D. dissertation, Wesleyan University.

Wallis, Roger, and Krister Malm. 1984. *Big Sounds from Small People: The Music Industry In Small Countries.* New York: Pendragon Press.

Waterman, Chris. 1990. *Juju: Social History and Ethnography of an African Popular Music*. Chicago: University of Chicago Press.

Waters, Anita M. 1989 [1985]. *Race, Class, and Political Symbols: Rastafari and Reggae in Jamaican Politics*. New Brunswick: Transaction Publishers.

Weber, Max. 1978. *Economy and Society*. Ed. Guenther Roth and Claus Wittich. Berkeley: University of California Press. Trans. Ephraim Fischoff et al.

Wilcken, Lois. 1991. *Music Folklore and Haitians in New York: Staged Representations and the Negotiation of Identity*. Ph.D. dissertation, Columbia University.

Wilentz, Amy. 1989. *The Rainy Season: Haiti since Duvalier*. New York: Simon and Schuster.

Williams, Raymond. 1977. *Marxism and Literature*. London: Oxford University Press.

Yih, David. 1985. *Music and Dance of Haitian Vodou: Diversity and Unity in Regional Repertoires*. Ph.D. dissertation, Wesleyan University.

Discography

Various. *Assali, Zeklè, Pirogue, Masterdji.* Shap, vol. 1. R. Francis Entertainment. 1987.

———. *Konbit: Burning Rhythms of Haiti.* A&M Records CD 5281. 1989.

———. *Caribbean Revels: Haitian Rara and Dominican Gaga.* Smithsonian/ Folkways SF 40402. 1991.

———. *Jazz and Hot Dance in Martinique.* Harlequin HQ 2018. N.d.

———. *Rhythms of Rapture: Sacred Musics of Vodou.* Smithsonian/Folkways SF 40464. N.d.

Atis Endepandan. *Ki sa pou-n fè* (What is to be done?) Paredon P-1031. 1975.

Ayizan. *Dilijans.* Ayizan Productions BMI 664. 1984.

Bossa Combo. *Haïti, que j'aime.* Dato Records LP DAT-101. N.d.

———. *Accolade.* Mini Records MRS 1069. 1978.

Boukan Ginen. *Jou a rive.* Green Linnet/Xenophile records XENO 4024. 1983–84.

Boukman Eksperyans. *Vodou adjae.* Mango Records 16253 9899-2. 1991.

———. *Kalfou danjere.* Mango Records 162-539-927-2. 1992.

———. *Libète (Pran pou pran l!).* Mango Records 162-539 946. 1995.

Caribbean Sextet. *Caribbean News.* Delta Records DR 2014. 1984.

Manno Charlemagne. *Konviksyon.* Alternative Culturelle STLP 314227. 1984.

———. *Nou nan malè ak oganizasyon mondyal.* Kako Productions KST 1915. 1988.

———. *La fimen.* Kako Productions KA 1915. 1994.

D. P. Express. *David.* Superstar Records SUP-111. 1978.

Jean-Michel Daudier. *Soley la* Shap Musique 1. 1986.

Gérard Dupervil. *Vous en souvenez-vous? Gérard Dupervil interprète les chansons imortelles de Dodòf Legros.* Mini Records MRS 1082. 1979.

Duval, Pierre-Louis. *Nwèl Lavalas.* [No label, no catalogue number.] 1990.

Ensemble [Cadence Rampas de] Wébert Sicot. *Cadence Rampa.* Ibo Records ILP-122. N.d.

——. *Zeponis.* Ibo Records ILP 129. N.d.

——. *Gina.* Mini Records MRS 1058. 1977.

Ensemble [Compas Direct de] Nemours Jean-Baptiste. *L'As du Rhythme.* Ibo Records ILP-124.

——. *Musical Tour of Haiti.* Ansonia ALP 1280. N.d.

——. *Les Trois Dangers.* Ibo Records ILP-127. N.d.

——. *Ti Carole.* Ibo Records ILP-130. N.d.

——. *Haïti Cherie.* Ibo Records ILP-131. N.d.

——. *Nemours-New-Sound.* Ibotone/Anson Music Center AMC 1201. 1966.

Les Fantaisistes de Carrefour. *Haïti.* Ibo Records ILP-143. 1968.

Jacques Fattier and Haïti '86. *Dechouke.* Institut Francais d'Haïti IFH001. 1986.

Frères Parent. *Operasyon Dechoukaj.* Michga Records 002. 1986.

——. *Veye-yo.* Michga Records 011. 1987.

——. *Chemen limye.* [No label.] LP 1388. N.d.

Gacin Garçon. *Nout tout se legliz: Solidarite, fòk sa chanje.* [No label.] GG003. 1987.

Gemini All Stars de Ti Manno. *Exploitation.* Musique des Antilles LP 4677. 1981.

——. *Sort Tiers Monde.* Chancy Records and Tapes CLRP 8016. N.d.

Ibo Combo. *Ibo Combo.* Tam Tam Records 102. N.d.

Jazz des Jeunes. *Super Jazz des Jeunes.* Ibo Records ILP 113. N.d.

——. *Saturday Night in Port-au-Prince.* Marc Records MDVG-203. N.d.

Farah Juste. *Lespwa.* FJ Records LPFJ-5231. N.d.

——. *Alelouya pou Ayiti.* Michga Records M-019. 1987.

——. *La Voix des sans voix.* [No label, no catalogue number.] N.d.

——. *10ᵉ Departement.* Tida [no catalogue number.] N.d.

Fédia Laguerre. *Operasyon dechoukaj: Fo yo vin-n Jugé.* [No label.] ADL-4812. N.d.

——. *Le Soleil luit pour tous* (12″ single). [No label, no catalogue number.] 1987.

——. [with Fritzner Pierre]. *Operasyon Lavalas.* [No label.] FP 001. N.d.

Magnum Band. *Expérience.* Marc Records Marc-310. 1979.

——. *Adoration.* Mini Records MRS 1140. 1983.

——. *Tèt-ensem.* TIDA Records TIDA 35719. 1987.

Manno et Marco. *Lapli.* Marc Records Marc 309. N.d.

Master Dji [Georges Lys-Herard]. *Politik pa m.* Bwa Patat Records 90001. N.d.

Gérard Merceron (Haiti 2000). *L'Energie Mysterieuse* GM Records ST-002. N.d.

——. *Tèt san kò: La nouvelle musique Haïtienne*. GM Records. GM-003. 1980.

Emeline Michel. *Douvanjou ka leve*. Shap Musique 1002. 1987.

Rodrigue Milien et son Coumbite Creole. *Rackêt*. Gayrleen Records LP 1367. 1981.

Mini All Stars. *Pure Gold: Quinze titres d'or de Nemours Jean-Baptiste*. Mini Records MRS 1126-1128. 1981.

——. *Raraman*. Mini Records MRS 1191. 1986.

Mizik Koral Tèt Ansanm de Jan Rabel. *Nou se lavalas*. Alternative Culturelle STLP 314229. N.d.

Mizik Mizik. *De ger*. Hibiscus Records 191348-2. N.d.

Mystic. *Merci*. Esprit Records and Tapes ES0001. 1980.

Toto Necessité. *Haiti libere*. Michga Records 003. 1986.

Beethova Obas. *La Chante de liberté*. Ch. Obas Productions 001-1. N.d.

——. *Si . . .* Ch. Obas Productions 001-2/Déclic Communications. 1994.

Orchestre Septentrionale. *Bwe Kayman*. Maxnelle Records MH 001. 1987.

Original Shleu-Shleu. *Poté colé*. Rotel Records 3367. N.d.

Papa Jube [John Altino]. *Liberasyon*. Melodie Makers MMI 1023. 1993.

Ram. *Aïbobo*. CinéDisc 12191. 1993.

Rara Machine. *Break the Chain*. Shanachie Records 64038. 1993.

——. *Voudou nou*. Shanachie Records 64054. 1994.

Sakad. *Rebati kay la*. Sakad Records, SK 001. N.d.

Shleu-Shleu. *Haiti, mon pays*. Ibo Records ILP-139. 1967.

——. *Tèt chove à New York*. Haiti Records SS-001. N.d.

Skah Shah #1. *Les dix commandements*. Skah-Shah Records 201.

——. *Van libète*. Pas de Shah Productions PRS-1102. 1987.

Solèy Lévé. *Ayiti démin*. Soley SOS 003. N.d.

——. *Chansons et poésies patriotiques*. Soley SOS 001. N.d.

System Band. *Ou tronpe m*. Machiavel Music SY-101. 1987.

Tabou Combo. *Baissez-bas*. Tabou Combo Records and Tapes TCLP 7985. 1980.

——. *Ce konsa ce konsa*. Tabou Combo Records and Tapes, TCLP 8015. 1982.

——. *Respect*. Mini Records MRS 1039. N.d.

Jose Tavernier and Mini All Stars. *My Twenty-Five Years in Music*. Mini Records MRS 1139. 1982.

Jean Yves Volcy. *Chansons d'hier et d'aujourdhui*. Gayrleen Records LP 1368. N.d.

Kiki Wainwright. 23 *nèg vanyan*. Michga Records M-014. N.d.
Zèklè. *Ce ou minm*. Zèklè music ZR 701. 1983.
———. *Stop*. Zèklè Productions ZR 104. 1984.
———. *San mele*. Nouvel Jenerasyon Records NJ 11. 1993.

Interviews

André, Yvon "Kapi"; August 1987, New York.*

Bazile, Chris; May 1988, Boston.

Beaubrun, Theodore "Lolo," Jr.; New York, 1990.

Boyer, Yves, "Chiko"; New York, 1990.

Cameau, Anderson; August 1987, New York.*

Chancy, Georges Loubert; August 1987, New York.*

Charlemagne, Emmanuel "Manno"; September 1994. [Conducted by Mark Dow.]

Charles, Cinna Octavius "Ti-Blanc"; August 1988, Cap-Haïtien.

Daniel, Gérard; August 1987, New York.*

Déjean, André and Fred; March 1988, Pétion-Ville.

Denis Jr., Raoul, Bobby Denis, Hans "Pirogue" Peters, and Réginald Policard; July 1988, Port-au-Prince.

Denis, Robert "Bobby"; August 1988, Port-au-Prince.

de Pradines Morse, Emerante; July 1995, Port-au-Prince.

Derenoncourt, Ronald "Aboudja"; July 1995, Port-au-Prince.

Dessalines, Charles; 1986. New York.

Duverger, Marc; November, 1986, New York.*

Duviela, Serge; June 1987, New York.

Juste, Farah, and Dr. Jean-Claude Desgranges; February 1989, Miami.

Franck, Ricardo "Ti-Plume"; 1993, New York.

Henry, Jean-Gesner "Coupé Cloué"; 1986, New York.*

Henry, Jean-Gesner "Coupé Cloué," and Guy Montreuil; March 1988, Port-au-Prince.

Herisse, Jean-Robert "Pòki"; March 1988, Port-au-Prince.

Joseph, Jean Yves "Fanfan Ti-Bòt"; June 1988, New York.

Koleksyon Kazak; January 1992, Miami.

Lalanne, Wagner; February 1988, Miami.

Lamothe, Gérard Tacite; October 1986, Los Angeles.*
Lamothe, Henri-Robert; January 1988, Miami.
Lévy, Nicole; May 1988, Brooklyn.
Martial, Fritz; May 1988, New York.
Martino, Robert; February 1988, Miami.
Michel, Alfred, and Adrien Jeannite; August 1987.*
Michel, Alfred; March 1988, Port-au-Prince.
Morisseau, Guesley "Ti-Gous"; May 1988, New York.
Pascal, Alix "Tit," and Pierre "Bobo" Ciné; June 1988, New York.
Pasquet, Alix "Dadou"; February 1988, Miami.
Paul, Fred; November 1991, Long Island.
Pierre, Jean-Baptiste "Baba"; March 1988, Port-au-Prince.
Similien, Jules "Toto Nécessité"; February 1989, Miami.
Smith, Ronald; November, 1986, Brooklyn.*
St. Aude, René; 1986, Brooklyn.* June 1988, New York.
St. Victor, Jean Michel "Zouzoul"; May 1988, New York.
Tabou Combo (Jean Yves "Fanfan Ti-Bòt" Joseph, Yvon "Kapi" André,
    Herman Nau, Elysée Pyronneau); 1990, New York.
Tavernier, José; February 1989, Miami.
Toussaint, Johnny Frantz "Ti-Frè," and Jean Michel "Zouzoul" St. Victor;
    August 1987.*
Ulysse, Fito; March 1988, Carrefour, Haiti.
Verdier, Jean-Claude; March 1988, Port-au-Prince.
Wainwright, Jeff; March 1993, Miami.
Widmaier, Herby; August 1988, Delmas, Haiti.
Widmaier, Mushi; July 1988, Port-au-Prince.
*Asterisks identify interviews conducted by C. C. Smith and Gérard Tacite
    Lamothe. Used with permission.

Index